Inside Animal Hoarding

New Directions in the Human-Animal Bond
Alan M. Beck, series editor

Inside Animal Hoarding

The Case of Barbara Erickson and Her 552 Dogs

Arnold Arluke
and
Celeste Killeen

Purdue University Press
West Lafayette, Indiana

ISBN 978-1-55753-432-3
    1-55753-432-2

Library of Congress Cataloging-in-Publication Data

Arluke, Arnold.
  Inside Animal Hoarding: The Case of Barbara Erickson and Her 552 Dogs / Arnold Arluke and Celeste Killeen.
     p. cm.
  Includes bibliographical references.
  ISBN 978-1-55753-511-5
  1. Erickson, Barbara (Sherry Barbara) 2. Obsessive-compulsive disorder--Patients--Oregon--Case studies. 3. Compulsive hoarding--Oregon--Case studies. 4. Human-animal relationships--Oregon. I. Killeen, Celeste, 1956- II. Title.
  RC533.A756 2008
  616.85'227--dc22
                              2008050332

Contents

Acknowledgments

We have many people and organizations to acknowledge. Celeste Killeen wishes to thank, for their invaluable assistance and input, Dr. Randall Lockwood, past Vice President for Research and Educational Outreach, Humane Society of Idaho; Dr. Gail Steketee of Boston University; Jane Nathanson, LCSW; Dr. Stephanie LaFarge, Senior Director of Counseling Services, ASPCA; and Dr. Irene Laudeman, Casa De Los Gatos Feral Cat Refuge. Many thanks to my writing group: Lydia Barbee, Coston Fredrick, Kelly Jones, Frank Marvin, and Dave Schneider for their input and patience. Thank you, Eileen Dingeldein, for teaching me how to listen; Debby Morrow for showing me how to put one foot in front of the other; and Steven Mayfield for your guidance. Thank you, Vaughn, for keeping me fed so that I could write. Last of all, thank you Sherry "Barbara" Erickson for sharing your life story with me.

Arnold Arluke is grateful to the Hoarding of Animals Research Consortium (HARC) for over a decade of collegial stimulation and support with this topic. Dr. Gary Patronek, its founder and director, along with Carter Luke, Dr. Ed Messner, Jane Nathason, Michelle Papazian, Dr. Randy Frost, and Dr. Gail Steketee, have all helped to further our understanding of the nature of animal hoarding and how best to intervene in these cases. Funding from the Kenneth A. Scott Charitable Trust and the Research and Scholarship Development Fund at Northeastern University also paved the way for some of the research behind our book, as did the practical support of the Massachusetts Society for the Prevention of Cruelty to Animals (MSPCA). Finally, I owe many thanks to Dr. Allan A. Rolfe for spotting hoarding cases in the news and to Lauren Rolfe for constant support and encouragement.

"Although the case of a dog being violently killed is shocking, in a hoarding case the suffering can be felt by hundreds of animals for months and months on end."

Randall Lockwood, Ph.D.
United States Humane Society

"I don't view the Ericksons as evil people. I think they started something from the goodness of their hearts that got outrageously out of hand."

Barbara Hutchinson, President
Second Chance Animal Shelter
Payette, Idaho

"My daddy said when I was little, 'One 'a these days, Sherry, someone's gonna kill you for talkin' so bold.' And I said, 'Well, let 'em try.'"

Sherry "Barbara" Erickson

Introduction

By the late 1990s, Barbara and Robert Erickson acquired hundreds of dogs—many dehydrated, starved, and sick—in their disheveled home, in Oregon. The Ericksons were neither an animal shelter, nor a breeder. They certainly were not everyday pet owners. They were what used to be called "collectors," or more recently, "animal hoarders."

Animal hoarders are people who amass dozens or even hundreds of cats, dogs, and other assorted creatures, purportedly out of concern and love for them (Lockwood 1994), only to become overwhelmed and unable to provide even minimal standards of nutrition, sanitation, and veterinary care. Law enforcement agents, animal control officers, housing officials, shelter workers, and veterinarians often find these animals in pitiful condition, chronically underfed or even starved, living in inadequate, overcrowded housing, and sometimes harboring painful diseases, behavioral problems, or physical impairments (Campbell and Robinson 2001). They also find hoarders and those living with them to be socially isolated and to suffer ill health. Sanitary conditions frequently deteriorate to the point where dwellings become unfit for human habitation. Floors may buckle from being soaked with urine and feces, and the air may be difficult for investigators to breathe without protective apparatuses. Although disturbing to almost anyone else, hoarders fail to acknowledge the deteriorating condition of the animals (including disease, starvation, and even death), the household environment (severe overcrowding, very unsanitary conditions), and the negative effect of their behavior on their own and other household members' health and well-being.

In terms of loss of life, destruction of property, and impact on the community, on a smaller scale, animal hoarders produce problems that parallel

1

those created by natural disasters. As with natural disasters, dealing with hoarding cases can cost tens of thousands of dollars, or more, to the community. Legal fees alone can become burdensome to those public and private agencies that prosecute these cases. Certainly, the cost in labor can be staggering when one considers how much time these cases can consume for those working in law enforcement, social services, humane welfare, public health, and housing—all of whom are likely to be called into action to rescue animals, people, and property.

It is daunting to understand why animal hoarders behave as they do, what they think and feel, and how they can be best managed, given the challenging and complex nature of such cases. Many audiences, each having a different interest in and knowledge of animal hoarding, pose these questions. Some audiences are very familiar with hoarding, including but not limited to academics, policy makers, or humane officials, while others are not. Given this diverse readership, addressing these questions calls for an unconventional approach.

To this end, we want to give readers an up-close-and-personal view of one of these cases—that of Barbara Erickson—while also putting it into a more general framework about animal hoarding. The result is a book that is a union of different, but complimentary styles of writing and analysis–one journalistic, the other academic.

The first part of the book is an in-depth portrait of Barbara Erickson that tells her story and captures her voice. This case study section opens the world of animal hoarding to readers, recording the interplay of roles between Barbara Erickson and her husband, neighbors, townspeople, law enforcement authorities, veterinarians, humane society workers, and one of the authors. Written by a journalist in a nonfiction novella form, this highly personal examination of animal hoarding brings to life all the important details of such cases—the characters, the action, the context—that one would experience if involved in them. We hear the pleas, demands, and concerns of Barbara Erickson herself as well as the frustration, sympathy, and anger of those with whom she came in contact.

The second part of this book deals with the Erickson case as one of many animal hoarding incidents, albeit an exceptional (but by no means a unique) example, given the enormous number of animals involved and the scale of their rescue. Written by a sociologist, this broad discussion relates the Barbara Erickson story to what is currently known and understood about animal hoarders—who these people are, what causes their behavior, how they are dealt with, how they think about themselves, and why so many of us find them both disturbing and interesting.

We do not claim to provide *the* explanation for why animal hoarding occurs or how *exactly* hoarders should be managed. To do so would be premature. Instead, we hope our dual approach stimulates further discussion about this problem, if not new research into its causes and consequences, so we can better answer the above questions.

PART ONE: The Barbara Erickson Case

Prologue
Celeste Killeen

On January 23, 2003, deputies from the Malheur County Sheriff's Office converged on a small farmhouse near the outskirts of Harper, Oregon. Their action—a rescue—came after months of complaints by neighbors of a wretched, foul-smelling odor wafting from the property. Based on preliminary investigation and rumors, the deputies expected to find fifty to one hundred dogs living on the tiny farm. Instead, on that cold, overcast, winter day, the officers found over five hundred diseased and emaciated dogs suffering under conditions that could only be described as otherworldly. "I love my babies," Barbara Erickson, the owner, told the deputies. "...I protect them."

Her words were heartfelt, delivered with utter conviction. Yet, she had cast her beloved "babies" into an unimaginable hell—some living outside in the cold mud, while most were crammed into a small, two-bedroom house that had no heat, fighting for a place to sleep on tables and chairs, or on the feces-encrusted floor. Mange and upper respiratory diseases were rampant. The stronger dogs viciously competed for food and water. The weaker ones, starving mothers and their whelps, became prey.

I first met Barbara and Bob Erickson from a distance, watching the shocking television reports that described the rescue of their surviving dogs. For several days after the dramatic police action, the evening news was filled with images of wild-eyed, filthy animals, some too weak and sick to move, others seemingly trapped in a frenzy of barking and clawing. Animal care personnel worked around the clock washing, feeding, hydrating, and in some cases, burying the dogs. Reporters bit into the story, holding on like a dog to its bone. They interviewed law enforcement officials and veterinarians. They sought information from the Idaho Humane Society. They ran the chaotic video clips day after day, changing only their voiceovers. In time, they reported the decision to prosecute the dog owners.

But no one talked to Barbara Erickson.

I wanted to know more. I, too, had been horrified by the flickering images on my television screen. Yet, I was equally saddened by the inescapable picture of an anguished, old woman whose life had lost hope. Behind the bright lights of the camera and the newspaper headlines, hidden in Barbara's eyes and in those of her dogs, was a shared sorrow, a like sense of betrayal and loss.

Barbara Erickson's story was my best effort to present a factual account of how animal hoarding developed in one woman's life. I interviewed many people, searched public records, reviewed scientific studies and articles, and spent hours upon hours educating myself about animal hoarding and compiling the information I had gathered into a readable story. What I learned in this process surprised and challenged me.

Several people can experience and remember the same event in very different ways, even when they have no obvious agendas. So how do I determine and present the truth? I found few and fairly nebulous guidelines for this process and relied heavily on my own common sense and desire to present what I learned about animal hoarding in the most factual and understandable way possible. In some scenes, I presented the most likely version of events and offered a rebuttal for the person whose views differed greatly. In other scenes, I blended the reports of several people to offer a conglomerate version of events. In still other instances—the chapters about Barbara's childhood—I created a scene around sketchy information to portray the essence of what happened according to Barbara, her relatives, and the people who knew her.

What I did not do was probe Barbara to remember and reveal every minute detail of her painful past. Instead I let her talk. I took her story and made the best attempt I could to fact check and corroborate it, then I developed a scene to portray the events.

Some events, though verified by Barbara and others enough to satisfy my own skepticism, have not been included in the story because they were so egregious I felt a need for actual court records as documentation before I was willing to offer the information for print. Barbara was not willing to share with me the aliases she used at the time, and thus I could not obtain the documents, so I chose to omit those events.

And so the story began.

Chapter One

I froze as the stagnant smell seeped into my car. A few days earlier, I had glanced over a pot of boiling cinnamon water to see a television screen filled with hundreds of frantic, barking dogs. The tangled notion of animal hoarding described in that newscast piqued my curiosity, leaving a trail of unanswered questions that, once followed, had led me to this horrific place. I'd been told what to expect. I was prepared, I thought. But now, in the face of it—the smell and the squalor—I wanted to run.

I slid the seat back for legroom and pulled on a brand new pair of knee-high, rubber boots. I grabbed my camera, opened the car door, and stepped out, one foot after another. A few feet away, the front gate opened to a make-shift walkway of empty dog food bags that had been trampled into the mud. Otherwise, the yard was a wasteland kneaded by hundreds of tiny paws, each imprint forming a murky, orange puddle. I hopscotched across the empty bags toward a once-white, clapboard house, holding my breath against the pervasive, acrid smell. As I drew closer, hundreds of muddy paw prints became visible, tracking up the sides of the house to hip level. Higher yet, the roof sagged and dirty brown cobwebs drooped from the eaves. A foul, malodorous cloud hung over it all.

At the end of the walkway, I jumped from the last dog food bag onto the bottom plank of the steps, clomped up to the porch, and tugged at the screen door. It was boarded and locked.

"I never had a key since they moved in."

The voice belonged to the landlord, Verda Palmer, armed with a walking stick in one hand and a tissue in the other. She'd come up the steps behind me as I peered through one of the sediment-encrusted windows. A smile flashed across Verda's worn face. She wore her usual baseball cap, this time held in place by a red-and-black, plaid scarf that she'd tied under her chin. "The back door's jammed shut, but they broke a window on the right side of the house," she said, pulling on the door handle. "You can get in there if you want, but we'll have to go around." She shrugged, tucking a lock of gray hair under her ball cap.

I braced myself and stepped off the porch, following Verda as we slogged through the mixture of mud and feces to a pathway carved through the dense pile of rubble abutting the house. Aged spruce trees stood in a row along the fence. Their drooping branches brushed the eaves of the house, fashioning a canopy overhead. We tromped along, using surface roots as stepping stones. Verda poked at the debris with her stick. "There's my fan I let them borrow last year," she mumbled. She stopped to lift a piece of dank carpet and probed the plastic beneath. "This used to be a nice place until the Ericksons come along," she added. The tiny house—Verda's rental—was in Harper, Oregon, a place I had never before visited, even though it was only a couple of hours from my Boise home.

"When was that?" I asked.

Verda sighed. "About five years ago," she said. "After the old tenants moved out, I was cleaning the house with my friend, Helen Dawson, when Barbara stopped by and asked if she could rent it. She looked nice and pleasant, and she had a wad of money in her hand. She said she would plant a garden and take good care of the house and yard. She offered me four-fifty a month, more than I ever got for the place before."

I paused to snap a picture of the house. "Did she tell you about the dogs?"

Verda shook her head. "Barbara said they had three dogs, her *babies*, but they would stay outside. So, I said 'okay.' Come to find out, they had thirty dogs."

I made my way to the rear of the house, while Verda rummaged through the trash. In the backyard, the grounds were divided into pens using plywood shelters, lean-tos, and tarps strung across the corners of the fence. Large plastic bowls, empty and gnawed, were scattered about. A scrawny cat lay in the path, lifeless in a glove of mud. I stepped over it and went on until a pair of over-turned, cracked wading pools forced me off the path and into an obstacle course of broken appliances: refrigerators, stoves, washing machines, and dryers—all smeared with paw prints. Mattresses strewn about the yard absorbed the sewage like giant sponges. Enormous dunghills of faded dog food bags filled with feces blotted the area. One pile bore the decomposing bodies of seven dogs, and more animal remains spilled from a bag split open by the rain.

Shocked by the corpses, I spun away and tripped over a mattress. For a few seconds, I scrambled to stay upright, performing a clumsy waltz across the rubble until gravity won out, and I pitched forward. The ground was rushing at me, and I twisted sideways, reaching out with one hand to break my fall while holding my camera high in the air with the other. For a moment, I kept my eyes closed. When I opened them, my face was mere inches from the mud. I was nearly prostrate, frozen in a sort of one-armed push-up, moisture seeping through the woolen fabric of my glove.

I considered calling out to Verda, but pride won out. I twisted and pulled one leg under me, pushed hard, and lurched to my feet, wrestling my glove off and flinging it aside. I looked about sheepishly and breathed a sigh of relief. No witnesses. Verda was still poking about at the side of the house.

The fall unnerved me, withering my resolve, but after taking a moment to gather my courage, I inched forward, the mud sucking in my boots with a *squoosh* and letting go with a *smack*. My pace quickened as I got the hang of it. At the far corner of the house, I spotted the broken window Verda had described. It was covered with damp cardboard—easy entry if I took out the shards of glass. I looked around and found a rake stashed next to a freezer draped by a feathery tent of cobwebs. Gripping the rake like a lance, I charged forward. The cardboard ripped and popped away from the window frame. After knocking away a few jagged pieces of glass with the rake head, I cautiously peeked inside and was hit with a malodorous blast of fecal ammonia that exploded from the window like a fire. I staggered backward, and, for the briefest of moments, thought about turning around, running back to my car, and screeching off as fast as possible.

Instead, I gulped a final breath of outside air, straddled the windowsill, and eased into the darkness. Inside the ice-cold house, I stopped after a couple of steps, waiting for my eyes to adjust. I couldn't see a thing. A few seconds later, the house still pitch black, I was again ready to turn and run, but I hesitated because I needed pictures.

With little aim, I raised my digital camera and snapped a picture. The image of a table appeared on the camera screen. I stepped to the right, took another shot toward the floor, and realized that I had found my guide through the house. Each picture produced a glimmer of what lay ahead. I slowly edged forward, accompanied by flashes of light from my camera, soon finding myself in the Ericksons' living room, where a small metal chair faced the television. The only other furniture was a card table piled high with homemade cages. The floor, once crowded with dogs, was covered with brown paw prints and trampled-on waste. Garlands of cobwebs hung from the ceilings and doorways.

I stopped, slowly rotating as I shot several pictures. For a few moments, the only sounds were the click of the camera and the soft shuffle of my rubber boots on the floor. The silence was broken by a scampering sound. I froze, holding my breath, listening, wondering if it were a dog left behind or perhaps a mouse or cat.

I began again, working my way through the house by following the images that flashed across the camera screen. I took several pictures of the kitchen counter—a crowded display of empty food containers, rotting produce, dirty ashtrays, air fresheners, crumpled cigarette packages, and dog-grooming products, all sprinkled with mouse droppings. A hallway, gated by an excrement-slathered sheet of plywood, led to the back rooms of the house. I crossed to the opening and shoved the plywood aside. Halfway down the narrow hall, I found a bathroom where cans of hair spray, bottles of shampoo, and air fresheners were scattered across the gold-speckled Formica counter, along with an uncapped tube of toothpaste and an overturned can of Comet. Two cracked and smudged mirrors hung on a wall painted candy cane pink. A small shelf above the sink held an ironically tidy display of shaving soap and cologne along with several small jars of face cream and an economy-sized jug of Drano. Across the room, a shredded shower curtain hung from a crooked rod. The filthy tub was filled with clutter, and a dry toilet, ringed in rust, sat in the corner.

In one bedroom, a lacy cobweb draped the window, trailing across the wall to an empty bed frame. In the next room, I found another bed frame and two dressers, one cluttered with dirty clothes and newspapers, along with an orange gasoline can and a pellet gun, the other a sort of dressing table topped by a mirror smeared with paw prints and, oddly, a pristine, blue cruet that seemed terribly out of place in a house where gloom and sadness lurked in every corner. Dog food dishes were scattered across the floor, all empty except one that held the partial remains of a Chihuahua.

I continued through the house, snapping pictures until the welcome image of the back door flashed onto my camera screen. Wasting no time getting to it, I grabbed the doorknob and jerked. Verda was right. The door was jammed shut. From a blackened corner, I heard a low howl as a gust of wind whistled under the eaves. At the same time, it seemed that the distant skittering sound had returned and was closer. My heart quickened, and I pulled again, harder. The door gave a bit, but stayed closed. A wave of panic swept over me, and I propped one foot against the jamb, gripped the doorknob with both hands, and pulled as hard as I could. The door heaved and groaned.

Wood splintered and the door burst open, allowing a rush of outside air that now seemed fresh by comparison.

I stepped onto the porch and looked around. Verda had made it to the backyard and was rummaging through the debris. She waved her stick when she saw me.

"There's a dead dog on the comforter over there." She smiled wryly. "I unrolled it 'cause I thought it might be Bob." Barbara's husband.

I followed Verda's gaze to a pink-and-blue, flowered comforter at the base of a freezer chest near the back door. There, between the folds, lay a decomposing dog, his dull black fur matted against a grid of ribs. I tiptoed through the mud and kneeled next to the corpse. "How curious," I said. "...in the commotion of living with hundreds of dogs, someone took the time to wrap up this one when he died." I covered his body with the damp shroud.

"Look at this." Verda had opened the lid of the freezer. She held a tissue to her nose and stepped back as I stood to look. Inside the freezer were countless, reeking packages of greenish-gray beef, pork, ham, and chicken, all ripened by three days without electricity. "There's more meat in here than they could eat in two years, and their stove don't even work," Verda said with disgust. She slammed shut the lid. "Every time we replaced it, the mice chewed through the wires."

"What's in that shed over there?" I asked Verda, already putting distance between me and the vile freezer.

Verda straightened. "Let's go see," she said. She offered me a tissue from her pocket before leading the way toward the back of the lot by weaving through the rubble: a rusty, gray car; a van filled with black trash bags and food wrappers; a charred, smelly garbage pit. We reached the shed, where I stopped to snap another picture. The shed was falling apart, its tattered shingles curling upward, trapping twigs and branches that had fallen from the surrounding trees. The unpainted wood siding was warped and splintered, as was the plywood door. A sheet of notebook paper, framed in duct tape and graced with formal handwriting, had been posted on the door, "This is private property. Stay to hell out!"

Verda pointed at the sign. "That's how Barbara is," she said. "This just makes people *want* to break in."

I grabbed the door handle and pulled. It didn't budge. "The door is nailed shut around the edges," I told Verda. "You wouldn't happen to have a pair of pliers in your truck?" It was a stupid question, I knew. Verda laughed.

"Oh, I have a whole tool box," she said, already heading back to her pickup. "Wouldn't go anywhere without it," she added, throwing a grin over her shoulder. I watched her trudge through the mud until she cleared the corner of the house, then looked at the sign again. "Stay to hell out!"

I almost laughed. After viewing all the video footage of Barbara Erickson, I could picture her carefully scripting the note and overseeing husband Bob as he nailed the door shut and posted the sign. Above the door, several bent, rusty nails were partially driven into the lintel. I reached up and tugged on one. It didn't give.

"This'll get it for you." Verda had returned, waving a pair of pliers in one hand.

With the door pried open, we found a cache of furniture covered with years of dust. Couches, tables, televisions, chairs, lamps, and dressers were piled nearly to the ceiling. I took a picture.

"They moved it all out here when the dogs took over the house," Verda said. She ran a hand across a Queen Anne coffee table. "This is nice stuff. Nicer than anything you'll find in *my* house." I snapped another shot, muffling a laugh when I saw a touch-lamp. Verda looked up, her tiny, dark eyes searching for an explanation.

"It's just the lamp," I said. "I had one like it, once. My husband and I thought we had found a unique treasure. Within a year we saw touch-lamps sprout up like weeds...at K-Mart, at yard sales. They were everywhere."

Verda studied my face. She understood. I had grabbed a piece of normalcy from the past—anything to take my mind off the devastation, even if only for a moment. I wanted to stay where I was, just outside the shed, the only place where we'd not found anything gruesome. Verda chose that moment to shut the plywood door. "Let's check out the barn over there," she said.

We crossed to the barn and peeked through the cracks in a warped, rotting door at another wall-to-wall stockpile of dog food bags, filled with feces.

"You couldn't pay someone enough to haul this away." Verda shook her head and snorted. "This place used to be alive with fruit trees, flowers, a lawn." She turned away and blew her nose into her tissue. "I rented it just to help people out. Now I don't know what I'll do."

I wasn't sure what to say. It was hard to believe that this car wreck of a house had ever been habitable. "Did the Ericksons stay up on the rent?" I asked politely.

Verda sighed. "The first couple years they paid on time. After that, every dollar was eaten by Barbara's babies."

I looked at the dilapidated house, the plywood porch tacked onto unpainted siding, and the sagging cobwebs around dark, foreboding windows.

The horror I'd found inside remained fresh in my mind. "The dogs seem to have consumed every inch of space in the house," I said, "and every ounce of energy, too."

We began to walk, not stopping until we reached the front of the house, where Verda bent to scrape her boot against a cast-off, metal cabinet. "Barb was always asking me for money," she told me, examining the bottom of her boot. "Said she was due an inheritance from her dad. Supposedly, he had a ranch in Washington that was held up in escrow, and she was just waiting for the money." Verda looked up at the house, her eyes wet with tears. "'Course it never happened. Barb was full of stories. After a while, it was just easier to give in."

Verda pulled a snapshot from her pocket. "This is what the place used to look like." She stepped closer to me and held up the picture, her fingers trembling. "See how nice it was…all painted, with grass." She began to describe her little rental, recalling long-lost details. With the picture to help, I could now imagine the house as it must once have been. Much like Verda, I suspected— solid, corner-true, and unmade up. She sighed again. "I was operated on for cancer, and my sister was terminally ill, so I just stopped paying attention."

Verda climbed into her weathered, white pickup. "I haven't been inside, but just from the smell the Sheriff said it'll have to be burned. I don't see how anyone can live there now." She started her truck and ground it into gear, tossed me a wave and rumbled off into a waning, sunless day. Behind me the house waited, but I kept my eyes on her pickup, watching it shrink into the distance.

I turned to go back, but instead went to my car to grab a notebook and pen. I scratched out a message asking Barbara to call me, afterward forcing myself back down the path of dog food bags and up the crumbling steps to the door. I slipped the note into the doorjamb and ran back to my car, where I pulled off my mud-caked, rubber boots. Resisting the urge to toss them into the yard, I wrapped the boots in a plastic bag and threw them into the trunk, then jumped into my car and followed Verda into the approaching darkness.

Chapter Two

For several weeks after the rescue, newscasts showed video clips of barking dogs crammed into pens, their lost eyes riveted on the camera. Mug shots of Bob and Barbara Erickson, disheveled and exhausted, filled the screen. They were charged with criminal mischief, animal abuse and neglect, and destruction of property. Reporters interviewed experts and wrestled with jargon. An unfamiliar label became part of local, water cooler gossip: Animal Hoarders.

I was skeptical. I knew how easy it was to label people. Ten years earlier, I had been a guardian ad litem for Ada County—a court-appointed legal advocate for children who had been neglected or abused. I'd met mothers who had ignored the needs of their children while feeding their own drug habits and fathers who had used their children as sex toys, afterward beating them nearly to death. I could never accept what had happened to the children, but diligent investigation almost always showed *why* it had happened. In the case of the Ericksons, the television and newspaper accounts had produced a simplistic trail of events. They had shown videos of mangy, hungry, dehydrated dogs, living in excrement, some injured or too weak to move. They'd spoken to police officers and animal experts and psychologists. But no one had talked to Barbara.

The rescue—a reported success because the dogs were removed and the Ericksons jailed—had devastated both the dogs and the Ericksons. It had cost the community. The financial burden, borne by taxpayers and benefactors, eventually grew into the thousands. Could the intervention have been timelier? Could the community of animal advocates, law enforcement officers, and social service workers have delved more deeply, learned more about the Ericksons and the phenomenon of animal hoarding? Could anything have

15

been done before the population of dogs had grown to over five hundred? I wanted to find out. I was haunted by images: the poor dead pup who had been rolled up and left behind; the out-of-control dogs; the anguish in their eyes; and the mug shot of Barbara, her face filled with the same anguish. I knew I had to tell the story.

At her arraignment, Barbara Erickson proclaimed her innocence and remained in jail, unable to make bail. Her husband, Bob, pled guilty to the same charges: animal neglect and abuse and destruction of property. With the guilty plea, he was released on his own recognizance, returning home the same day where he found the note I'd left on the door. He shared it with Barbara, and, with her consent, called me. Barbara wanted to talk. I phoned her at the Malheur County Jail, where she was allowed one five minute call per week.

"I want to write your story," I told her, expecting that she would need time to think about it. Instead, she agreed immediately. She wanted to be heard, to be somehow vindicated.

"I never hurt my babies," Barbara insisted. "The fact is I protected them. I did it for them. I couldn't turn them out on the highway to be killed."

The desperate tone of her voice surprised me.

"They made me out to be some criminal...said I abused them dogs. Oh, they're crooked, Honey. I've known that for a long time."

"I think it's important for the whole story to come out," I said, trying to get her back on track, "and I'd like to write a book about what happened... and about your life."

A hearty laugh bubbled over the line, followed by a deep, raspy cough.

"Well, it'll be one helluva story," she said. "And I want everybody to know that house was a mess because old Verda never took care of it like a landlord should. We was all winter without any heat and had to..."

Barbara was suddenly cut off, our five allowed minutes apparently over. Still, I was pleased with our first interaction. She'd seemed more than willing to talk.

I called a publishing attorney who put together a contract that I mailed to Barbara, along with a letter explaining the journey we were about to take together. A long week passed before I received a call from Barbara. I sat on the edge of my bed, holding the phone, while Barbara prattled on about her dogs. The contract and the story seemed far less significant to her than the prospect of a friend to talk to. She offered to name her next Chihuahua puppy after me. Finally, I heard the words I'd been waiting for. Barbara was eager to get started on the book and had already mailed the contract.

Chapter Three

A week after receiving the signed contract, I called Barbara who was still in jail. She'd talked with her court-appointed attorney, Manuel Perez, who had served up some fast-food advice: *Don't talk to anyone.* Nonetheless, Barbara and I agreed to keep in touch. We would talk weekly, but never about the case until after the trial, scheduled for six months later. With the rules set down, I began our first telephone interview by asking Barbara for her maiden name. "Sherry Hawkes," she replied. Oddly, she seemed unsure about the spelling.

I was confused. "But people know you as 'Barbara,'" I said.

Barbara hesitated. "I took that on when I moved to Oregon," she explained, "just for a change."

I asked for the phone numbers of relatives and friends who might be available for interviews. Barbara told me she had no contact with any relatives, except a brother, Mikey Hawkes, who could not be reached because, "He works on special assignment with the FBI." Besides, Barbara said, even though her friends were supportive they didn't want their names disclosed or their phone numbers given out. Frustrated with Barbara's stonewalling, I gave up for the moment. Acquaintances would have to do. A few days later, I drove to Coleman Service—the hub of Harper, Oregon—to sniff around.

After reaching Vale, the Malheur County seat, I drove southwest on Highway 20 until I came to Harper, a gathering of some fifty ranches that was nearly lost in the rolling hills that surrounded it. Once there, I quickly found Coleman Service, a lonely building on the highway, stirring up a poof of dust as I pulled around the gas pump and eased up to the front of the store.

Brian Coleman, a slight man with dark eyes and a clean and tidy finish, had walked the same path as his father and grandfather, spending much of his life pumping gas and pouring booze. He ran Coleman Service, an all-you-need establishment, and he knew everyone in Harper, their comings and goings, and even mentioned with matter-of-fact credibility, "Here, you know what people are going to do before they do it."

This wasn't the first time I had met Brian, a principal figure in the small community. Several days after the dog rescue, I had driven to Harper to investigate, stopping at Coleman Service. When I'd mentioned Barbara Erickson, Brian's brow had furrowed. He had looked hard into my eyes, holding his gaze until I began to squirm. I'd felt that he was testing me, trying to figure me out. Even after he started to talk, his words were issued cautiously, as if I were a foreign emissary from a hostile nation.

The small store was barely large enough to accommodate its two-stool, scrub-worn, Formica counter and brown vinyl-upholstered booth. Even so, a large, gleaming cooler, wider than the door had been, was somehow tucked into a corner. When Brian saw me, the reticence he'd shown during our first meeting was gone. He hustled out from behind the service counter and shook my hand as if I were an old friend. He led me through a door at the back of the store that opened into a small apartment.

"Make yourself at home," he said, indicating the kitchen table. I sat and looked around. The living quarters were spotless and pure 1970s remodel— brown carpeting, brown-and-beige linoleum, almond appliances. The warm aroma of freshly baked cookies filled the small apartment.

A bell dinged, and Brian scurried outside to pump gas. I picked up my tape recorder and trailed him, stopping inside the tiny store where a man and a woman were nestled into the corner booth. As I came out of Brian's apartment, the couple stopped talking and appraised me without awkwardness. The man, his thinning, gray hair flat on his head, offered me the usual, small-town nod and looked down, fingering the brim of a huge cowboy hat he'd set on the table. Its band was darkly stained with sweat. The woman had a medium build and wore jeweled, drugstore glasses. When I looked at her, she reached up and pushed a curl off her cheek, displaying obviously home-done, red-polished nails, one broken to the quick.

"You're writing that book, aren't you?" The man waved me over with a calloused hand. I nodded, easing onto a stool at the counter. The man tapped a pack of cigarettes on the table, going on before I could say a word. "Well, don't believe anything that dog-woman tells you. She can tell a lie quicker than I can tell the truth."

"I'll keep that in mind," I said, glancing at my recorder. The couple's eyes followed me. "Just making sure it's on," I explained. The man continued. They were local ranchers and had known Barbara and Bob Erickson well, although they were not friends. Her name was Audrey; I never got his.

"Barbara is very intelligent," Audrey told me. Completely at ease, she perched on the edge of the booth with her legs neatly crossed. "She has a good vocabulary, and she speaks on a wide range of topics, so she is evidently well read and good at telling people what they want to hear. She reads people pretty well."

The rancher took a sip of coffee. His hands were gigantic, his finger unable to fit through the handle of his cup. "She *uses* people," he said with a sigh. The rancher lifted his chin and nodded as I heard the door behind me open and close. I turned to see a man who could have been the rancher's brother or son—same hat, boots, and jeans, same face, wind-blown and leathery. The man nodded at us on his way to the coffee pot behind the counter. He poured himself a cup and sat on the stool next to me, facing forward.

Audrey waited until the man was seated. She lifted her large glasses and rubbed the side of her nose with one finger. "She would sit in here for hours, sometimes," Audrey told me, "and when a stranger walked in, she'd strike up a conversation like they was old friends. The next stranger comes, she ignores him...like she somehow knew when a person was not favorable toward her."

Brian returned to the register eying a handful of cash, which he immediately thumbed through, his lips whispering each number.

The rancher picked up his cowboy hat and slid out of the booth. Standing, he towered over me. Apparently, my interview with them was coming to an end. "Barbara is very opinionated," he said. "She will come right out...just right off the bat...whether it be politics or her animals, or whatever...she will say it like it is."

"Most of us don't have the education or knowledge to deal with someone like her," Brian added, "the way she will not take 'No' for an answer. The way she can—when confronted—just have a response that quick." He snapped his fingers.

"Her mind is sharp," the rancher added, "and you can never quite figure out what's truthful and what's not."

Brian went on, and Audrey and her rancher husband again sat, listening. "The owner of The Merc over in Adrian, Oregon walked in here one day and asked me if I knew the woman using the pay phone outside. I knew her name, all right, but at the time, I'd never spoken to her. 'Don't give her any credit,' he told me. Seems she owed him for some dog food."

Brian shook his head.

"It was Barbara Erickson," he said. "A couple months later, Barbara pulled up for some gas, and I went out to wait on her. She immediately hit me up for credit. I said, 'No. I'm not going to do it.' But Barbara is unlike any person I've ever known. She was adamant. She was going to get what she wanted."

Brian paused and looked into my eyes wearing the same expression he'd offered me at our first meeting. "I have come to know a lot about her," he said. "She is pretty headstrong, but I can be, too. We butted heads out there...'No... Yes...No.' She made promises...'I will pay you back in a day or two,' she said, but I kept saying, 'No, I will not.' Eventually, I turned and walked into the store here, but Barbara was right on my heels. I'll never forget it. Come right in with me, and we had more than a little bit of a set-to."

He stopped and studied his shoes. When he didn't go on, I jumped in. "What happened?" I asked.

Brian shook his head again and laughed. "She won," he said. "I weakened." He cocked his head to one side, every neatly-clipped, burnt umber hair in place. "She has tenacity. Most people will not have a comeback for you. She always has a comeback. I said, 'Barbara, we'll both be upset when you can't pay, and things between us will deteriorate.' And she said, 'Oh, but we're good enough friends that I would never let that happen.'"

Brian laughed without humor.

"You would have thought we'd known each other for years...the way she spoke of me as a friend." He paused, his mouth open, searching for the right words. "Looking back, Barbara probably knew within minutes of meeting me how she could get her way," he said.

The rancher and his wife stood to go.

"I will say this," Brian finished, "for a couple of years she was good about her charging. She made her payments."

"I wonder if that was part of the con," the rancher said. He handed some money to Brian. "This is not Barbara's first rodeo. I don't know if she purposely set out to con you, but as her population of dogs grew and money became tighter..." He didn't finish.

"I'm torn about it," Brian said, "because the finger points both ways. It's easy to say that it's Barbara's fault, but the finger also points back at me, because I allowed it."

The rancher nodded. He held out a large, nicked-up hand for his change, not counting it. I watched him leave with Audrey, then looked across the counter at Brian—a careful, decent man, a man more concerned about being righteous than right.

"My grandfather bought this land and the building for twelve hundred dollars," Brian said. "He taught my father, who taught me, that we provide a needed service, and we do it honestly. That was the number one thing for my grandfather. For my father and me, too."

"How do you think he would have handled Barbara?" I asked. I set my tape recorder on the counter. Brian looked at it for a moment before answering.

"When confrontation happened over a bill or a credit issue, my dad was ready for it," he said. "I think he thrived on it. My mom handled those situations with a little more tact. Don't get me wrong. She was dead-set and resolute in her ways, but she left people with a sense of dignity. I tried to incorporate her way when I dealt with Barbara."

Three teenage boys burst through the door, leaving it wide open. One of them, all pimples and squeaky voice, caught Brian's disapproving glance and kicked the door shut with his foot, carrying out an exaggerated bow as his two friends browsed the cooler for sodas. He quickly joined them, and they each found a Coke, holding it up for Brian to see. Just before flopping into the booth the doorbell clanged, and a white-haired man in soiled coveralls and a seed cap stood at the door eyeing each person as if taking a head count. The man crossed the small room with a noticeable limp, poured himself of cup of coffee, and took a seat at the counter.

"You must be the writer," he said. I looked at him, and he smiled, showing me a full set of coffee-stained teeth.

"Brian's been on the nursing home board in Vale for fourteen years," the old man said, looking at me. "I don't think anyone has ever thought of Brian Coleman as being a taker, he's more of a giver."

Brian sniffed as if to dismiss the remark. "I seem to be geared toward older people," he said. "Probably because my parents were older. I like being around the elderly, sharing experiences, talking. You know, just being with them."

"You accepted Barbara when other people in Harper shut her out," I said.

Brian thought for a moment. "We're pretty close-knit here in Harper," he said, "and believe me, everybody knows what everyone else is doing. But when outsiders like the Ericksons move in, it clams people up."

"Especially people like the Ericksons," the old man chipped in.

"I think maybe you would call it a rural mentality," Brian said.

I interrupted before the old man had a chance to begin another story. I was there to find out about Barbara. "What did the local people think about all the dogs?" I asked.

Brian answered for both of them. "We knew there were a lot of dogs, but we didn't know how many. I once heard my cousin—he's their neighbor—anyway, he thought there might be a hundred dogs there. We had no idea there were over five hundred."

"Nobody did," the old man added. He shook his head. "People wondered how they could afford to feed all them dogs. Rumor was they sometimes gave them road-kill to eat."

"No one was ever allowed inside the house," Brian said. "Barb came out to the front yard before you made it to the door, and the Sheriff couldn't do anything as long as the outside dogs were fed. My cousin, Don Coleman, complained to the health department. Oh boy, Barbara didn't like that."

He made a face.

"Don helped in the dog rescue, too. He knows more than I do 'cause he drove past the Erickson house all the time. Maybe you should talk to him."

Brian continued to talk, but it was mostly to rehash the same story. People knew. They complained. Nothing could be done. The gossip faded in the summer and resurfaced when winter forced the dogs penned outside to live in the cold and the mud. I stayed an hour longer, said my goodbyes, and headed out.

During the drive home, I thought about what I'd learned about Barbara Erickson in Harper, contrasting it with the reactions of people back in Boise. "In her next life," one of my friends had told me after watching a video of the rescue, "that woman should have to come back as one of her own dogs. She should suffer like they did." I thought about Brian Coleman, his compassion, and ability to accept Barbara, to show respect. Maybe she *had* suffered the way her dogs had. Maybe Brian could see it.

About twenty miles north of Harper, my stomach began to grumble, so I stopped off in Vale, pulling into a local eatery that was fronted by a hand-painted sign: BigBurger. Inside, two men roosted in one of the booths, gabbing with the waitress as I looked over the menu. I was hungry and ready to forget about Barbara Erickson and Harper, Oregon and dogs for more than a little while. The voices next to me rose and fell. Then, I heard a name...*Erickson*. I put down the menu and perked up, leaning toward the two men.

"I had to go into their house a few years ago to fill their oil," one of them said. "I worked for Consumers Co-op back in them days, and you couldn't walk anywhere in that house without stepping in dog shit."

"Oh man, I'm trying to eat here," the friend grumbled, his mouth full of food.

"I don't know how they could live like that, with all those dogs," the waitress offered. She was in her early thirties, neatly dressed with a pony tail and good posture, too old to be a college-girl waitress, but too young to have already settled on BigBurger. Her nametag was handwritten, Lois.

"Their bed frame was propped up against the wall, 'cause of the dogs," the oilman continued, "so who knows where they slept. And you wouldn't believe it...they had dogs on top of the dining room table and on every chair in the place."

"Did you call the sheriff or the humane society?" Lois asked in a soft voice.

"Hell, no." The oilman picked up his greasy burger. "There's nothing you can do."

Lois made a tight line with her lips and puttered off, clearing a cup and ashtray from the counter before slipping through the battered saloon doors that led into the cafe's tiny kitchen. The men watched her go, then went on talking.

But this time I wasn't listening. The oilman's words had angered me.

There's always something you can do, I thought.

Chapter Four

I drove back to Oregon the following week to meet with Don Coleman, Brian's cousin and an Erickson neighbor.

After reaching Harper, I drove past Coleman Service toward the Erickson house. I shivered as I approached. It appeared deserted and cold. The yard was stiff and crusted over after several days of sunshine. I headed down Coleman Road, which was little more than a dirt path meandering through hills covered by dried grasses, some faded and green, others amber or yellow. Driving slowly, I searched among the empty hills for signs of a dwelling. After a series of hairpin turns, the road became even more bumpy and uneven, and I had to fight the wheel of my Volkswagen Beetle, bouncing over large, sharp chunks of gravel for several more miles. Rounding another bend, several out-buildings appeared next to a tidy field of hay, and I was soon angling my car onto a groomed dirt driveway nestled between two hills.

It was obvious that I'd come to a working ranch. As I slowly drove toward the house, I had to dodge a rumbling tractor and a pair of ranch hands who reined in their skittish horses to make way. The driveway stretched up a low hill, swerved to the left, and finally opened into a grassy yard that fronted the house, an A-frame built by Don and his father that had huge, tinted, scalene windows and a two-story wing on one side. A stone walkway led to a redwood staircase extending up to the second floor entry of the wing.

I parked at the edge of the grass, grabbed my recorder and a notepad, and stepped out of my car just as a man on an all-terrain-vehicle came roaring up behind me. He was dressed like he belonged on a Western calendar: huge cowboy hat, rumpled chambray shirt, denim jeans, and dusty boots. The man climbed off his ATV as if dismounting a horse and approached me, one hand held out.

"Don Coleman," he said. "I've been expecting you."

Don Coleman was much like his cousin Brian—quiet, straightforward, and efficient. Without another word, he led me to the side of the house and up the solidly-built stairs. He held the door open, following after me into an expansive country kitchen that adjoined an equally spacious dining area. Don Coleman's home, like the rest of his ranch, was wide open and inviting. I was immediately drawn to a pair of huge windows that revealed a panoramic view of the wide Oregon sky hanging over pristine hills and fields. From this high vantage point, I could see the entire ranch.

"Quite a view," I said, as I walked back to the kitchen.

Don motioned to the chair he'd pulled away from his large table. I lay my notepad and tape recorder on the edge of its Maltese lace runner and took a seat.

"Can I get you a cup of coffee?" he asked, as he walked into the kitchen.

"No thanks," I answered, pulling off my coat.

Don joined me at the table. "Brian said you like to tape these deals," he said.

I laughed and pushed the "record" button. "The tape recorder has a better memory than I do," I said. Don Coleman studied my recorder just as his cousin had done. "So, tell me about the Ericksons," I started. A few moments passed, making me wonder if he'd reconsidered the idea of an interview. Leaning on his elbows and gazing out the window, he began.

"I had to pass by that place every day," Don said, "had to stop in front of their house to check my mail." He wrinkled his nose. "I hated it—that smell and all the barking. Sometimes, the dogs would be yapping, and Bob'd shoot one of 'em with a BB gun. They'd yip and bite the dog next to 'em." He shook his head. "I'd see Barbara hobbling around in the yard with all them dogs, but I never met her until the day she chased down my pickup."

Don paused, allowing a tight-lipped, crooked smile.

"You mean her *dogs* chased your pickup, don't you?" I said.

Don laughed. "No," he went on, "Barb chased me, even though she gimps like hell. She saw me coming and waved me down, then jumped into the passenger seat. 'I need a ride to Coleman Service,' she told me, big as life. 'You goin' that way?' Seems Bob had the car. Barb was pretty pissed about it. 'He shoulda known not to take it today,' she told me."

Don laughed again. "She says to me, 'I need it to go to Idaho where I practice law.' She thought Bob was down in Vale drinking beer and gambling.

She wanted to use Brian's phone to call him. She was probably right, too. Dog shit Bob used to get drunk over in Vale all the time. He shoulda been hauled in for drunken driving more than once, but nobody wanted to arrest him 'cause he stunk too bad. Anyone else woulda been in jail."

He hesitated as if waiting for me to respond. "What did you do when Barbara jumped in your truck?" I asked.

Don cocked one eyebrow, a smile on his face. "Have you *met* Barbara?" he asked.

"We've spoken," I said.

Don shook his head and issued a grunt of amusement. "Well then, you know that she ain't one to take 'No' for an answer. I took her to Coleman Service."

That had been his first face-to-face meeting with Barbara, and his cousin Brian had gently ribbed him after he drove up with the "dog woman." It was only fair. Don had been doing the same to Brian for weeks. As I listened, Don told me about it:

"Getting to be good friends with your neighbor?" Brian asked, winking at Don's father, Frank Coleman, who sat in the corner booth.

"That's the first time I met her," Don said, nodding at his dad. He pulled a stool from the counter and sat. "She just hopped in my truck and said she wanted to go see her boyfriend, Brian." He cackled at his own joke.

"You're the one who's been up at her house," Brian countered.

They went back and forth at each other, trading viciously hilarious barbs, a ritual that dated back nearly to the cradle for these two old friends. Frank broke it up.

"What's she doin' with you?" he asked his son.

"She's looking for Bob," Don answered. He paused. "And you know what? She says she's a lawyer." He was answered by loud laughter from Frank and another of Brian's customers, a thin-faced greyhound of a man with grease under his nails and long, straight hair. Brian merely smiled.

"I seen them building more pens," Don said, "They headed out in an old van and come back with more dogs...twenty or thirty, at least. I'll tell you, I didn't think the smell could get worse, but yesterday they burned a big pile of dog shit and threw a couple of the dead dogs on it."

"Oh, man!" the greyhound man whined. "You gotta be kiddin' me!"

Don was starting to answer when the door banged open. The three men's abrupt silence was matched only by their newfound fascination with the Formica countertop. Facing forward, they hunched over their coffee cups, eyes downcast.

"Smells like dog shit in here," Frank said under his breath.

Barbara Erickson hesitated, her gray hair whirling about her face, a ratty muffler wrapped around her neck. She didn't come in, instead holding the door ajar as she appraised Frank Coleman with bold, fierce eyes. "Smells more like cow shit to me," she snapped, slamming the door shut. Burning a look into their backs, Barbara limped to the cooler, still muttering, "Or horseshit, or maybe it's just bullshit." She grabbed a Coke from the cooler, set it on the counter, and smiled warmly at Brian. "How you doin' today, Brian?"

Brian smiled back, ignoring the wheezy snickers coming from the counter area. "Just fine, Barbara. How's your hip in this weather?"

"Oh...not good," Barbara answered, handing him some change. She seemed pleased that he'd asked. "The doctor said I need a hip replacement, but, shoot, I can't afford it." Barbara glanced at the men sitting at the counter. "I got babies to feed, and I'll never let them go hungry no matter how bad my hip hurts."

The register clanged. Brian took a coin from the change tray and gently laid it in Barbara's palm. "Can't the doc give you something for the pain?" he asked.

Barbara snorted with disgust. "He gave me some pain pills one time, and it took me three days to get over it. I had a sick baby to take care of—a little Chihuahua I named 'Teeny-Weeny' cause she fit in the palm of my hand— and the pills made me forget what to do. So, I said 'No way.'"

Brian shut the drawer and nodded. "It's gotta be tough, taking care of all those dogs."

"Well, I'm a tough broad," Barbara answered, her face flushed with pride. She crossed to the door and turned, glaring at Frank Coleman and the man at the counter, afterward slamming the door behind her.

Laughter erupted from the men inside the store. "I heard that Ray Huff went out there and cited them," Frank Coleman said. "Barb held a BB gun under his chin and threatened him."

"There's not much intimidates her," Brian said.

"She got so she hated me," Don recalled as he finished his story, "because I called the health department and the sheriff's office to complain. The Sheriff couldn't do nothin'. Later, I heard they—Barb and Bob—had come here from Adrian, Oregon. Bill Cummings—he was the chief of police in Nyssa—he said they went by maybe four different last names." Don chuckled and shook his head. "One of the names they used was Wilson 'cause they lived on Wilson

Lane. They finally got kicked out 'cause of the dogs and not paying their rent. Bob Derby—he's a vet in Nyssa—they got into him for quite a bit of money, too. Something like eight hundred dollars."

I glanced toward the window where a low-hanging sun told me that it was about four o'clock. I needed to get going.

"She and Bob smoked like hell," Don offered. "You would think they'd both get diseases from that and living in that dog shit. They had no heat, either. I figured some winter they'd die or freeze to death. Far as that goes, Bob might have died, and no one would ever know. Nobody was ever allowed inside the house. Barb wouldn't even let the paramedics in. Couple times she was having trouble breathing and called an ambulance and *walked* out front to *meet* them."

"What about Bob?" I asked. "What part did he play in all this?"

Don leaned back in his chair, arms folded across his chest, his lips pursed. "He went along with whatever Barb wanted," he said after a moment. "She told people that Bob had Alzheimer's, and he was kinda slow. I guess Bob sometimes complained about having all the dogs, but if anybody asked, he'd claim they couldn't afford to spay them."

As Don went on talking about Barbara, he seemed more concerned than angry. "She spent hours sitting in Coleman Service, talking to Brian," Don said. "She'd smoke cigarettes and tell stories about spending time in Korea and Vietnam or nursing John F. Kennedy back to health when he was shot in World War II. No one ever believed her, but Brian would listen."

"She seemed closer to Brian than anyone," I said.

"Yeah," Don replied. His face brightened, and he continued. "She'd bring him coconut cream pies that she made herself, and they *were* really good. She said it was 'cause they were made with real coconut milk." Don laughed and slapped his knee. "I told Brian that she used dog milk! He couldn't eat 'em after that."

Not long after, I was bouncing back up the road, thinking about Don's story. Behind me, the Coleman ranch was again hidden by hills that made long shadows as the day approached its end. I was eager to make it back to Boise before rush hour but stopped for a moment and grabbed my notepad. Don told me he'd notified the health department and the sheriff's office several times, and I was curious about the details of the complaints. I made a note to get copies of the records. He'd also mentioned a name I'd heard before: Ray Huff.

Chapter Five

September 1926—Kittitas County, Washington.
Sherroni Nonoma Hawkes slid into the hands of a midwife and gulped her first breath of sweet orchard air. It was September 15, 1926 in the fruit-picking county of Kittitas, Washington. Born the second child of Almon and Rose Mae Hawkes, Canadian Cree Indians, she was their "Shining Star Over Big Water." Five more children would follow: Bonnie, Shirley, Loretta, Virginia, and Mikey, joining Sherry and older brother, Al Junior. Scratching out a hardscrabble existence, the Hawkes family lived in a tumbledown, seven-room house with Almon's parents—Grandpa and Grandma Hawkes—in the farming community of Badger Pocket. There, they eked out a living raising sheep and chickens and selling fruit from their small orchard. A large vegetable garden added to the usual family dinner of boiled chicken and home-canned fruit.

When Sherry was three-years-old, the Great Depression hit with America's farmlands among the most affected. Still, Almon and Rose Mae managed to stay on the farm even after the development of cold-climate apple varieties caused their own fruit sales to fall off. By the mid-1930s, increased competition from counties to the north had resulted in lower demand for the Hawkes's crop. However, it also meant abundant stores for canning, a process performed by Rose Mae and Grandma Hawkes that could take as long as a month. Sherry and Al Junior were enlisted as helpers, spending many days retrieving fruit from the cool stock cellar under the farmhouse.

Al Junior flung open the trap door to the cellar, releasing a bouquet of fruity aromas. A ladder dropped into the darkness below. He watched as his little sister, seven-year-old Sherry, put her foot on the first rung. She wore her brother's old shoes. Without looking, she started down into the tomb of unsold apples, the ladder creaking and swaying

31

with each step. Al Junior followed, navigating the steps above her so quickly, he caught her finger between his brand new Oxfords and the splintered edge of the rung.

"Oweee!" Sherry cried. She yanked her hand back and dropped to the cellar floor. Immediately, she scrambled to her feet, shaking the straw and sawdust from her dress. "You clodhopper," she yelled at her brother. "I'm tellin' Mom!"

"Aw, quit your whinin' and hold out your apron," Al said.

Sherry obeyed, fashioning a makeshift hammock with her oversized apron. She waited as Al rolled a handful of apples into the apron, and another handful, and another. Finally, with a satisfied grunt, Al tied the calico corners together and sent her up the ladder. With one hand gripping her apron, Sherry began to climb. Her finger throbbed as she grabbed each rung, but she kept going. Nearing the top, she squinted against the sunshine, at the same time feeling an apple drop from her heavy bundle. She looked down to see it just miss her brother's head and thump to the earthen, cellar floor. Sherry smiled and eased her grip on the apron a bit more. The other apples tumbled out, one after the other, bombing Al who waited below. He howled as an apple hit him in the face and ducked away, disappearing into the darkness. Sherry knew a moment later he would be clambering up the ladder, but it was too late. She had already bolted from the cellar and into the adjacent cornfield, bubbling with glee right down to her second-hand shoes.

Sherry ran as fast as she could, not slowing until Al's cries had faded into the crackle of the dried cornstalks that brushed her face and chest and arms as she raced along. The afternoon sun had warmed the field, releasing the perfume of autumn, and Sherry took in great gulps of musty-sweet air, running until her sides hurt. Finally, she stopped and listened, not moving. There was no sound. Al was not chasing her. After a few moments, she sat and examined her finger. The cuticle was red and swollen, and there was a smudge of dirt on the knuckle. Sherry stuck her finger in her mouth, afterward wiping it on her apron. Minutes passed. All around, there was silence. She was safe. The cornfield had taken her in.

With Al and chores abandoned, Sherry remembered her snake family, a nest of blue racers she'd found near the pond the day before. I need to check on them, she thought, and the ducks, too. Have they left for the season? There was much to be done. Sherry jumped to her feet and clomped down the furrow between the stalks to the edge of the field. Once there, she hesitated, eyed her surroundings like a wild animal, then sprang forward through the underbrush over a rotting, fallen cottonwood and into the tall bunchgrass that surrounded a small, muddy pond. She had gone to her thinking spot.

Sherry looked under the cottonwood log, but the racers were nowhere to be found. Next, she looked for the mallards. They, too, were gone. Standing waist-deep in the grass, mesmerized by the gentle splash of water against the bank, she looked across the gently rippling pond. Often, on warm days, hours would pass before she left this spot, but a cooling breeze made her shiver, and she remembered what had happened in the apple cellar. Her brother would be mad when she returned, her mother, too. She had chores for Sherry to do. Sherry sighed, knowing that she had to go back.

After checking under the cottonwood log one last time, she reluctantly began the long walk home, trudging along sadly, dragging her feet in the dust. As the warm sun overhead and the fluttering breeze made her forget what awaited her, Sherry began to skip, slowly at first, then faster and faster. She twirled and skipped all the way back to the house. Once there among the peach trees in the backyard, her brother and chores were forgotten. Her twirls turned into lengthy spins. She twirled and spun until she was dizzy, fell to the ground, and rested on her back in the soft grass, waiting for the trees to stop dancing around her.

"Sherry, come help me with this floor."

Her mother's gravelly voice shot out the back door of the shabby farmhouse. Sherry stood and grabbed the small trunk of a peach tree. She peeked through the branches at her mother's face. Rose Mae Hawkes had a look that meant business. Queasy from spinning, Sherry stumbled across the wild grass lawn to the porch. She swung open the screen door and was met by flies and the smell of damp wood. Dirty water sloshed about in a bucket just inside the door, a thin coating of foam the only evidence that soap had ever been added. She pulled Al's old shoes from her dainty feet, eyeing the blisters they left behind before stepping onto the damp floorboards.

"Here." Sherry was handed a scrub brush. "Get those corners and edges," her mother demanded, a cigarette bobbing precariously between her lips.

Sherry dipped the brush into the bucket, trying to keep her fingers out of the dirty water. Within seconds her hands were wet, and every cut and hangnail stung from the lye. "Oweee!" she cried. "How come Al don't have to help?"

There was no answer, prompting her to look up and scan the room. Her mother had left, gone like the snakes and ducks at the pond.

Sherry worked on the floor's unpolished corners and edges for what seemed like the whole afternoon. Once finished, she stretched her hand above her head as far as she could and dropped the brush into the bucket. Water splashed onto the floor. Sherry ignored it, listening for footsteps and the voices of her mother and her brothers and sisters. The house was silent. She was alone.

Still barefoot, Sherry padded on cold, wet feet to the back bedroom she shared with her three sisters. For once, the room was empty. She plopped onto her bed and melted into the mattress. The damp hem of her dress clung to her raw knees like a pair of cool bandages. Sherry didn't mind being alone. It was quiet. A soft breeze fluted through the room's only window, gently lifting its gauzy curtains. Her eyes closed and she pulled her quilt up to her chin, snuggled in, and let go of the day.

"I'm gonna take a nap with my little baby, Sherry."

The muffled voice crept through the cracks in the door. Sherry stiffened and ground her eyes shut. The door creaked open, then closed with a click. She heard footsteps and curled up under the bedcovers, waiting for the familiar, awful smell—a sour mixture of alcohol, tobacco, and sweat.

Her grandpa slid under the quilt, and in one fluid move, embraced her from behind like a spider taking its prey. She felt his hands on her body, his hot breath against her neck, his whispers that didn't make words. Her body began to jerk. She whimpered for help, but the heavy door remained closed. The jerking took on a rhythm, and Sherry buried her face in the pillow, letting her mind drift until she was floating on the breeze that had lifted her curtains, lost in the safety of a dream—outside, far away from her room, watching a scrawny mama cat as she bobbed through the tall grass, her kittens rolling along behind her, pouncing on each other, stopping occasionally to keep an eye on Mama.

When he was done, Grandpa rolled over, and Sherry heard the zip of his pants as he wriggled under the quilt. His smell made her gag. She lay motionless, waiting, listening carefully. When his labored breathing had turned into a snore, she slipped down the hall to the bathroom holding her damp panties against her bottom. Perched on the toilet—a bench with a hole in the middle and a pot positioned beneath—her pink feet curled inward as the pee stung her tender flesh.

Outside the bathroom door, she heard a familiar clickety-clack sound. Dog toenails were tapping the wood floor. It was Lady, a two-year-old collie, and Buddy, a German shepherd. Lady nudged open the bathroom door, and the two dogs bounded in. They danced around Sherry, licking her knees and looking for fun. Sherry hopped off the toilet and led her playmates out to the backyard, where the dogs began to frolic among the hens. She grabbed a stick from the woodpile and raced to the barn. Joyously, Lady and Buddy chased after her, leaving chickens squawking in the dust.

Inside the barn, Sherry flung the stick to the top of the haystack and followed the dogs as they scrambled through the hay. Buddy found the stick first, gripping it proudly in his mouth, spinning wildly to keep it from Lady. With a laugh, Sherry pounced on him and pulled the stick away. Holding it high, she sat down at the very top of the haystack, throwing the stick toward the barn door. In a flurry, the dogs disappeared, chasing each other into the yard as tiny flecks of hay drifted through the air and landed on Sherry's dress. A moment later, Lady reappeared at the barn door with the stick in her mouth. Up the haystack she came, her tail wagging. At the top, the collie curled up at Sherry's side and gnawed on the stick. Sherry gently stroked her long fur. Buddy soon followed, wandering in and scaling the haystack like a mountain climber. He found a resting spot next to his two friends. Protected by her dogs, Sherry fell back onto the hay and slept.

For two more years, Sherry Hawkes was visited in bed by her grandfather. She kept her mouth shut. At nine-years-old, she began sleeping in the barn. Lady and Buddy and a quilt warmed her through the long nights.

"What's my baby Sherry doing out here?"

Her grandfather stood at the threshold of the barn door, silhouetted by rays of afternoon sun. "You come inside now," he cackled.

"No!" Sherry fired back at him. She reached out to her dogs. "Daddy said I could sleep out here."

Lady sat on one side and Buddy on the other, standing guard over her like Chinese Fu Dogs.

The old man scowled. "Don't sass your Grandpa, now," he growled. He climbed to the top of the haystack. "Give me your hand."

"No," Sherry whimpered, clinging to her dogs. "I'm gonna tell Daddy."

Her grandfather had made it to the top of the haystack and was not too out of breath to issue a contemptuous snort. "Oh, no you won't." He pointed a wrinkled finger at her face. "I'll tell everyone you're a liar. Sherry, the little liar, makin' up stories again." He laughed, fisting his hands into his hips. "Now, get up," he ordered.

With low, rumbling growls, the dogs eyed the old man.

"No," Sherry squeaked.

"Don't you sass me, you little skunk," Grandpa Hawkes thundered. He grabbed her hand. With his movement, Lady stood and growled, her teeth bared.

"Get outa here, varmint," Grandpa roared. He flung an arm at the dog. Lady dodged and cowered, but Buddy's throaty rumbles erupted into barks, and he lunged forward. Canine teeth found flesh. Grandpa shrieked and flailed, breaking free of Buddy's grip only to fall backward off the haystack. Lady, her courage regained, leaped on him, pinning Sherry's grandfather to the ground, her teeth at his throat. Realizing he was in a serious fight, Grandpa Hawkes swung his arms frantically, catching Lady on the side of the jaw with his fist. Her wail pierced the air as she was knocked away, and Grandpa Hawkes used the opening to scramble to his feet. He glanced at Sherry, and, for a split second, her heart jumped into her throat. Without a word, the terrified old man ran as Buddy leapt from the haystack and chased him back to the house, barking angrily until the door had been slammed shut and locked.

Back in the barn, Sherry remained motionless, her mouth agape, dress clutched tight in her fists. Lady climbed up beside her. Together, they waited. After a few moments, a familiar figure appeared in the doorway below. It was Buddy. His tail wagging furiously, he bounded up the haystack into Sherry's embrace, and she smothered him with kisses.

Outside, the day began to lengthen, and with it, the sun's rays flattened, al-

lowing cold and darkness to fill in the corners of the barn. Sherry shivered and settled more deeply into the warm hay. Lady and Buddy snuggled in beside her. Sherry hugged them, closing her eyes and listening to their breathing, to the distant beat of their hearts. Evening passed gently into night, and the barn remained quiet and safe. Her grandfather did not return. All around the farm, autumn chill was settling in, bringing a moon that, later that night, would reach fullness for the second time in a month. But Sherry never saw it. Long before its pale, blue light was cast on the hay, she had at last relaxed alongside Lady and Buddy, surrendering to her two friends who whimpered and licked her face as if cleaning an open wound.

Chapter Six

Ray Huff turned out to be an inspector from the Malheur County Health Department. "I went out to the Erickson house the first time in 1998 and found about a hundred dogs in the yard," he told me when I phoned him. His voice was soft, almost inaudible.

"What was it like inside?" I asked.

There was a long silence, but I could hear his breathing and the shuffling of papers. He was still on the line.

"Who are you again?" he asked, louder this time. It reminded me that I was following a live case. Barbara and Bob Erickson were going to trial eventually. Ray Huff would probably be called to testify. Anything he said to me might come back to haunt him. I understood his concern. I had worked court cases and knew the drill. I introduced myself again, reiterating how I'd gotten his name and number and explained my contract with Barbara. Then, I played my trump card.

"I really respect your caution," I told him. "I've worked in the court system as a guardian ad litem and have seen how cases can be messed up when officers talk too much."

There was a pause. Finally, he spoke. "Like I was saying, I found about a hundred dogs in the yard, but the Ericksons wouldn't let me in the house. That Barbara Erickson was a real character, I remember. Told me she was a vet and a lawyer."

I scribbled notes, listening to him describe what he'd found.

"The animals in the yard seemed to be cared for. They had straw to lie on, shelter provided by makeshift sheds, and food and water. But there was dog poop everywhere. So, I warned the Ericksons to remove the waste."

"Did they comply?" I asked.

"They agreed to clean up twice a week," he answered. "It was all I could do at the time. I couldn't go in the house without a search warrant."

I wanted to ask why he hadn't pursued a search warrant, but he went on.

"I'll send you a copy of the file. If you have more questions, just call me."

A week later, I found a thick manila envelope folded and crammed into my mail box with an official return address: Oregon Department of Health. Handwritten in large, blocked letters was my name. It was misspelled, but I didn't care. Ray Huff had come through. I headed for my office, pulling at the sticky flap of the envelope.

According to the documents, neighbors had called the Oregon Health Department in 2000 and 2001 to complain about the smell coming from the Erickson farm. Each time, Huff investigated, afterward ordering the Ericksons to remove the waste. A new complaint filed in April of 2002 led to a citation for violating a Malheur County ordinance by "committing or permitting to be committed the accumulation of putrescible solid waste from September, 2001 to March, 2002." The violation carried a fine of five hundred dollars. When the Ericksons removed the waste, Huff dropped the fine.

I sighed, stretching out the ache in my back. I was disappointed. Ray Huff's information was new, but still offered no explanations. *Why had it happened? How had it been allowed to happen?* I gathered up the papers and tossed them onto my desk next to a steadily growing stack of interview transcriptions. Somewhere up there lay the un-transcribed tape of my interview with Don Coleman. I leaned back on my elbows, recalling my trip to his ranch—the rolling hills and fields of hay, the panoramic view from his living room window. I remembered something else from our interview—Don had called the sheriff to complain. I jumped up and went to my desk.

A few pecks later, the homepage of the Malheur County Sheriff's Office popped up. The Web page was standard issue—an easy scroll-down with no hyperlinks to other sites. A properly idealistic mission statement ran the length of the page with pictures of the department's officers zigzagging within the blocks of text. Sheriff Bentz struck a pose for the first picture. He was leaning on his elbows, hands folded over a stack of papers. His drawn-down mustache and the slope of his shoulders brought to mind Wally the Walrus. In a good cop-bad cop scenario, I had him pegged as the good cop.

Undersheriff Wolfe held the second spot on the page. He'd been photographed while sitting in an oak armchair behind his desk. In the picture, he was talking on the phone, his back at a perfect right angle to the floor, the pronounced line of his jaw and the level width of his shoulders reminding me of a *GQ* model. His dark brown hair, close-cropped on top and buzzed over the ears, matched his eyes and uniform, completing an image that stood in stark contrast to his desk, where a jumble of papers and post-it notes surrounded a bulky gray monitor, leaving little space for the phone and tape recorder. More paper hung from a corkboard on the cinderblock wall behind him.

Keeping my eyes on Wolfe's photo, I called the number at the bottom of the Web page. To my surprise, he answered the phone himself. When I explained the reason for my call, he jumped in before I could finish. "I remember this case well," Undersheriff Wolfe said. "It's not one I'm likely to forget." His voice was as clear and sharp as his Web site photo as he went on, easily recalling specific details.

He had received several complaints about the Ericksons, beginning in 1997 when they'd moved to Adrian, Oregon, a farm town on the Idaho border, directly west of Harper. "One guy told me he'd bought a sick puppy from Barbara," he remembered. "He was worried about the health of the other dogs, given the stink. Barbara wouldn't let him inside their mobile home."

"Did you investigate?" I asked.

Wolfe didn't answer for a moment, making me afraid that I'd offended him.

"Yeah," he said, finally. "We got a call from a fella who said a couple was living on his property without permission. It was over by the Owyhee River." Wolfe cleared his throat and continued. "Me and my deputy went out there, to the river. They—the Ericksons—anyway, they were living in a camper-trailer." He went on, and I listened without interrupting, visualizing the scene in my head.

"Well, well—that's none other than Mrs. Erickson," Brian Wolfe said as he climbed out of his patrol car. Deputy Jim Wood, an ex-Marine whose heavy eyebrows pulled attention from a crew cut that was little more than five o'clock shadow, exited the passenger side and adjusted his thick, leather utility belt.

"The dog woman?" he said.

Wolfe nodded. They'd gotten an earful about Barbara and Bob Erickson from a number of locals, and he'd seen the couple around town, but this would be his first face-to-face meeting. Wolfe scrambled down a shallow embankment and approached the camp, his eyes quickly finding the Idaho license plate near the rear door of a small aqua-and-white travel trailer that was hooked up to a muddy pickup. He made a mental note of the license plate number. They'd picked a good spot, Wolfe thought. The Erickson's trailer was nestled under a pair of towering pines that gently swayed in the cool breeze. The nearby Owyhee River spilled over smooth rocks, creating a soothing rhythm.

As the two men drew nearer, a dozen or so small-breed dogs began barking. Their yaps alerted the other dogs, and the gentle sound of the nearby river was soon lost in a cacophony of yowling and woofing.

"Whoa," Deputy Wood said, raising his hands to his waist. "I feel like bait in a fishing hole."

Wolfe chuckled and was about to reply, when a door swung open and slammed against the side of the trailer, making a sound like a gunshot. Wolfe and Wood jerked, their hands instinctively reaching for their sidearms, their eyes fixed on a wild-eyed woman with long, frizzy-gray bangs and no makeup. She wore fuzzy slippers and a faded housedress. A small, plastic whistle dangled from the heavy shoestring she'd looped around her neck. It was Barbara Erickson.

Barbara paused in the doorway, glaring at the officers. She shut the door and awkwardly descended the two metal steps, moving through her riled pack, soothing them. "It's okay, baby," she murmured, reaching out to pat bobbing heads. Bob Erickson stood in black coveralls near the cab of their pickup smoking a cigarette, a large bag of dog food at his side and a blank expression on his face. After studying the officers for a few moments, he snuffed out the cigarette and began filling a row of plastic pans with dog food, ignoring the commotion around him. By now the whole pack of forty to fifty dogs were up and moving. They scurried about the campsite, barking and jumping, some running to the food dishes, others dashing toward the officers.

Wood issued a low whistle. "How many damned dogs do they *have*?" he asked. Wolfe didn't answer. The two men picked their way through the mounds of dog excrement, warily eyeing the dogs that circled them. Barbara watched, arms crossed over her chest, eyes narrow, a tight smile on her face.

"You can git your hands off them guns," she called out. "These dogs won't bother you."

"Mrs. Erickson," Wolfe called out. "I'm…"

"You don't know who I am," Barbara interrupted. She stepped forward, pointing a finger at his nose, but Wolfe didn't give her a chance to say more.

"Ma'am, I need to see some ID and the registration on your vehicle," he said. All around him, dogs were jumping and barking, but he kept his eyes fixed on Barbara. For a few moments, it was a western standoff. Neither was about to give in. Barbara broke first.

"Bob!" she yelled, looking straight into Wolfe's eyes. Behind her, Bob glanced over his shoulder as a pair of dogs tried to jump into the bag of food he was holding. He had the same blank look as before, something Wolfe would learn was typical.

"Get the registration out of the glove box, and grab my purse from the front seat," Barbara commanded. Her words were heavily enunciated. She watched her husband until he'd set the bag on the ground and headed for the truck. "He can't hear very well," she explained, grimacing at Wolfe who had pulled a small tablet from his jacket and was noting his observations that the pack appeared to be fed and cared for.

Deputy Wood nudged his arm, a salacious grin on his face. Wolfe followed his eyes to a pair of mating dogs rutting around in the dirt. He made another note that the pack will continue to grow.

"How many dogs do you have here?" Wolfe asked.

"I don't count 'em." Barbara bent to scoop a pup into her arms. "I just feed 'em and water 'em and love 'em." She kissed the dog on its head and let it scramble from her arms. The pup ran to the dog dishes and wriggled between a pair of larger mutts, trying to get at the food. Barbara watched him, a soft smile on her face. After a moment, she looked back at Wolfe, and her smile disappeared. She jabbed at the air with her finger. "Besides," she snapped, "there's no law in Oregon sayin' how many dogs you can have."

Wolfe smiled and nodded. A veteran officer, he knew better than to argue. "Well, you're right about that," he said. He glanced at Wood, then took a step toward Barbara, his movement casual, like a lion-tamer approaching one of his charges. "In Malheur County, you can have as many dogs as you can reasonably care for," Wolfe said.

"Here they are." The voice was Bob's. He'd returned from the truck with his ID, the vehicle registration, and Barbara's purse. He handed them to his wife and faded back. Leaning against the trailer, he lit another cigarette.

Barbara flung her purse over her shoulder and fished through it until she found her billfold, an oversized wallet bulging with frayed papers and envelopes but no money. She plucked her ID from a small pocket and handed it to Deputy Wood along with their truck registration and Bob's ID. Then, she stuffed her billfold back into her purse, glaring all the while at the deputy. Wood ignored her, turning and walking back to the patrol car. As he radioed to check for outstanding warrants, Barbara turned her attention back to Wolfe.

"Why are you out here harassing us?" she demanded, "Run out of coffee and donuts?"

"We got a call from a citizen," Wolfe said.

"Bob, get me a cigarette," she yelled. "I can't take this harassment!"

Wolfe took a deep breath. "Did you know you're on private property here?"

Barbara issued a dramatic cough in response, a great, gurgling thing that was followed by a gasp. For at least a minute, the coughs came in waves, leaving her out of breath. When finally the paroxysm stopped, Barbara dug through her purse to retrieve a cough drop.

From behind, Bob spoke. "Here ya go, Honey," he said, holding out an already lit cigarette. Barbara reached out, taking the cigarette between scissored fingers and bringing it to her lips. She sucked hard on the filter, allowing the thick stream to flow from her nose and mouth. Her face was as gray as the smoke.

"Are you all right?" Wolfe asked quietly. Barbara ignored his question, instead gesturing toward the bubbling river.

"This don't look like private property to me," she said, spitting out the words. She plopped down on the metal steps of the trailer and was immediately joined by a scroungy white terrier that jumped into her lap. She dandled the dog and ruffled its ears and touched his nose with her own. "Nobody owns that river," she said, still nose-to-nose with the terrier. Before Wolfe could respond, something caught his attention. His hand instinctively moved to his gun as he watched Bob open the door of pickup and lean far into the cab.

Wolfe felt something at his elbow. It was Deputy Wood, holding the Erickson's documents. "All clear," he whispered, eyeing Bob. The two officers rested their hands on their guns. They relaxed when Bob emerged from the truck with a bottle of water, a grin replacing his usually vacant expression.

Bob crossed to them and handed the water to Barbara. She looked up at him and smiled. "Thank you, Honey," she said in a gravelly voice. She spat her cough drop into the mud and a growling frenzy immediately broke out at her feet. Barbara watched it for a moment, then took a long drink as Bob waited patiently. When she'd finished, Barbara held out the bottle without looking. Bob took it, replaced the cap, and headed back toward the pickup where he resumed feeding the dogs, a fresh cigarette dangling from his thin lips.

Wolfe sighed. They were stalling.

"The owner wants you out of here," he said.

Barbara scowled. "Then he can come down here himself, and we'll see about it." She slapped her knee, and with the sound, several dogs tried to jump into her lap.

"No," Wolfe said, his voice steady and cool, "You need to pack up your things and move on. You're trespassing."

A few moments passed. Barbara stared at the ground, gritting her teeth, her cigarette held between violet lips. "Damn cops around here," she mumbled. Wolfe watched as her mouth continued to move, carrying on a silent conversation that he felt certain was not going in his favor. Barbara grabbed the handrail and pulled herself up with a loud grunt.

"Bob!" she yelled, her voice coarse and loud, making the dogs scatter. "Let's get to hell outta here!" Barbara took a long drag from her cigarette, dropped it to the dirt, and snuffed it with the toe of her fuzzy slipper. "We don't need this harassment," she added, glaring at Wolfe.

Bob appeared from around the front corner of the trailer. "Open that door," she ordered him, flinging an arm toward the trailer. She watched her husband lumber up the rusty steps, shouting after him. "And then go get the doggie bowls!" She elbowed her way past Deputy Wood and was met by a mass of furry, upturned faces. "Poor dogs wasn't even finished eating," she muttered.

Wolfe looked at his deputy and shrugged as he turned to head back to the patrol car. A shrill whistle made him jump. He whirled around, his hand again on his gun. Wood was grinning at him.

"She got ya," he said, wiggling an eyebrow toward Barbara who gave her whistle another toot. At the sound, even more dogs appeared, and Bob began herding them into the trailer as Barbara doddered over to the fire pit to fold up their frayed lawn chairs.

"You think just 'cause you have a piece of tin on your chest you can stick your nose where it don't belong," she said to Wolfe.

He remained silent. They were complying. That's all that mattered.

Twenty minutes later, Wolfe watched the Ericksons climb into their truck as Wood kicked at the cold ashes in the fire pit. Bob started the engine, and they slowly pulled out, the pickup groaning and creaking as it hauled their swaying trailer down the washboard road. A few moments later, they had disappeared behind the trees.

Wolfe shook his head as he and Wood walked back to the patrol car. "She's a feisty one," he said.

About a year after the encounter at the Owyhee River, citizen complaints began to trickle into Wolfe's office. The Ericksons had sold some puppies infected with parvovirus, and the dogs had died within several days of the sale.

"Barbara refunded the money," Wolfe told me, "but a lot of those folks were concerned about the other dogs in her care. I investigated each complaint, but the Ericksons wouldn't let me enter the house without a search warrant." He paused, awaiting the obvious question. When I remained silent, he answered it for me. "There wasn't enough probable cause to justify a search warrant. I had to look at the dogs that were actually in her care. None of the dogs we saw at the river looked sick, and there were signs of food and shelter. I couldn't get a search warrant to look inside the trailer without evidence that the outside dogs were being abused. I didn't see that."

A few seconds passed.

"I wish I had," he added forlornly.

Wolfe went on, explaining the current Malheur County ordinance that allowed residents to have as many animals as they could adequately care for. The ordinance fell short of protecting animals hidden from sight. I was disheartened, but Wolfe offered a glimmer of hope.

"The county is passing an ordinance that requires a kennel license if you harbor twenty dogs or more," he said. "Kennels are subject to inspection, so we'll be able to go inside a house, make sure it's sanitary for pets. That was the biggest problem with the Ericksons. We were never allowed access to the house where the living conditions were worse."

Undersheriff Wolfe didn't have much more to say. Complaints continued through the spring of 2002, when he called the Oregon Humane Society (OHS) who sent two undercover agents to the Erickson home under the pretense of buying a dog. They were invited into the yard, but, like Wolfe and the health inspector, they were not allowed to enter the house. The agents reported that the outdoor dogs were not overcrowded and had no visible wounds or signs of illness. The Ericksons had provided adequate food, water, and shelter. Once again, the scene lacked enough evidence of neglect to justify a search warrant.

Chapter Seven

In our contract, Barbara had agreed to once-per-week interviews and complied by calling me from a pay phone. After her release from jail, she and Bob had supposedly rented a hotel room but provided me no phone number. When I asked the name of the hotel, Barbara hedged. I suspected they were living in one of their vehicles, which raised yet another question. Undersheriff Wolfe had described a pickup and a trailer. I'd seen the trailer back at the Harper residence, surrounded by overgrown weeds, its tires flat and cracked. When I pulled the creaky door open, I found it stuffed with empty dog food bags and trash. Don Coleman had talked about a brown van they'd loaded with dogs. Supposedly, there was another vehicle—a Vega station wagon. It didn't make sense. Barbara was scamming for credit all over Malheur County, yet they owned four vehicles, plus the storage shed filled with furniture that Verda and I had discovered. I jotted a note: *Source of income? Inheritance? Government? What?*

Barbara's calls came randomly, sometimes collect. Mostly, she sounded cheerful and optimistic about her future, but at times tearfully bemoaned life without her dogs. She often shared anecdotes or complained about Verda. Now and then, she'd ask how the book was coming, and I told her who I had most recently interviewed. One afternoon, as Barbara launched into about the tenth retelling of the same story, I interrupted.

"I spoke with Undersheriff Wolfe on the phone," I said.

After a moment of dead silence, Barbara issued a snort. "That Brian Wolfe," she growled. "He's the instigator of it all. He's been tryin' to get me since we first come to Oregon. He told us that we couldn't stay in *his* county."

Her breathing was increasingly rapid and wheezy.

"That's illegal and against the law," she fumed.

I imagined her snapping at Wolfe's ankles like one of her unruly pups.

"It's not *his* county, and we weren't botherin' *nobody* down there by the river. We had us a little piece of land with a trailer on it and were mindin' our own business. He don't have any right to tell people to get out. That's against a person's constitutional rights." Barbara blathered on about Wolfe's cocky demeanor, her words rushing forth like water over a broken dam. "He's just tryin' to make a name for himself," she said, "actin' like a big shot. He don't care who he hurts." She paused and issued a thunderous cough followed by a sniffle. "He used his badge to kill my doggies," she gurgled.

I remained silent for a moment, taking it all in. I could almost see Barbara standing at the pay phone, her hip hurting, feeling embattled.

"It's all so sad," I offered.

Barbara said nothing for a moment. "That's okay. I had a friend report him to the FBI. They said he's liable for one hell of a lawsuit for telling us we had to leave *his* county." Her voice had become louder and more strident as if the act of throwing words into the air somehow gave them the ring of truth.

"Um-hum," I replied, although I knew Barbara didn't need a response. This wasn't a conversation. It was a monologue, and she simply needed an audience.

"Oh, you bet," she said, "and he don't know who he's dealin' with. I may be old and crippled, but I'm not one to be pushed around. The FBI told me they wanted to get Wolfe, but I told 'em, 'Don't do anything just yet.'" Barbara lowered her voice to a conspiratorial whisper. "I'm not at liberty to give out any more information," she confided, "but I do know that the FBI is tryin' to get rid 'a crooked courts here in Oregon. And CBS wants the story."

The phone seemed hotter against my ear, and I laid my head on my desk. I felt like a kid in school waiting for the last bell. Barbara abruptly took off in a new direction. "Hey, what does that Wolfe say about me? I bet he don't like me." Barbara stopped and waited for me to respond.

I stretched my back and sighed. "You know, he seems genuinely concerned about you," I said.

"Well, he knows not to mess with me," Barbara replied, her voice louder and more confident.

"I think he saw you as a person who wanted to help animals," I said. "The number of dogs just got to be more than any two people could handle alone."

"Oh, it wasn't that bad," she quickly responded. "Bob and I had a routine and everything." She didn't talk as her breathing quickened, followed by a tumble of angry words. "We was fine till Wolfe stuck his nose in it. And he made up a new name...animal hoarder. I wasn't an animal hoarder 'cause I sold the puppies and hoarders don't let their doggies go. But I didn't give 'em to just anyone. We'd keep 'em 'cause everyone has a right to live."

I mentally paged through the usual nonsense Barbara offered up as excuses: the cost to feed an unsold litter versus the cost to spay and neuter; bringing new puppies into the pack when the old ones hadn't sold yet; keeping ailing dogs alive as if death was worse than suffering. It all seemed so hopeless. I was suddenly wishing that someone would come to the door and give me an excuse to get off the phone. But then, Barbara offered up something new.

"Sara Sharette always wanted me to hand 'em over to her."

I grabbed a pen and began scribbling on a notepad. "Now, who is Sara?" I asked.

"I wouldn't trust her," Barbara advised. "She thinks she knows it all, and she don't know nothin'. She was probably workin' with Wolfe to get my dogs. She's with Second Chance." I wrote down the names and drew circles around them.

"Barbara, I have to go," I said. I was anxious to find out about Sara Sharette and Second Chance.

Chapter Eight

Summer 1935—Kittitas County, Washington.

The apple crop had been a good one, and Almon Hawkes was about to keep a promise he'd made many times over.

"Let's go you kids! We're goin' fer ice cream!"

From her room at the back of the house, nine-year-old Sherry heard the thump and clatter of feet joined by squeals of delight. She ran out into the narrow hallway and was nearly run down by Al Junior.

"Git yer shoes on," he shouted as he ran backwards. "Daddy's takin' us fer ice cream!"

Sherry couldn't believe it. The promise so often made was about to come true. She quickly pulled on her shoes, visualizing the little soda shop in nearby Ellensburg. Sherry loved the shop with the giant, pink ice cream cone painted on its huge, front window and the cheery, candy-striped awning overhanging the sidewalk. "Served With A Smile," the scooped lettering on the window promised.

Not bothering to tie her shoes, Sherry dashed through the house and out into the yard where the rest of the family waited by their old truck. It was a balmy day, the sky clear and cloudless. Chickens wandered about the yard, pecking at the ground while somewhere behind the house, a lamb cried out. Sherry looked around for Buddy and Lady. Maybe her father would let them come, too.

Little Bonnie toddled up to Sherry, giving her a gap-toothed grin. "We're gettin' ice cream!" she said, hugging herself with delight. "Daddy's takin' us fer ice cream!"

"I know," Sherry answered, looking around for her dogs. Al Junior came up from behind and gave her a shove.

"Served with a smile!" he shouted, following it with a great horse laugh.

Sherry glared and shoved him back.

"You kids get in the back, and quit hittin' each other or you won't get no ice cream," *Rose Mae yelled. She narrowed her eyes at the two oldest of her brood. Saying nothing, she climbed into the passenger seat of the truck.*

"Served with a smile, served with a smile," *Al Junior sang. Sherry ignored him, looking instead at her father.*

"Was it a good crop, Daddy?" *she asked.* "Was there lots of apples?"

Almon Hawkes lifted Bonnie, setting her down inside the rear bed of the truck, then studied his oldest daughter. He seemed confused. "We ain't gone to market yet," *he said.* "There ain't no apples sold."

Sherry was bewildered. "But you said we'd only get ice cream if the crop was good."

Almon Hawkes hesitated, a puzzled look on his hatchet of a face. Slowly, a grin spread across his nut-brown features. He dug into his pocket and pulled out a thin roll of greasy dollars. "Oh, I got it covered, little girl." *He waved the money in the air.* "This here trip's compliments of Buddy and Lady." *He winked at Grandpa Hawkes, who had appeared from the other side of the truck.* "Ain't that right?" *Almon said. He and his father erupted in laughter that doubled over the old man in a cough.*

"Whoa...you all right?" *Almon said. He motioned to his wife who climbed out of the truck and crossed to Grandpa, putting a handkerchief to his lips. When she pulled it away, it was stained red.*

"Served with a smile. Served with..." *Al Junior chanted, spinning in circles until Sherry grabbed his arm.*

"What does that mean?" *she asked him.* "'Compliments of Buddy and Lady.' What does that mean?" *Her voice was trembling.*

Al Junior stopped spinning and shook his head to clear it. He grinned at his little sister. "Dad sold 'em," *he said,* "and now we get ice cream." *He pulled his arm away and ran toward the truck.*

Sherry didn't move. She watched her brother as he leapt onto the rear flatbed. Near the cab, her mother stood beside Grandpa Hawkes with husband Almon on the other. The old man sagged in their arms.

...Daddy sold them!

Sherry felt faint, the sky overhead swirling, the ground trembling beneath her feet.

...Daddy sold them...Buddy and Lady...Daddy sold them!

She sank to the ground and pulled her knees to her chin, rocking back and forth, a low moan escaping her lips that became louder and louder, until she could no longer contain it.

"No!" *Sherry cried out.* "No!"

The plaintive cry made her mother look up.

"No!" Sherry cried out again, sobbing.

"Quit makin' a scene," Rose Mae snapped at her. Your grandpa's just coughin'. He'll be fine."

Sherry stared at her mother through watery eyes. "No!" she shrieked. "...Buddy! ...Lady! You sold them! They're gone!"

Rose Mae straightened, her brow wrinkled. Her eyes darkened as she understood. She glanced at her husband. His eyes were downcast, but his jaw throbbed with anger.

"You ungrateful, little..."

"Not Buddy and Lady," Sherry wailed.

"They bit your grandpa," her mother hissed, her face hard and narrow. "They woulda bit one of the young'ns, if we'd kept 'em. How woulda you liked that, if they bit Mikey." She went on without waiting for a response. "Quit yer blubberin'! You're nine years old. Act like it." She glared at her daughter, but for once, Sherry was unafraid, pointing her chin at her mother and glaring back.

"How could you?" she cried, her body shuddering.

Rose Mae released her grip on Grandpa's arm and reached her daughter in three, lightning-quick strides. "Stop yer bawlin' or I'll..." Without further warning, her hand crashed into Sherry's face. Sherry crumpled to the ground, but Rose Mae wasn't finished, thumping her on the back with the heel of one fist. "Stop yer bawlin'!" she shouted over and over until Almon pulled her away. "Stop yer god damned bawlin'!"

On the ground, Sherry opened one eye. Near the truck, her grandfather was on his hands and knees, a long string of rusty spittle hanging from his lips. Her mother stood a few feet away, pointing a long finger at her husband, her face as lethal as a rattlesnake. Rose Mae ran forward and gave Almon a shove that nearly knocked him down. She pointed again, her finger so close, it seemed to be touching his nose.

"Whatta we gonna do with her?" she screamed. "Why can't you do somethin' about her?

Al Junior, always happy to see his sister in trouble, had climbed down from the truck and now edged closer to watch. Without warning, Rose Mae Hawkes abruptly whirled and grabbed him, pinching his ear between her fingers and giving it a painful tug that sent him sprawling in the dirt.

"Git in the damn truck!" she shrieked.

Seeing the fat tears in Al Junior's wide eyes, Sherry felt the beginning of a smile. She remembered.

"My Buddy," she cried, grinding her eyes shut. "My Lady." A moment later, she felt hard, rough arms gathering her up.

"Shut the hell up," her father's voice roared.

Almon carried his daughter into the house and rolled her unceremoniously onto the kitchen floor. Still wailing, Sherry curled into a ball, never hearing her father's heavy footsteps, nor the bang of the door slammed shut with such force, it shook the thin windows of their house. A few moments later, the truck's engine growled and tires spun with the scattershot sound of gravel thrown against the house, but Sherry remained deaf. On the floor of the Hawkes kitchen, a storm of sobs ripped through her, making her stomach twist and her chest ache.

This is what it's like to die, she thought.

Sherry Hawkes slept for what seemed a long time. She dreamt of her friends: Buddy jumping in the grass to snatch a butterfly; Lady licking the tears from her face when Henny Penny died; the two dogs chasing each other around the barn, the ever-present stick in Buddy's mouth. In her dream, she ran her fingers through Lady's soft fur, felt the warmth of Buddy's body as he lay next to her, guarding her in sleep.

When she awoke, the room was dim. Outside, the sounds of daytime had faded save the distant call of a magpie. The curtains fluttered gently. Sherry lay on the floor where her father had left her, the smell of damp wood filling her nostrils. She lifted her head from the floor and winced from a sharp pain near her eye. Untangling her legs, she leaned on one arm, ignoring the exposed nailhead that dug into her palm. Her eyes wandered, following the long shadows slung across the kitchen floor, she listened intently. The darkened house was still, no bantering children or clattering dishes. No rumbling coughs.

Sherry stood and crossed to the door, looking out through the torn screen at a low-hanging sun that was casting its last faint rays at her feet. The yard was as deserted as the house, the chickens roosting in their coop, the sheep scattered somewhere behind the barn. Sherry took a deep breath, then issued a soft, thready whistle through gapped teeth. There was an immediate response, an almost inaudible thumping followed by a distant rumble. She caught her breath in a gasp. A second later, her hopes were dashed. The yard remained deserted. Her friends—her only friends—were gone. Her whistle had been answered by hope and the grumble of an empty stomach. Nothing more. The others—her mother and father and brothers and sisters, her grandfather and grandmother—were somewhere in Ellensburg, perhaps still at the little soda shop with the painted window.

She clenched her teeth, forming a hard knot in her jaw. Her father had waved the money in her face. Her mother had beaten her because she'd mourned her lost friends. Al Junior had taunted her, and Grandpa Hawkes...well, may God hurl a lightning bolt into the old man's chest.

"It doesn't matter," Sherry said aloud. She shoved open the screen door and

dashed toward the barn. "It doesn't matter," she shouted to the deserted farmstead as she scaled the haystack, kicking up a flurry of alfalfa dust. At the top, she sat watching the small blades of hay that drifted through the air and landed on her dress. Again, she whistled, but no one came. Sherry called out.

"Buddy! Lady!"

A barn swallow rustled its feathers from a dark corner above her, but there was no other sound. Below, the wide barn door was open, and she suddenly wished she'd closed it behind her. They would be home soon. It was getting darker, and they would all be home, rattling up in the old truck and piling out, filled with good cheer... and store-bought ice cream. All of them. Grandpa Hawkes, too.

From far away, Sherry heard a cry, a long, agonizing yowl that gripped her gut and tore at her heart. She covered her ears with both hands, but the yowl simply became louder and louder. Throwing herself backward onto the hay, she tried to burrow under it, her eyes ground tightly shut. The eerie cry became louder yet, and she opened her eyes, searching the darkness for the terrifying creature, her heart pounding like a timpani, her head exploding. She tried to scream, and only then did she realize that the sound was coming from her own lips.

In time, the old truck bounced back into the yard long after the sun had hidden behind the hills, allowing night to creep back into the apple orchards. Full bellies and tired eyes found comfort in their warm beds. No one looked for Sherry.

The following day, Sherry awoke before sunrise, a chill in the late summer air. She was cold and reached out for Buddy and Lady. Her hands found only the scratchy hay, and she remembered. They were gone. Sold to buy ice cream. Outside, a rooster crowed, and as if on cue, chickens appeared on the barn floor below the haystack, clucking like little busybodies as they scratched at the dirt. Almost immediately, a pair of scrawny cats dashed from a corner scattering the chickens in a flurry of feathers and cackling. Darting through the door, the cats spanned the open ground in a flash and disappeared into tall grass. Sherry had to pee.

She climbed off the haystack, crossed the yard to the house, and eased open the back door, lifting it slightly to dull the squeaking of its un-oiled hinges. Just inside the house, Sherry heard a distant snore and the creak of a bed. She tiptoed to the bathroom, rubbing the goose bumps that covered her arms and legs as she perched on the toilet. No softly padded feet appeared at the crack under the door. No happy, long-eared faces waited outside.

Heading back to the kitchen, Sherry found a bucket of apples near the sink. Tying up her apron to make a sling, she filled it with apples, grabbed a sweater from the hook behind the door, and eased back onto the porch. Holding her breath, she crept down the wooden steps and ran through the barnyard and onto the road. She ran past neighbor Mackners' house and past the hayfield next to it. She ran without slowing, almost without taking a breath, not stopping until it was no longer possible to see her from the Hawkes farm, even if one were standing on the roof.

By noon, Sherry had covered several miles, making it all the way to where the highway paralleled the tree-lined Yakima River. It was hot at midday, and she made her way to the river's edge where she pulled off her shoes and bit into one of the pilfered apples. Sitting by the river under a canopy of leafy branches, she began to relax. Her eyelids drooped, and she gave in to the sweet smell of the dogwoods and the hypnotic slosh of the lazy, wide river.

From behind, a familiar growl broke the spell, waking her. Sherry jumped to her feet and quickly ducked behind a tree. A moment later, she caught her breath and dropped to the ground, her eyes tightly shut.

Did he see me?

The sound had come from a familiar sight—her father's truck with its spinning, red wheels. He would be furious, Sherry knew. With harvest over, Almon Hawkes needed to get his crop to market. This was no time to be out searching for his crazy, head-in-the-clouds daughter.

Did he see me?

The truck roared as it drew nearer, the high whine of a loose fan belt abrading the soft, bubbling melody of the river. Sherry cringed and curled up into a ball, waiting. Then, the sound changed. The whine abated, and the grumbling of the engine grew fainter. Sherry opened her eyes, lifting her head slightly. Although the engine noise was still audible, the sound was dissipating.

He didn't see me!

Sherry jumped up and ventured a look. Far up the road, Almon Hawkes's truck swayed under its load of Jonagold apples, picking up speed as it moved away.

September brought a full week of rain and an early frost. Humidity and the drafty farmhouse tormented Grandpa as he struggled to breath. His hacking and sputtering filled the air as Rose Mae and Grandma forced the children to tiptoe about the house, trying not to disturb him. Sherry had returned home after two days away, only Grandpa Hawkes acknowledging her absence. "Looky what the cat dragged in," he cackled before dissolving in a fit of coughing. He'd collapsed that night and had since been too weak to visit Sherry's bed. With her father at market and Grandpa Hawkes sequestered in a back bedroom, Sherry felt safe for the first time since Buddy and Lady had been stolen from her.

She was spending more time with her grandmother, a stormy-haired woman who often seemed lost in her own world. Like Sherry, Grandma Hawkes had a deep love for animals, carrying on long conversations with the chickens as she scattered their feed on the ground or rummaged about in their nests for eggs. Sherry had once seen a grainy photo of her grandmother as a young girl, hair pull back tight, her expression Victorian-grim, but with a soft sadness about her eyes, almost as if she knew even then that her future lay with the grizzled, old man who became her husband, living in a broken-down house with a sullen, brutish son and a hateful, gravel-voiced daughter-in-law, ignoring the squeak of the springs as her husband eased out of their bed in the dead of night and the sounds that followed in the next room, as well.

"You gonna go to town and get some shoes today?" Sherry asked her Grandma. She sat on her grandmother's bed. Grandpa Hawkes was not there, having managed to get himself as far as the couch in the living room. Grandma Hawkes gave Sherry a puzzled look. She smiled and nodded when she understood. Sherry had watched her pull a Mason jar from a closet shelf. The elder Mrs. Hawkes's meager savings— some loose change and a few, wrinkled dollar bills—were in the jar. She studied her granddaughter and said a prayer aloud.

"Your Grandpa had a bad night," she said with a tremble in her voice.

Sherry said nothing. She had watched her grandfather shuffle slowly to the bathroom between naps that grew longer each day. Serves him right, she thought. Maybe he'll end up like Henny Penny...just an old chicken in somebody's pot. Sherry smiled, and immediately regretted it. There were tears in Grandma's eyes. For all his sins, she still loved him.

Grandma Hawkes screwed the lid back on the now-empty Mason jar. Afterward, she held up the money in one, thin, veiny hand to show Sherry. "I'm going to town to find him a doctor," she said.

Sherry shuddered. Yes, Grandma still loved him. Worse yet, she was about to bring him back to life.

"He has pneumonia," Al Junior told Sherry, unable to hide the excitement in his voice. He'd eavesdropped on the conversation between Doctor Whitmore and their grandmother. "He might even die," he added, almost gleefully.

Grandma Hawkes's few dollars had been enough to get the doctor out to the farm. He'd glided up to the house, driving a car that seemed to ignore the potholes and rocks that peppered their driveway. Erect and dignified, Doctor Whitmore strode into the house without knocking, smelling of soap and hair pomade, the cleanest man Sherry had ever seen. If the squalor of the Hawkes home bothered him, he hid it well with nary a wrinkle of his perfectly straight, patrician nose. He'd gone directly to Grandpa's room without being told where to find him. With Grandma and Rose Mae hovering outside the door, he'd carried out an examination that lasted only a few minutes. He reappeared in the hallway, dark-eyed and serious. Speaking under a veil of whispers that only Al Junior hiding in the crawlspace below could hear, he'd swallowed Grandma Hawkes's tiny hands with his own, his lips hardly moving.

He took a pad from his heavy, leather bag, wrote on it for less than a minute, and handed the instructions to Rose Mae.

"Try to make him comfortable," Sherry heard him say.

He'd reached out and squeezed Grandma Hawkes's arm, nodded at Rose Mae, and then was gone, his low-slung, un-dented late-model car easing up the driveway and onto the road, where it gathered speed and disappeared over the horizon.

Doctor Whitmore's visit triggered a rush of activity around the house. Grandma concocted mustard plasters that she applied to her ailing husband's chest. Rose Mae sat at the bedside, wiping his face with a cold, damp cloth for hours on end. The children scuttled about quietly, hardly speaking. Meanwhile, visitors began to show up, nearly all of them bringing food. The Hawkes family was awash in pies and loaves of bread and roasted chickens.

After a few weeks, Sherry was roused one morning by the sound of her mother's laughter. She jerked upright, immediately awake.

Grandpa must be better!

She cocked her head, listening, waiting for his knock at the door. After a few moments, Sherry sank back into the pillows, covering her head with the blanket.

The mustard plasters must have worked!

She began to cry, slow tears at first, then great drops that spilled from her eyes, making a dark, wet circle on her pillow. She began to wail, so loudly she didn't hear her bedroom door squeak as it was pushed open, nor the voices from the kitchen that grew louder.

"Wake up."

A hand was on her shoulder. Sherry curled up more tightly, but the hand was relentless.

"Wake up, Sherry! Yer havin' a nightmare! Wake up!"

Sherry clutched her covers, but the hand was stronger, pulling them from her grasp. She felt someone grip her arm, jerking her upright.

"Wake up, Sherry! Stop bawlin'! I need you!"

Sherry sighed. It was no use. She'd have to give in.

"I'm awake," she said, her voice sounding tiny and far off.

"I need your help. Grandpa died, and I need you to wash his bedsheets."

Sherry blinked and looked up. Her mother towered over her wearing a strained expression.

"I don't have time for your crap, today. Now, get up!"

Sherry blinked again, her heart pounding, struggling to find a response that never came. When her blank-faced daughter remained motionless and silent, Rose Mae Hawkes straightened and raised one hand as if about to slap her. Then, slowly, she lowered her arm and sighed.

"Fer Chrissakes, Sherry," she said. "Yer grandpa is dead. Now, get up!

Chapter Nine

"Before the rescue, *I* was Second Chance," Sara Sharette said the first time I phoned her. "The animals were at my house, the phone was at my house. *Everything* was here." Sara's words came out like gunfire. She paused as if to reload, then continued. "Every penny Second Chance had, I raised for them, including all the money from the rescue. The whole rescue was my doing. I called the Sheriff. I called the news media. I did the whole thing from square one." Sara's voice rang with contempt.

"That's quite an accomplishment," I said

Sara took a deep breath, and her voice softened. "We couldn't have done it without the news media getting the word out," she said, sighing, "but the board didn't like me calling them. So, after the rescue, they replaced me. Now they're paying someone to do what I did for free."

"After all the work you did?" I asked.

Sara hesitated. She didn't speak for what seemed a full minute, and I could almost see the knot in her jaw as she fought to control her emotions. She didn't have to say it. The board of Second Chance had done a number on her, and she hadn't gotten over it.

"They said it was unprofessional to call the news media before the rescue even happened," she told me. "They were unhappy because I didn't notify them first." The pitch of her voice rose. "Mind you, the board had never been involved in anything. They'd never even been to an adoption event. They were totally uninvolved until money came into the picture."

As Sara spoke, I could feel her disappointment. "As soon as we had all the new donations, they kind of pushed me aside," she said, sighing. "You know, it was the media that saved us. We had volunteers before we delivered the dogs because the story had been publicized."

I waited a moment before going on. I'd clearly touched a nerve, one that lingered close to the surface. "I'm sorry you lost your position," I said. "Undersheriff Wolfe mentioned that you were very helpful in the investigation leading up to the rescue.

The mention of the Malheur County law officer seemed to help.

"How is Brian?" Sara asked, her voice warmer and more controlled. "I haven't seen him in forever."

"He's well, I think," I answered. I felt guilty. I'd never met Brian Wolfe in person. We'd spoken only over the phone. "He mentioned that you knew Barbara Erickson before the rescue."

There was a pause, as Sara took a deep breath and released it. "Yes...I knew Barbara," she said. "I remember the first time I ever saw her." I imagined her slowly shaking her head. "It's been two years," she said, quietly, "hard to believe." As I listened, Sara recounted a day she'd not forgotten.

Sara Sharette was headed to Wal-Mart. Once again, Second Chance, the animal shelter she managed, had run out of paper towels and cleaning supplies. Second Chance —a non-profit corporation—had been founded in 2001 by Barbara Hutchinson at the request of the Payette, Idaho city council after a local citizen began trapping and shooting feral cats, causing an outrage by inadvertently executing a few luckless neighborhood pets, too. Hutchinson had been selected as president, a post she still held, and a board of directors duly elected. After that, the real decision-making—how to house and care for the animals, fundraising, and administration—had been left to Sara under Hutchinson's guidance. The board kept a cool distance, something Sara wasn't sorry about.

Sara found a narrow parking place in the huge lot and eased out of her car. As usual, the lot was packed. Dodging a few cars with cranky drivers trolling for spaces, she headed for the giant retail warehouse, marveling at the vision of Sam Walton, a shopkeeper from Arkansas, who turned a ridiculously simple idea into a household name. She thought about the thin wallet and thinner checking account she used to supply Second Chance, wishing she had a tiny fraction of the Walton fortune.

Sara stopped and laughed, ignoring the angry horn that blared at her from behind. Parked near the tall, glassed entrance to the store was a brown Vega station wagon with a crude, handmade sign propped against one fender. It was the sign that had made Sara laugh: "Chawawas for sale."

Ignoring the disgruntled lot troller behind her, Sara headed for the car, a grin still on her face. As she drew closer, her expression changed. The battered car seemed to be packed with dogs, its paw print-smeared windows muffling the hysterical chorus that came from inside. Sara squinted, trying to assess the condition of the animals through the car's filthy windows.

"You lookin' for a pup?"

Sara jerked with surprise. A frizzy-haired woman wearing cotton pajamas had seemingly materialized from thin air, standing at the rear of the car with a smile on her face almost larger than the tiny puppy she held.

Sara managed a tight-lipped smile in return. "Hi," she said to the odd woman. "I'm Sara. I'm with Second Chance." She tugged on her T-shirt, which sported the shelter's name. "Have you heard of us?"

The woman considered the lettering on Sara's T-shirt for a moment, then looked up.

"I'm Barbara," she announced in a whiskey-and-cigarettes voice. She moved her dog's paw in a tiny wave, "and this here is little Baby." The scrawny Chihuahua in her arms trembled, burying his head in the woman's elbow. Sara nodded, at the same time moving to get a better look inside the car. Fortunately, Barbara had opened the station wagon's rear window to allow air.

"Wow, you've got a lot of dogs in there," Sara said. "Are they all Chihuahuas?" Ignoring the overpowering odor coming from the vehicle, she stepped closer and looked in. More than a dozen pairs of eyes peered back. Sara leaned forward and touched the tailgate, and the dogs cowered, drawing back. Then she backed away, one hand over her nose and mouth. If Barbara appreciated Sara's disgust, she hid it well.

"Oh, they're mostly Chihuahuas," she said in a bright voice, "and they all have their shots and papers and everything."

Sara clenched her jaw, scanning the car. Barbara was partly right. There were a few Chihuahuas, but also terriers and small, mixed-breed dogs, including one bug-eyed, brown-and-white mongrel that seemed determined to breed a smaller Chihuahua with Sara watching. A few of the dogs had bald patches where their fur had been amateurishly cut off, a tell-tale sign of un-groomed animals. Sara had seen it before. In long-haired breeds, thick, tangled rasps of hair formed unless they were regularly combed. Once that happened, the only solution was to cut out the tangle.

"Yeah, some a' these is purebreds," Barbara boasted.

Sara stared at her, unable to mask her disbelief. Fortunately, Barbara used that moment to cuddle the tiny pup in her arms, kissing the top of its head. It gave Sara just enough time to gather herself. To help these poor dogs, she needed to stay calm. Still, the chaos inside the small station wagon had her teetering between tears and fury. Sara pulled her hand away from her mouth and looked into Barbara's pale, blue eyes.

"Are you getting any buyers?" She was trying to keep her voice upbeat, but the sound of it seemed distant and tinny inside her head.

"Oh, I don't have a problem sellin' 'em," Barbara answered. She leaned over to put the puppy back into the car and grinned. "One week, I made two thousand dollars."

Sara nodded. "Well, this is the place to do it." She gestured at the steady stream of shoppers going in and out of the wide Wal-Mart entrance. "You'll never get more foot traffic."

Barbara followed Sara's eyes. After a moment, she spoke with greater ease, as if she'd decided that Sara was trustworthy. "Yeah, and I don't let 'em go to just anybody," Barbara said, fumbling with a cigarette. "If I don't like the looks of someone or my babies don't like 'em, they stay right here." She added a tight-lipped nod.

A few minutes had passed, settling Sara's nerves a bit. She again peered into the car. A tiny, trembling pup hid behind an empty food bowl, a crusty, yellowish goo filling up both eyes and tracking down the sides of his nose. Sara reached in and retrieved him. "This little guy isn't doing so well," she said.

Barbara offered a blank look in response, the still unlit cigarette between her fingers.

"Some dogs are prone to eye problems," Sara went on.

Barbara shrugged. "Oh, that's Teeny," she said, putting the cigarette to her lips and lighting it. She took a deep puff and exhaled a cloud of white smoke. "His eyes are just like that. It's in the breed."

Sara nodded. "You have quite a pack here," she said. "I bet they keep you busy."

Barbara glanced at the dogs. "Oh, yeah, bathin' and feedin' 'em and we play-play at certain times." Sensing an audience, Barbara's voice became louder, ringing with pride. "I take them behind the Texaco station...let them run and run."

"That's a lot of work for one person."

"Oh, my husband helps. We have a routine, so it's not that bad." Barbara shifted her weight with some difficulty. "I gotta check on my other babies," she said, tossing her cigarette to the pavement and snuffing it with the toe of her shoe. She turned and slowly made her way to the front of the car, limping and swaying. Sara followed. "Bad hip," Barbara said when she saw the inquiring look on Sara's face. "Doc says I need a new one." She sighed and shrugged her shoulders, gesturing at the car, "but I got mouths to feed. I can't afford it." She offered Sara a weary smile, then pulled open the car door. Inside, cordoned off from the rear of the car with chicken wire, were another dozen dogs.

"These here are my older babies," Barbara said, picking up a listless Chihuahua. "I've had 'em for years and years." She slid into the passenger seat and looked up at Sara. "Some a' these babies is twenty-one and twenty-two years old. Jocko here is nineteen." She rubbed the little Chihuahua's head. It didn't move, although Sara could see some eyelid fluttering. Most of the dogs in the front seat were apparently asleep. A black terrier with a graying muzzle lifted its head from the seat, his lips protruding. He had no teeth.

Sara furrowed her brow. "Do your dogs get regular care from a veterinarian?" she asked.

A flicker of suspicion crossed Barbara's face. She stepped out of the car, blocking Sara's view of the inside, her movements considerably more spry than earlier. She closed the door and faced Sara, holding one of the listless Chihuahuas. The smile was gone. "I went to vet school, so I know how to take care of 'em myself," Barbara said, lifting her chin. "I give 'em their shots and everything. My baby girl here, I took her to a vet, and they *blinded* her. So, I buy vet supplies from the Co-op and tend them myself." Barbara bowed her head and kissed the sickly dog. She didn't speak for a few moments, petting the dog and murmuring in his ear. Sara wondered if she'd pushed too hard.

Sara glanced at her watch. She'd have to get back to Second Chance soon, and she still had her shopping to do. She studied Barbara, waiting for her to begin talking again, but Barbara remained silent, petting the little Chihuahua, her eyes downcast. Sara took a deep breath and released it. There was nothing more she could do for now. She turned and retraced her steps, Barbara trailing along with the dog still in her arms. At the back of the car, Sara glanced at the license plate, making sure she'd gotten it right, then caught her breath as she wondered if the car may have been stolen.

A smile crossed her lips. Barbara—at least seventy years old with her cotton pajamas and arthritic hip—didn't look like much of a car thief. Sara shook her head and again glanced at her watch. "Well," she said, "I guess I should..." Barbara spoke up.

"Baby Girl, here, she got bit in the throat by one of the mothers," she said, "and I took her to the vet down at Four Rivers to see what they could do about the little holes in her throat. They told me to put her to sleep 'cause her food and water ran out the holes. I wasn't gonna let 'em kill her, so I got some triple-antibiotic, and I filled her little holes and put a big bandage right here."

She pointed at a cluster of four scars on the dog's scrawny neck. Sara nodded, squinting against the morning sun that glared off the windows of

Barbara's car.

"I kept her right with me all the time, in a box on the table," Barbara said, her voice growing louder. She seemed to be enjoying herself, eyes settling just over Sara's shoulder as she went on. "I kept watchin' her. Heck, in four days, when I changed her bandage, them holes was healin' over. Baby Girl ate real good then, and, by golly, she got well."

Barbara paused, and her eyes returned to Sara's face. Sara knew it was her turn to respond in the little drama that Barbara was playing out. "Wasn't it painful?" she asked.

Barbara shook her head, sending her hair flying around her face. "Oh no!" she replied, waving at the air with one hand, "she wasn't in any pain. I felt her little throat, and she never winced or cried or nothin'." Barbara shrugged. "It's like when I get a cut, and it don't bother me 'cause I can heal up in no time. Well, I took Baby Girl back to the vet, and they looked at her holes. 'You wanted to put her to sleep,' I told them, 'but I healed her and you couldn't.'"

Telling the story seemed to energize the old woman. She stood more erect, her shoulders back, a flinty look of defiance in her face. It was at least the third or fourth personality change Sara had seen in their few minutes together, and she felt the distant beginnings of a headache. Keeping up with Barbara's rambling and mood swings was proving to be a formidable challenge.

"Then they put some medicine in her little eye 'cause it was swollen," Barbara continued, holding the Chihuahua up for Sara to see. "I think it come from the throat problem 'cause your muscles and nerves cross each other there. After that, her little eye turned funny, and then she went blind." Barbara snorted. "They *blinded* her in one eye."

Sara became aware that they were not alone. She glanced around and saw small clusters of people watching, all keeping their distance. At the entrance, a burly security guard eyed them, his legs widespread, a black flashlight as big as a baseball bat dangling from his belt. Sara offered him a sheepish grin. He narrowed his eyes in response.

She turned back to Barbara. "Maybe I could help you, Barbara," she said. She fished around in her purse, retrieving a brochure. "Here's some information about Second Chance. We're a no-kill shelter for animals."

"I don't need no help."

"I know you don't right now," Sara said gently, "but down the road, if you needed help with anything—vet care or dog-sitting—let me know. My number is on the front." She held out the brochure for Second Chance.

"I don't need no help," Barbara said again, although she took the paper from Sara's outstretched hand.

"I know," Sara said.

"I'm fine," Barbara replied.

Over the next few months, Sara spotted Barbara several times, parked outside Wal-Mart with her dogs. "Eventually, she traded in that little wagon and bought a van," she told me as we wrapped up our conversation. "Barbara thought her animals needed more room, but instead she added more dogs. They were just as crowded."

"I was also trying to earn her trust," Sara said. "I hoped she'd come to Second Chance on her own."

In January 2003, Sara's efforts paid off. The answering machine at Second Chance had a convoluted message from Barbara Erickson. She had three terrier-mix puppies to hand over for placement.

"You must have been happy to get that call," I said.

Sara didn't speak for a moment. "Barbara had never given up any of her dogs, no matter how hard she had to struggle to care for them."

"So giving up three was a good start," I offered, "right?" Although we were talking on the phone, I could almost see Sara shaking her head.

"No," she answered, her voice flat. "It meant that conditions for her dogs had worsened."

Chapter Ten

August 1940—Kittitas County, Washington.

"You get room and board here," Carl Mackner said, "and not much more." His words were tough, but he'd already decided that he liked the look and size of this kid with the thickly calloused hands, his shoulders busting out of a threadbare flannel shirt. The boy was big, but not very smart—a perfect hired hand. "Times are tough right now," Mackner warned his new employee. "You'll have to work hard for every mouthful."

"Thank ya, Mr. Mackner," the boy said, squinting under a tattered straw hat. Mr. Mackner recognized the hat, an old one he'd lost a few months back over by the Yakima River. A cougar had spooked his horse, nearly throwing Carl before dashing off in a panic. By the time he'd settled the mare, his hat was far behind. He never went looking for it, something that made his wife happy. "That hat got to smelling so bad, my wife wouldn't allow it in the house," he later told Almon Hawkes over a beer.

"You'll be working dawn to dusk with barely time for a meal," Carl went on. He was pleased. The kid looked confused, but grateful. As long as he was fed, he'd not ask for money, something Carl clung to as tightly as the kid now gripped the hat he'd pulled off his sweaty head.

"I'll do you right, Mr. Mackner." The nineteen-year-old put his hand over his stomach. "Haven't eaten since yesterday, but I expect to work first." He grinned, a lopsided effort that made him look even dimmer. Mackner softened.

"You can stow your gear in the barn," he said. "It's the best place to sleep in the summer. Nice and cool. After that, go on up to the house, and Grandma can round you up a biscuit."

"Thank ya, Mr. Mackner. Thank ya."

Across Ruby Road at the Hawkes' place, thirteen-year-old Sherry grimaced as she picked through the straw looking for freshly laid eggs. She hated this chore. It felt like pilfering. Hens should be allowed to hatch their eggs and raise their brood, just like people, Sherry thought. But eggs had become the common currency of the area since hard times hit, and Ma was out of sugar. Sherry shooed the chickens aside, methodically plucking eggs from the nests as the dried droppings crunched under her feet. It only took a few minutes to fill a small handbasket, and after apologizing to the frazzled, indignant hens, Sherry headed across the road to the Mackners'.

"Got some eggs for you, Mr. Mackner," Sherry called out to Carl who was out in the field next to the house, pitching hay into a wagon. He stopped and waved before wiping his brow with the back of one hand and resuming his work. Sherry pranced up the wooden steps and pounded on the door to the Mackner house. She could hear muffled voices through the cracks.

The door opened to Grandma Mackner's smile. Strands of gray hair had pulled loose from the bun on her head and were fluttering about her face. Her eyes were clear and lively, crinkling unapologetically as her smile widened. "Well, look at you, Sherry," she said warmly. "All covered with flour. You look like a ghost."

Sherry handed over the basket of eggs. She quickly swiped at her face with the edge of her apron. "Ma needs a cup of sugar," she said. "We was wonderin' if you have some to spare." She held up the tin cup.

"Oh, the Lord provides," Grandma Mackner said. She stepped back, motioning at Sherry to come in, but the girl didn't move as Grandma Mackner crossed the expansive kitchen to a cabinet that stood next to the washing tub and pump. Pulling a large can from the cabinet, the old woman dipped the tin cup in and filled it with grainy, white sugar. When she looked back, Sherry stood, framed by the doorway, staring at the stranger who sat hunched over a plate of food at the end of what the Mackners called their kitchen table, an old warped door that was balanced across two tree stumps. A rusty hinge still hung from one cracked, unpainted edge.

Grandma Mackner laughed. "That there is Ralph Halstad," she said to Sherry. "He's helping Carl with the hay."

Sherry didn't speak, but Ralph looked up and winked as he continued to shovel food into his mouth, the makeshift kitchen table wobbling with each spoonful. He was older than Sherry, tall, with a thatch of blond waves that hung over his brow. His shoulders were broad and his hands large. If not for the yellow teeth and wolfish eyes, he might have been handsome. Sherry crossed her arms over her breasts and stared at the floor.

"Here ya go, Honey," Grandma Mackner said, handing the cup of sugar to Sherry.

"Thank you, Ma'am," Sherry answered. She took the cup and left, pointing

*her eyes at the floor, away from the Mackner's new hired hand. They'd not exchanged
a single word.*

The season of sunshine was about to tip over into autumn, creating a cool mist on
the surface of the water, as Sherry stood motionless in the tall bunchgrass next to the
pond. On the tiny beach across the water, a large summer beetle lay on its back, legs
flailing, struggling to right itself. The beetle's season was nearly over, too. Night frost
would soon visit the orchards and fields, ending the beetle's life if the chickens and
geese didn't get him first.

Sherry closed her eyes and let the breeze tease her with sweet smells: dried leaves
and pine needles, ripe apples fallen from their branches, the rotting cottonwood log.
She was at her thinking spot, her safe haven. She swung around. She'd heard a soft
rustle in the underbrush behind her. There was nothing there, but a moment later,
she heard it again.

...Al Junior!

She clenched her fists. Sherry was thirteen-years-old now, almost fourteen,
and nearly as big as Al Junior, who was small for his age. There was no more running from him. She could stand and fight. The rustling grew nearer and louder,
making Sherry angry. He knows better than to come out here, she thought. This is
my place! It belongs to me!

A boy lurched out of the tall grass, nearly tripping over the cottonwood log.
Gathering himself, he straddled the log and sat. Ralph Halstad had been working
for the Mackners long enough for Sherry to develop a serious dislike. The hulking,
muscular Ralph, his lurid slash of a grin baring brown, pointed teeth, took every
opportunity to leer at the shy, blossoming neighbor girl, his pale, lifeless eyes running
across her body like a snake about to swallow a mesmerized canary.

"There y'are," he said, "out here all by yerself." He grinned.

Sherry stepped back and studied the ground for a moment. Then she looked up.
His unexpected appearance had taken her by surprise, but she quickly recovered, fixing
him with slitted eyes. "This here's private property," she said. "You ain't allowed."

Ralph snorted with laughter, making Sherry brave with anger.

"You can't stay here. You need to get on back to the Mackners'."

Ralph laughed again. He spat a thin stream of tobacco juice onto the ground.
"I don't see no signs," he said. "How do I know this here's your property?" He swung
his other leg over the log, but remained seated, facing Sherry.

"How do you know it ain't?" Sherry countered. It wasn't what she'd wanted
to say, but this tall, mean-looking boy was making it hard for her to think.

Ralph casually locked his fingers around one knee and leaned back, giving her
a look of frank appraisal. His eyes narrowed. "How do I..." He didn't finish. Instead,

his eyes widened and he threw his arms outward, flailing at the air as if trying to take flight. Baffled, Sherry remained motionless, staring at him as Ralph's lupine expression disappeared and was replaced by the look of a drowning man. She took a step forward, reaching out, but it was too late. Ralph teetered precipitously for only a second longer before toppling backward off the log, landing with a crash in a nest of dried sticks behind it.

For a moment, all Sherry could see of him were the bottoms of his boots, one displaying a rather large hole that framed a piece of ragged, heavy burlap.

"You got a hole in your boot," she snickered. "Matches that big ol' hole in your head."

She gathered her skirt and sprinted toward the back of the pond where the grasses gave way to a narrow strip of gray, sandy beach. If she could put the pond between them, he'd never catch her. He could chase her around that pond all night if he wanted, and if he tried to cut through, the pasty muck of the waterbed would trap him until long after she'd made it back to the farm.

Wait 'til I tell Mr. Mackner, she thought, just as she felt Ralph's nails digging into the tender skin of her arm. She was lifted up and slammed into the ground. Just as quickly, Ralph Halstad was atop her.

"Now you just calm down, Girl," he panted. "I ain't gonna hurt you." He put his forearm across her neck, and she fought to breathe. "We're gonna have a little fun," he whispered. He smelled of stale tobacco and rancid sweat and tooth decay.

"No!" Sherry screamed, kicking one leg from under him. He quickly shifted his weight, and she was again pinned tight to the ground.

"Yer a buckin' little filly," he laughed, ignoring her screams.

"Daddy!" Sherry cried out. "Help me!"

She gasped for air as Ralph buried his fist in her belly, driving the wind from her lungs. Tiny thread-like fragments floated before her eyes, and the sky seemed to darken.

...Buddy! Lady!

Still unable to breathe, Sherry felt her heart slowing as Ralph's arm pushed against her neck.

...Buddy! Lady!

The sky turned black.

When she awoke, muddy sweat dripped into her eyes. A weight was on her chest, but at least she could breathe. Above her, Ralph Halstad grunted as he lunged into her over and over. With each thrust, Sherry felt a stab of pain in her lower belly. She blinked and shook Ralph's foul sweat from her eyes. He had pinned her to the ground on her back, her legs shoved open as he squirmed atop her.

"Hold on," he moaned, pushing harder against her. "Hold on..."

She felt the knife-like pain again, and realized that he'd not taken off his pants, merely unzipped and freed himself. His huge belt buckle was ramming into her pubic bone, cutting into her skin with each brutish thrust of his hips.

"Hold on," he groaned, his face wet and contorted.

She closed her eyes and waited for it to end.

Long after Ralph Halstad had stuffed himself back into his pants and disappeared into the bunchgrass behind the cottonwood log, Sherry awoke to the sound of a squawking duck. She lay on her belly at the edge of the pond, her fingers just touching the cold water. Lazy ripples lapped at the shoreline, playing a mother's lullaby. Her head ached.

The sun had moved to late afternoon, and the ducks were settling in for the evening. They wanted her to leave. Sherry watched one of them for a moment—a highly indignant mother duck. She waddled about angrily on the opposite side of the pond, quacking furiously as if to scold Sherry. As if to say, "This is my place! It belongs to me!"

Thirteen-year-old Sherry Hawkes stood and gathered up her dress before easing into the frigid pond. The mud of the bottom sucked at her feet, but she continued forward, one step after another, until the water lapped at her hips. Some time later, as evening turned into night, Al Junior came and led her back through the field, one hand on her arm. They didn't speak. Sherry never again returned to the pond.

Chapter Eleven

July 2000—Coleman Service, Harper, Oregon.

Verda Palmer leaned over the table at Coleman Service, head in her hands, a wrinkled and shredded tissue woven through her fingers. Brian Coleman was in his usual place behind the cash register. Barbara had just left after bending Verda's ear for what seemed like hours. Verda sighed.

"I might as well let them stay there," she said without looking at Brian. "They aren't paying rent, so maybe they'll pay for the upkeep."

"You gotta do what you think is right," Brian replied.

Verda sighed again, dabbing at her eyes with the tissue. It had been nearly a year since the Ericksons had paid their rent. In the meantime, her once tidy, little house had deteriorated inside and out. It was sagging at the eaves, windows were unwashed or broken, and the yard was a sea of mud. The flowers she'd long-ago planted were dead. Then, there were the dogs. Part of it was her fault, Verda knew. The electrical system—a homemade network of substandard wires—had shorted out, starting a fire in the attic. There were other problems, things a landlord should look out for and take care of. But her sister, Sophie, was sick. Cancer, they'd told her. And arguing with Barbara was just too hard. Besides, even if she could successfully evict the Ericksons, it was going to cost thousands of dollars to bring the house up to code.

The bell on Brian's door clanged, and a stalwart woman bustled in. She had pinned her brown braids to her head, forming a crown. Helen Dawson, a longtime Harper resident, struggled under the weight of a huge bag of tomatoes. Crossing to the cash register, she plopped the bag on the counter with obvious relief and grinned at Brian.

"There's more where these came from," she said.

Brian peeked in the bag and issued a low whistle. "Nice ones," he told Helen. She nodded at Brian, at the same time glancing at Verda. What she saw wiped the grin off her face. "You okay?" she said as she crossed to Verda and pulled up a chair. She settled in, smiling at Brian when he brought her a cup of coffee.

"You look like you just saw a ghost," she said.

Verda gave her a tight smile. Helen was an old friend and a plain speaker. "I was talking to Barb Erickson," Verda began.

Helen leaned back in her chair, grimacing. "Say no more," she said. "I don't know how the two of you can stand talking to that lunatic." She tossed a look at Brian, shaking her head. If listening, he didn't show it.

"Maybe so," Verda said, "but today, she told me some things I just don't want to believe."

Helen laughed. "Now you're catching up with me," she said. "Barbara never says anything I believe."

Verda looked at her without answering, and Helen swallowed her grin. "I'm sorry, Verda," she said. "I shouldn't poke fun." Neither woman spoke until Helen broke the silence. "What'd she tell you?"

Verda looked across the small room at Brian who pointedly busied himself reorganizing the cash drawer. His eyes were dark, and his mouth drew a tight line. Verda swiveled her eyes back to Helen, studying her. What she was about to tell would be in the gossip mill by suppertime, she knew. Still, she had to tell someone. Verda took a breath and released it. "Barbara told me that she had a baby when she was fifteen years old," she said, her voice nearly a whisper.

"Fifteen?" Helen responded, her mouth open.

"That's what she said," Verda answered, nodding.

Neither spoke for a moment. "Fifteen years old?" Helen said.

Verda nodded sadly.

"My dad woulda *killed* me," Helen snorted.

"Her *dad* got her pregnant," Verda whispered. "And he took the baby when it was born. She said he might have tried to sell it...or worse."

"Indians'll do that." Helen said, "they'll sell their own children."

Outside, yet another battered, long-bed, Ford pickup eased in next to the gas pumps. Brian was instantly moving. Verda watched him go, waiting until he'd pulled the door shut behind him. "She labored for three days and almost bled to death when it was born," she told Helen. Verda dabbed at her eyes with the wrinkled tissue. "She was probably too small to have a baby."

"I wonder if it even survived the labor," Helen said, shaking her head sadly. "I mean...well, gosh...three days of labor...it was probably stillborn, don't you think?"

"Not according to Barbara," Verda replied, immediately regretting her choice of words. She ignored the skeptical look she was getting and went on. "Barbara thinks her father might have killed the baby. She never saw it again. She doesn't even know if it was a boy or a girl." Her throat tightened, and she fought back tears. Helen reached across the table and put her hand on Verda's. Neither spoke for what seemed a long time.

"After that she could never have kids," Verda said. She glanced out the window where Brian was making his way back to the store.

"You know," she said, "I think Barbara has been missing her baby ever since."

After a tearful Verda Palmer told me about her conversation at Coleman Service, I tried to coax more from Barbara, but she vehemently denied ever telling Verda or anyone else about a pregnancy. "I never wanted children," she huffed to me. "I had enough nieces and nephews to last a lifetime."

Barbara went on in a voice laced with anger. "Verda keeps asking questions. I told her I was raised to keep my nose out of other people's business. But Verda keeps wantin' to know about my past."

In a later conversation with me, Barbara claimed to have had uterine cancer, necessitating a hysterectomy. Another time, it was a gunshot wound to the abdomen while serving with the navy in Vietnam, again resulting in a hysterectomy. Each story was told with utter conviction as if she believed them herself. I didn't know what to think. Certainly a history of uterine cancer was more plausible than a war wound. I tried to find a military hospital record or evidence of enlistment and service in the United States Navy for a Barbara or Sherry Hawkes. As expected, I met a dead end. It was part of an all too familiar pattern—trying to tease out the truth from Barbara's blurred memories.

Chapter Twelve

October 1941—Kittitas County, Washington.

Fifteen-year-old Sherry Hawkes groaned with exhaustion. She had been in hard labor for three days, banished by her father to a makeshift bed in the barn because her cries interrupted his sleep. Now, he stood just inside the barn door, leaning back into it, his greasy hair plastered forward, a look of utter confusion on his face as he stared at the ruddy, motionless infant lying in the straw between Sherry's legs. Just then, Sherry felt another contraction, and the accompanying pain muffled the sound of her father's gasp when the bloody afterbirth was delivered into the straw beside her newborn child.

Sherry lay back and closed her eyes. She'd done this alone, her mother gone now for several months, her grandma off to live with Aunt Alva. Even Al Junior was gone—to where, no one seemed to know. Only Almon was left. Her father. Her baby's father, too.

Almon Hawkes found a blanket and laid it on the floor. He bent to scoop up the lifeless form entwined in its own umbilical cord. He dropped the infant unceremoniously onto the sheet, then shoveled the afterbirth behind it, wiping his bloody hand on the straw. He never looked at his daughter who lay, still and silent, still bleeding, her face ashen.

"I'll get rid of this," he mumbled.

"You lying whore!" her mother had shouted when Sherry's belly began to round. She'd refused to believe that Almon Hawkes had slept with his own daughter.

"He made me be the wife when you was away! I had to run his bath and wash his back...wear your nightgown...sleep in your bed!" Sherry insisted. "He made this baby! Not me!"

Rose Mae answered Sherry's protests by beating her and forcing her to marry the neighbor's twenty-year-old hired hand, Ralph Halstad. The wedding had taken place without ceremony, before a judge who seemed only slightly less dim than the groom. "I do' for her," Rose Mae Hawkes had said, when her daughter failed to respond to the judge's promptings. She'd said it with satisfaction, as if sealing the last can of apples for the season. Sherry had lifted her eyes from the dull, uneven planks of the courtroom floor and glanced nervously at the boy standing next to her. Ralph, wearing a white shirt and jacket better suited to a man twice his size, had nervously fingered a foul-smelling straw hat by its mangled brim. He was one step away from prison for what he'd done, and he knew it. Besides, the baby probably was his. Rose Mae Hawkes seemed to think so. Sure, it had been more than a year since he'd raped Sherry Hawkes by the pond, but Ralph didn't know much about such things. Rose Mae Hawkes had shown up at the Mackner farm with a shotgun voice, and Ralph wasn't about to argue with her.

Sherry ran out of the courtroom that day, a married woman. She never slept with Ralph Halstad. He stayed at the Mackners', and she lived with her father. Her mother left the same day, October 28, 1941. Sherry never saw her again.

Following the birth of her baby, Sherry spent most of the month in bed, weak from the aftereffects of the unattended labor and delivery. Pain came, often in wrenching swells, filling the emptiness inside with spasms so consuming, she nearly forgot about her baby. Night after night, Sherry tossed and turned far into the quiet of the very early morning, drenched in sweat even though October in Washington often chilled the house nearly to freezing. A recurrent dream haunted her. In it, she roamed the orchard at dusk, frantically looking behind each sapling for her lost baby. On her hands and knees, nearly blind as darkness drank up the last rays of light, she felt her way along an endless row to the edge of the orchard, where her baby suddenly appeared, drifting in the air. In her dream, Sherry leapt up, reaching, only to suffer a stabbing pain in her abdomen, a pain that awakened her. Afterward, awake and alone in the dark, Sherry held her empty belly and cried out for the child she had lost. "Baby, Baby," she whimpered, having no other name for her child, never knowing if it had been a boy or a girl. "What happened to you? Where are you?"

Chapter Thirteen

Social Service records from the 1940s were not retained in Kittitas County, Washington, to verify the existence of an infant born to Sherry Hawkes. Likewise, there was no death certificate for the child, and hospital records that would have confirmed any postpartum medical treatment could not be found. My research turned up yet another name used by Barbara: Jo Ann Taylor. That gave me three names: Barbara Erickson, Sherry Hawkes, and now, Jo Ann Taylor. The real name versus the alias was anyone's guess. My telephone interviews with Barbara weren't much help. She remained elusive, offering up her personal history as a scattershot series of inconsistent anecdotes—the world according to Barbara Erickson—part truth, part myth, uttered with heartfelt sincerity and often just as faithfully rebutted a moment later.

"I skipped a lot of grades in school 'cause I studied all the time," Barbara told me one day. "I think I was in the seventh grade when I was ten. People made fun of me in school 'cause my mother married me off so young. So, I was already graduated out of high school when my Uncle Art Taylor—he was Daddy's brother and looked just like him—anyway, he came and took me to Las Vegas. I lived with him and my aunt for years, and he put me through college and nurse's trainin'. He sent me back to Virginia for school...and Maryland. All them places. There isn't any place I've missed."

"Where in Virginia?" I asked, my pencil poised. I was eager to get any records that could document Barbara's past life.

Barbara ignored my question. "We coulda bought land on the Las Vegas Strip for a hundred dollars an acre back then. I coulda been rich," she boasted, pausing before going on. "But Bob woulda gambled it away," she said.

"So when did you live in Virginia?" I asked again, stupidly persistent.

It was no use. Barbara was off on another tangent. Each time I tried to tweak out more about Barbara as Sherry or Jo Ann, she fended me off, launching into another story as unbelievable as the one just told. Despite Barbara's rambling and tall tales, certain things came through with a consistency that lent them the ring of truth. She may have been abused by her grandfather and, possibly, by her father as well. Her mother had deserted the family just after marrying off fifteen-year-old Sherry to Ralph Halstad. Al Junior left home before Sherry was married, and the remaining Hawkes children, save Sherry, were placed in foster care in the early 1940s. There was, indeed, an Arthur Taylor from Las Vegas, and Sherry had lived with him and his wife for a few years. I asked Barbara why her father's brother was a "Taylor," and not a "Hawkes." "He had his name changed," she told me. "Don't know why...that was just him."

Despite the attorneys' official allegations and Barbara's unofficial tall tales, one thing seemed certain—something that no one had yet put down on paper. A little girl, born in the apple country of Washington on the eve of the Great Depression, had been abused and ignored until the most tender lights of her heart were nearly extinguished. Abandoned by her mother, violated by the men who should have protected her, shunned by a society that sanctioned her parents' crimes, the little girl had grown up to become a woman named Barbara Erickson—a woman desperately running from her past.

Chapter Fourteen

Undersheriff Wolfe's voice was friendly, and I suspected that he'd probably checked me out with Brian Coleman. I'd not expected to hear from him again, and his phone call surprised me. "I know you're interested in these animal hoarding cases," Wolfe began, "and after we talked, I remembered a news story about some people over in Midvale, Idaho." He paused, as if expecting a response.

"I don't know about them," I said.

Wolfe went on. "I guess they were living with nearly three hundred dogs," he told me. "Marv Williams, the deputy over in Washington County, handled the complaint. The records are public, so you can get a copy from the court."

I thanked him for the lead, hung up, and called the Washington County Courthouse. A clerk answered, her voice warm and small-town friendly. Her name was Naomi. I introduced myself, half-expecting she would already know about me. I was beginning to learn how quickly news traveled among the folks in these farming communities. Naomi remembered the case and excused herself to find the record. I waited, listening to a distant conversation in the background. No recorded music. When Naomi returned, she had the file.

"It was in 1996, just as you thought," she said. I heard the flap of turning pages. "It was a couple." She paused. "The Ericksons. Erickson was their name."

"Barbara and Bob Erickson?" I asked.

"No...Sherry and Bob Erickson," Naomi replied.

"She goes by 'Sherry' sometimes," I added. I told her the whole story, the yard filled with feces and garbage, the forlorn little house, the huge pack of hysterical dogs. Amazingly, she'd not heard the story. No television, I was guessing.

"So...they've done it again," Naomi said when I was finished.

"It would appear," I answered.

Naomi agreed to mail copies of the Erickson file upon receipt of an administration fee. I waited for her to ask for my credit card number, but she gave me a reality check instead—a few counties in Idaho were not yet set up to accept credit cards. I wrote a check and slipped it into an envelope, afterward staring at the interview tapes scattered across on my desk, wishing that they could magically transcribe themselves.

After several evenings of tedious transcribing, I was ready for a change of pace. I called Deputy Marv Williams of the Washington County Sheriff's Office to talk about the 1996 rescue in Idaho. As soon as I mentioned the name Erickson, he said he knew the case well and agreed to share his experience.

"The initial complaint came from local feed stores," Williams told me. "They had received checks with insufficient funds from Sherry Erickson, which is Barbara's real name. We were investigating the allegations when a call came in from Frank Land, a landlord who claimed he evicted Mrs. Erickson. She left numerous dogs behind at his rental house. It was really sad. We pulled into the yard, and dogs were everywhere, scurrying around like a bunch of rabbits."

Williams paused, then went on before I could ask a question.

"I called the Idaho Humane Society (IHS) to ask for assistance. We went out to the Erickson farm, and what we found looked like a flock of gigantic birds had landed," he said. "There were dogs in every crevice. It was so unimaginable I took pictures because I didn't think anyone would believe me. Inside the house, you couldn't walk anywhere without stepping in feces. And the smell...whew, you could hardly breathe."

"Did you suspect a case of animal hoarding?" I asked.

"We had never heard the term 'animal hoarding,'" Williams said. "And Mrs. Erickson seemed to care about the animals. She even returned to feed them after the eviction. Things just got out of hand for her."

He went on, describing the scene in great detail. The Idaho Humane Society workers had been forced to snare the dogs one-by-one with catchpoles and transport them to the main IHS facility in Boise. According to Deputy Williams, some of the dogs were subsequently adopted, but most were euthanized after testing positive for parvovirus, the microorganism responsible for a highly contagious disease in dogs that impairs the immune system and attacks their intestinal lining. About thirty dogs avoided capture, only to be shot by neighbors of the Erickson's who feared the virus might infect their own dogs.

As Deputy Williams finished, he seemed to almost whisper, as if recalling aloud the Midvale rescue might awaken a few old ghosts.

"Do you remember the IHS person you worked with?" I asked.

I heard a shuffle of papers in response. "I have it here," he said. "It was the Director of Shelter Operations...Pat Vance."

I thanked him, and we said our goodbyes as I was looking up the number for the IHS in Boise. Pat Vance was still working there. She agreed to meet with me at her office.

Chapter Fifteen

June 1972—Rock Springs, Wyoming.

"Hell, no, I'm not married," forty-six-year-old Sherry Hawkes said to Malcolm, a regular payday drinker at the Astro Lounge in Rock Springs, Wyoming. The dark, cool bar was starting to fill up as the usual corps of pipefitters and ironworkers crowded in. They had been recruited from across the country to this windy hole-in-the-wall in western Wyoming to help construct the Jim Bridger Power Plant. A tough lot, long on talk and short on history, they drank hard, bragging about romantic conquests and improbably risky maneuvers on the scaffoldings that inevitably led to near-misses— all fatal if not for their quick thinking or bravery. Sherry, the bartender, egged them on as Merle Haggard belted out "The Bottle Let Me Down" from the jukebox, and quarter bets were placed at the pool table. The more the workers talked, the more they drank...and the more Sherry made in tips.

She'd been here a few months, her last job at a nursing home in Oakland, California. Non-construction jobs were hard to come by in the Rock Springs of the early 1970s, and bartending at the Astro Lounge had proved a godsend. With tips, she'd made enough to settle nicely into one of the local resident motels, along with her dogs. All fourteen.

"My husband, Paul Koch, died in sixty-three," Sherry told Malcolm. Paul and I were both in the Navy then, and he served with JFK. They were friends."

"JFK...the president?" Malcolm asked, as a broad-shouldered gorilla of a man slid onto the stool next to him.

Sherry drew a beer for the gorilla without asking what he wanted. Without a word, he tipped it back and took a long drink. "That's right," she said, giving Malcolm a tight-lipped nod. "The President. I met him when I was at the White House. When Paul died, they sent the FBI after me. They said, 'You are wanted in Wash-

ington, D.C.,' I damn near went crazy. They took me there, and I stayed overnight in the Blue Room. John F. Kennedy gave me Paul's medals and the big flag they'd draped over his coffin."

Sherry nodded at a couple who'd taken a pair of stools at the end of the bar. *"What can I get you two?"*

"I'll have a Bud," the man said. He turned to the woman who was applying another layer of lipstick. *"Whaddaya want?"* he asked.

"Same," she said, without looking at him. She eyed Sherry suspiciously. *"So you were in the Navy? I was in the Army until 1965."*

"I was a Navy nurse for nineteen and a half years," Sherry said, pulling up a pair of dripping bottles from the cooler behind the bar. She popped the tops and brought them to the couple. *"They give you six months good behavior to get out. The Navy does...the Army don't. I was a lieutenant commander when I come out."* Sherry set the two frosty bottles of beer on the bar and pushed them toward the couple. *"One-fifty,"* she said, grinning when the man gave her a five. *"I'll get yer change,"* she said.

"Keep it," the man replied, as she knew he would. The Jim Bridger Power Plant paid well.

Sherry turned and headed back to Malcolm's end of the bar. She didn't see the woman whisper into her boyfriend's ear. She didn't hear them laugh.

"Oh yeah, I worked at Oakland Knoll Naval Hospital," Sherry said, her voice getting louder. *"I worked at Great Lakes and Sandpoint...wherever they sent me. Paul and me weren't transferred together, so we'd have to make time...thirty days together at home, then one of us would have to go back. He was a hard-headed, German-American, but he had the most beautiful blue eyes you ever saw. And he loved pets."*

"Where did you train to be a nurse?" Malcolm asked.

"They taught me overseas...Korea and Vietnam," Sherry replied. She leaned against the bar, settling in for a long story. *"Some of us were trained to do minor surgeries like tracheotomy, appendectomy, removing bullets from patients. I saw so much horrible, bad stuff in the military, I still have nightmares. I was over there four times...Vietnam. You go for six months, then they send you home for three, then you can sign up for six more. But it was bad. I still can't talk about it. You had to be on alert all the time. One time I worked three days with no sleep. I needed toothpicks to hold my eyes open. When I finally got off duty, I slept twenty-four hours. After I woke up, my brain was just numb."* Sherry sighed, staring wistfully into space. Malcolm, a bit of a dim bulb, was hanging on every word.

Sherry Hawkes went on pouring drinks, serving beers, and rambling. Each story outdid its predecessor. Before long, a small group had gathered around Malcolm, listening.

"Yeah, I went to law school for two years, but decided I didn't want to be a lawyer 'cause that's when you start goin' into the courtroom. I told my classmate, Greg, I says, 'You know what? I won't be a good lawyer,' and he says, 'Why?' and I say, "Cause I'll be in jail all the time. I won't put up with no bullshit from those judges.'"

The windowless door to the lounge opened, permitting a quick sliver of sunlight. With it came Bob Erickson who quickly shut the door. He hesitated, allowing his eyes to adjust to the dark interior before taking his regular spot at the end of the bar. With shiny black hair and bushy sideburns, he looked like Elvis in coveralls. A member of the pipefitter's union out of Las Vegas, Bob had been in Rock Springs for two months working at the power plant like most of the men in the bar. "Got it made," he'd told himself at first. With a travel card for expenses and a job that took him away from the tangled trap created by an ex-wife and two teenage sons, an itinerant lifestyle had seemed perfect—good money, not much responsibility, no woman at the end of a hard day who won't stop talking. But soon, the quiet nights he'd initially enjoyed began to haunt him.

Bob straddled the red Naugahyde-upholstered stool at the end of the bar, singing the words to a tune he'd been humming all day, "All I need is a pocket full of beans and a new pair of jeans and a woman to wash and cook things." He waited patiently, until he caught Sherry's eye, then shot her a huge face-scrunching wink. She tossed him a flirty smile in return and immediately began mixing his usual: bourbon and Coke.

"Then I went to vet school for three years." Sherry poured a jigger of bourbon into a glass, talking over her shoulder to Malcolm and his buddies. "I quit before I finished. All I wanted was enough training to take care of my babies."

"Your babies?" Malcolm asked. At the end of the bar, Bob smiled.

"Oh, yeah," Barbara said, turning to face Malcolm. "I had quarter horses, a milk cow, three hundred chickens, lots of piggies, and fourteen dogs. And I loved every one of 'em. They all had names. I had a dove named Jerry, and some white Angora kitty cats, and..."

Sherry topped off Bob's glass of bourbon with a Coke. "Gotta go," she said to Malcolm and the boys, before making her way to Bob.

"Hi, Honey." Sherry set his drink on the bar and leaned over for a kiss. "How you doin'?"

Before Bob could answer, a cowboy announced his arrival with a great bellow of laughter, plowing up to the bar. Beer splashed to the floor. Bob's bourbon and coke ended up in his lap.

"Fill 'er up," the cowboy yelled, offering Sherry a grin that displayed nearly all his tobacco-stained teeth.

"You son of a bitch!" Bob snarled, pushing ice off his lap. "Watch what yer doin'!"

The drunk cowboy reeled back on his heels. Six feet tall and whiplash lean, he looked like he'd been in a scrape or two. "You got a problem?" he said, leaning toward Bob until they were nearly nose-to-nose. He'd not noticed that Bob had a pipefitter's thick wrists and bulging forearms. Bob was a forklift in coveralls.

As quickly as it had started, Sherry was around the bar and between the two men. "Back off," she warned, adding, "I got spike heels on and I know judo and karate."

The cowboy leered at her and threw his head back and howled with laughter. "You know judo? You know karate?" He laughed again, looking at Bob. "Can't you defend yourself?" he said. He crouched into the exaggerated pose of a martial arts warrior—knees curled, legs open, arms bent like lightning bolts, knuckles bared. "You gotta have..." he sneered at Barbara, "karate-lady do it for you?"

Bob never got a chance to answer. The man's comical position left him wide open for the kick in the groin Sherry gave him. The cowboy doubled up, issuing a gasp that sounded like air escaping a punctured tire. In an instant and with surprising ease, Sherry slammed him against the jukebox. His sweat-stained hat tumbled off, and Sherry grabbed a handful of hair, dragging him toward the door. Halfway there, she released her grip and gave him another kick, this one in his skinny butt. Retrieving his hat, she flung it at him.

"Now get out!" she ordered.

After Sherry's fight with the cowboy, her romance with Bob moved along more quickly. Soon, he was spending every moment off the job either at the Astro Lounge or in Sherry's cluttered motel room a few blocks away.

"You sure have a lot of dogs here," Bob said the first time Sherry brought him home.

"Oh, Honey, no little one is gonna starve around me," Sherry bragged. She picked up a dog and kissed it. 'Cause I believe every little creature has a right to eat. I even told the mice if they stayed out of the house I'd give them bread and milk. They like bread and milk."

Bob shook his head, chuckling. "You feed the mice?"

"Damn right," she said. "When I had my ranch, I had all kinds of animals. That was after Paul died in sixty-three. He had back surgery and never recovered. He was six-foot-three before the surgery and five-foot-eleven after it. They had to take a lot of his spine out. We'd only been married seven years, and he had insurance I didn't even know about until he died."

She put the dog back down and watched it scramble with some difficulty onto *the thin, chenille cover atop her bed.*

"I used it to buy six-hundred-forty acres. I had quarter horses, thoroughbreds, and of course, all my dogs."

Bob settled into his chair. He could see that Sherry was on a roll.

"This one hen I had...pretty little girl...she molted and never got her feathers back, so I knitted her a little pink sweater. And then I knitted her another one..."

Sherry talked, and Bob listened. It seemed enough for him. He didn't expect to be asked about himself. He didn't complain about the growing pack of dogs crammed into Sherry's room. One day, after a few weeks, Bob showed up at Sherry's door on a Saturday. He'd showered and shaved, and wore a new shirt and his cleanest dungarees. Before Sherry could speak, Bob jumped in, blurting out what he'd come to say before she could launch into one of her stories.

"They're dragging me out next week," he said in a breathless rush. "Next stop is Coal Strip, Montana. Will you marry me?"

For once, Sherry was speechless.

"Will you marry me?" Bob asked again. "I don't want to be alone."

Chapter Sixteen

With Bob's reassurance that she could keep her animals, Sherry agreed to go with him, but later told me during one of our phone conversations that she resisted the idea of marriage at first. "I've always been a loner, and I like it." They never discussed children, although the subject of Sherry's supposed hysterectomy must have come up at some point. "My doggies are my children," she told Bob.

A few days after Bob Erickson proposed marriage, Sherry found homes for her cats and birds in Rock Springs. She loaded her fourteen dogs into Bob's dusty car along with a few clothes and household items, and they were off. Bob and Sherry spent the next several months in Coal Strip, Montana, then returned to Bob's home base in Las Vegas. There, despite Sherry's reluctance, they were married in a chapel on the Strip. Bob giggled throughout the ceremony, prompting an annoyed Sherry to chastise him. "Do you wanna get married or keep laughin'?"

Over the next five years, Bob labored as a union pipefitter, mostly on the road, a lifestyle he'd come to prefer. Each turnaround assignment lasted several months, and Sherry traveled with him, bringing her dogs along. Bob worked hard on these assignments, and the fourteen hour days, seven days a week, offered plenty of overtime. With no permanent residence and Bob's travel card covering most of their living expenses, the Ericksons were able to amass some money. They slept in hotels on the road and in their station wagon while waiting in Las Vegas for Bob's next job. The pack of dogs kept growing, some rescued during their travels, others whelped in the back of the car. None were turned away.

Verda Palmer recalled for me an afternoon in 1998, about a year after

Barbara and Bob had moved into her rental house. Barbara was sitting in Verda's living room, reminiscing about her life on the road with Bob. "We had mattresses in the back of the car for the kids," she told Verda, "and built-in wires to hold their pans. They always let us know when they wanted to go potty, and we'd pull off and let them run and run and run. When we were ready to go, we'd open the car door and blow a whistle, and...boy, you had to stand back and get out of the way. Once in, they'd lie down and sleep. It was really nice. I had my Teddy Bear, but he died of old age. Then I had Scooter... he was a standard poodle. And Sunny...she wasn't a Great Dane, but I can't think of what she was. The paper boy gave her to me."

Barbara had stopped by Verda's house to complain. As usual, Verda offered her a cup of coffee before settling in for the afternoon. She knew that Barbara would smoke and talk into the early evening.

"In Vegas, they took the doggies away from us," Barbara claimed. She paused to take a sip of coffee. "I went to an attorney down there, a friend of ours. He called them people up and said, 'You better turn those animals over.' I had all their shot records and tags and everything. But they wouldn't do it."

"Why did they take them away in the first place?" Verda asked, nestling into her favorite chair. It sat precariously close to the wood stove in her living room and was surrounded by reading material, piled up on the side table and scattered onto the floor—books, magazines, and newspapers all within reach of her chair.

"Somebody made a complaint," Barbara said, issuing a snort of disgust. "We traveled in a big station wagon, the old-fashioned kind. And some nosy old bitch stuck her nose in it. Well, she got hers. She ended up in jail for narcotics. Anyway, I went down there and said, 'I'm takin' the dogs so you better damn well open the cages.'"

On and on it went, Barbara recounting the stories of her travels for Verda. In Bullhead, Nevada, she and Bob traded the station wagon for a large van that could carry their growing brood. A few months later, they were off again—Richland, Washington, Chugwater, Wyoming, wherever power plants were being built. Finally, in 1982, Bob took a permanent job sorting potatoes at the Lamb-Weston processing plant in Connell, Washington.

"He started having trouble rememberin' things around then," Barbara told Verda. She looked down at the nearly full ashtray next to her. "So, we left Connell in 1985 and went back to Vegas. Besides our doggies, we had two wolves, by then. We had a gray Lobo named Chief, and we had Princess, a Timberwolf. They had puppies, and the fire department and police department bought 'em. We had a bobcat, too. I can't remember his name, but he used to go in and out through our bedroom window."

"A bobcat?" Verda dug her nails into the padded arms of her chair. "I would have shot him right between the eyes," she said.

Barbara laughed. "Oh, no, you would'na shot him. He was the nicest cat. He use'ta sit with his paws on my shoulders and give me a smooch-smooch. We had a thunderstorm one night, and he jumped in the window and onto our bed soaking wet. And then there was Jerry the bird…"

As the shadows began to lengthen, Verda dozed off, but Barbara kept talking, gesturing with her hands for emphasis. Verda had heard it all before and had long ago accepted that Barbara's apocryphal accounts were a sort of mythology she'd created to lend her life spiritual power. Verda no longer made the mistake of trying to ferret out the truth. If one of Barbara's stories didn't make sense, she ignored it. If it did, she filed it away in her head, waiting to see if it would turn up again. In this way, two patterns consistently emerged: 1) the Ericksons were always on the move, and 2) nearly everywhere they'd lived, someone had filed a complaint with the authorities about their menagerie.

Barbara's tall tales, whether told to Verda or Brian Coleman or me, always stopped just short of the recent past. Not much was known about the Ericksons' life living near the Idaho-Oregon border, on one side of the Snake River, and then the other. From my interviews with Barbara, I learned that Bob had retired in the late 1980s. Afterward, they towed a trailer filled with dogs throughout southern Idaho for several months, camping along the way. The Ericksons followed the mountain rivers, drawn to the power of the whitewater rapids up north and the meandering flow of the southern lower forks, where the river spanned nearly a mile wide in places. They sought out remote stretches among the cottonwoods and white pines, where water lapping the banks offered a trough for the dogs and small clearings provided a place for romping. They stayed until someone found a reason for them to leave.

Barbara claimed to have lived in Wilder, Idaho for a time during her childhood, although I've found no record to verify that a Sherry Hawkes or Taylor was enrolled in school there. Nonetheless, Barbara was drawn to the rolling alfalfa fields and convinced Bob to rent a small house between Wilder and Parma. It would be perfect, she thought. A place where they could settle in with their dogs. They were there for four years, and on to Nyssa, Oregon, for the next four; then to a small farmhouse in the center of Washington County, Idaho, just outside a little town called Midvale.

The Parma house, Barbara told me one day, was burglarized and all her military and college documents stolen.

"You can request copies," I said.

Barbara issued a great horse's laugh. "Oh, Honey," she said, "I been tryin' that for years and haven't heard a thing. I went through senators and everything. I never got no answers, so I figured to heck with it. I'm tired of their bull."

"What about the colleges you attended?" I asked. I'd knocked on this same door before and expected the same answer.

"Oh, I can't even remember the names of the schools, it's been so long," Barbara said. I could almost see her dismissing the thought with a wave of her hand. She immediately took off in a different direction, telling me about the kennels she and Bob had constructed at the Parma house. Barbara prattled on, and I listened to her stories. This was how it went for most of our phone interviews. Sometimes, I poked or prodded for answers. Mostly, I just listened, pulled more deeply into her world, finding myself drawn closer to her.

Chapter Seventeen

It had been years since I'd visited the Idaho Humane Society in Boise, and I was pleasantly surprised by what I found. The remodeled building looked clean and fresh. The lobby was bustling: people lined up at the counter, dogs using their tails to tap out Morse code on the gleaming linoleum floor, smiling, chatty technicians working efficiently. The smell of newness surrounded us with nary a hint of animal odor.

Pat Vance, the Director of Operations, led me down a hall painted sea-foam green and lined with windows that allowed visitors to see into the small, individual offices. Vance's office was at the end of the hall. She led me in, motioning to a chair. "Have a seat," she said, smiling. Despite her title, Pat Vance's space was no larger than any of the others I'd peeked into as I followed her down the hallway, having just enough room for her desk and chair and a seat for one visitor. A counter filled with neatly aligned books and files ran the length of the window behind her desk. She edged past me and slipped into her seat. Leaning forward, she began to talk about the Midvale dog rescue in 1996.

"The state veterinarian requested our help," she told me, running one hand through her short, blonde hair, "because the facilities over in Washington County were too small to handle a rescue of that magnitude." She offered me a grim smile. "Three hundred dogs...they had about three hundred dogs on that property." She shook her head sadly. "We really aren't set up to offer extensive resources to communities outside Boise and Ada County, but we couldn't walk away from it."

Pat Vance settled back into her chair and studied the wall. When she didn't go on, I prompted her.

"What did you find?" I asked.

Her eyes darkened. I was becoming accustomed to this. Each eyewitness to one of the dog rescues seemed to have buried the experience somewhere and was reluctant to resurrect it. Flat expressions, tight lips, narrow eyes— it lasted merely a moment. Brian and Don Coleman and Verda Palmer had shown it, and I'd heard it in the voices of Undersheriff Wolfe, Sara Sharette, and Ray Huff.

"We drove to the property, quite a ways out of Midvale, back in the hills," Pat Vance began. "They had rented a farmhouse, and, apparently, the owner hadn't checked in for a long time. When he finally came by and found all the dogs running around, he called the authorities in Washington County."

"Marv Williams?"

"Yes," Pat said. "Deputy Williams. Anyway, Barbara was using the name 'Sherry' at the time."

"That's actually her real name," I offered.

Pat hesitated, nodding. "Is Erickson a phony name, too?" she asked.

"That one's real," I answered. "Did you talk to Barbara at the time?"

"Oh, yes. I thought I could talk her into letting me help without getting knee-deep into all sorts of trouble." Vance issued a humorless laugh. "She sounded normal at first, but things went downhill quickly. She told me she was a college graduate with five degrees. She claimed to be a lawyer and a vet. Wouldn't let me get a word in edgewise. After a few minutes, I knew that reasoning with her wouldn't work, so I stopped listening. We decided to capture as many animals as we could and come back the next day." She tapped a pencil on her desk as if counting. "We got about eighty dogs the first round," she added.

I asked the obvious question. "How were the dogs doing?"

Again, Pat studied the wall, pointing her eyes with such intensity, I found myself following her gaze. For a moment, we sat together silently, staring at her wall. Then, she sighed. "Every animal we were able to save had at least five of eight common conditions," she said, ticking them off one-by-one. "Parvo, roundworm, Demodectic mange, Cheyletiella mites, coccidiosis, Giardia, sucking mites, and ear mites. It was unbelievable."

Vance leaned forward, her face contorted and sad. "It was almost too horrible to describe. The best of them were dirty, matted, and sick. All were starving. One dog had wedged itself between the barn and a fence and the other dogs were eating him. He was still alive when we got there. We found half-eaten puppies, too. There were lots of animals with obvious genetic problems from all the inbreeding. Some of the dogs lived like wild animals, sleeping in underground dens."

My jaw was aching, and I realized that I'd been clenching my teeth as I listened to Vance's account. I'd not forgotten my first day at the Harper site, trudging through the foul mud, inching my way through the darkness of the icy house, finding the miserable dog wrapped up and left behind.

After a long pause Vance continued, "Sherry, or Barbara or whatever her name is, went on and on about how the dogs were her 'babies.' She claimed that she loved them and never let them inbreed." Pat said. "It was ridiculous. She's telling me this nonsense while dogs are breeding right in front of us."

She leaned forward, facing me. "We found dilapidated cardboard boxes with ten to fifteen puppies in them. The mothers were communally feeding them. If one jumped out, another immediately jumped in to replace her."

I'd never heard of such a thing. "Dogs nurse puppies that aren't their own?" I asked.

Vance nodded. "Dogs do what they need to do to survive."

She went on, telling me that Barbara had visited the Boise IHS facility several times after the 1996 intervention in Midvale. Each time, she attempted to get a few dogs released into her custody. When that was unsuccessful, Barbara sent in friends who claimed that the dogs were theirs. Vance hadn't been fooled. "I threatened to cite her friends for animal abuse," she chuckled. "That shut them down."

A month later, Barbara appeared in a Washington County Court as Sherry Erickson. She was facing multiple counts of animal neglect. The charges were dropped when she signed an agreement stipulating that she would refrain from selling dogs, spay and neuter the dogs currently in her possession, and allow a local veterinarian to make unannounced visits. Although she signed, Barbara remained uncowed. "That Mrs. Erickson is pretty nervy, I'll tell you," Pat Vance said. "I guess as long as her dogs were alive, she thought they were okay."

Vance paused as if trying to find the logic in Barbara's perspective. "There are worse things than death," she said quietly, nodding. "We euthanize animals all the time, and one thing is clear—animals don't fear death. They fear mistreatment and starvation."

A few weeks after Barbara's court appearance, the IHS filed a complaint against Sherry Erickson, claiming that she had more than fifty dogs at a residence in Council, Idaho. The Ericksons promptly moved to Oregon.

I thanked Vance for her input and returned home, emotionally spent. Face-to-face meetings made the story I was following seem more intense. The phone kept me one step removed, providing a shield that allowed me to gather information without the emotional punch in the gut. I was tired.

Chapter Eighteen

September 1997—Adrian, Oregon.

The Ericksons were again living in their trailer after being evicted from a rental in Nyssa, Oregon. They'd liked the little house on Wilson Lane and liked the name even better, using "Wilson" as an alias to write unfunded checks. After the local veterinarian and other businesses complained, Bill Cummings, the Nyssa Chief of Police, investigated and subsequently advised the landlord, Vern Hancock, to evict the Ericksons. No reports were made to the humane society about the animals even though Cumming was nearly knocked over by a blast of fecal ammonia when he served Barbara and Bob with their eviction notice.

Bob and Barbara didn't mind being evicted. It was time for a new start, anyway. They loaded their pack into the small travel trailer and soon found a good campsite near Adrian, Oregon, where they settled in while Barbara looked for a new home.

"I got us a house, Bob." Barbara closed the trailer door; afterward bending to accept kisses from her dogs.

Bob perked up. "That one near Harper?"

"That's right," she said, "and there's plenty of room for the babies and a big old barn and a couple'a sheds. I can plant me a garden again and everything."

"When we gonna move in?" he asked.

Barbara held up a set of keys and jangled them. "As soon as we want—and I told her my name was Barbara so don't call me Sherry."

Bob grinned. "Do I get a new name, too?"

Within a month, Bob and Barbara Erickson were settled in their new home in Harper, Oregon. They had a new landlord—Verda Palmer—and Barbara had al-

ready marked the quiet, neatly-dressed man who ran Coleman Service as a possible source of credit. They moved their furniture out of storage, hung some pictures, and placed knick-knacks on the shelves. With home cooking filling the air, they completed the transition from their old trailer by placing plastic over the carpet, afterward topping it with a layer of newspapers.

Bob went to work building plywood shelters for the outside pack that was sure to grow with the coming of spring. Barbara placed "Dogs for Sale" ads in the local newspapers, instructing potential buyers to call "PMs only between 1 and 3." The number listed was the pay phone at Coleman Service, where each afternoon during the appointed hours, Barbara sat patiently in her car, waiting. Interested callers were assured that, "The dogs are registered with papers to prove it, and they've had their shots." No one was allowed on the Harper property. Instead, Barbara arranged to meet them, usually in the parking lot of a vacant store next to the Wal-Mart in Ontario where the customers were accosted by a wild-haired, nonstop talker with a carload of barking puppies.

"We're gettin' too many dogs," Bob told Barbara one day. He'd just completed the construction of another pen. "How we gonna feed 'em all?"

Barbara was tired of her husband's complaining. She'd just settled down on the couch for a cigarette after throwing out the urine and shit-stained newspapers from the day before. Afterward, she'd cleaned the plastic with bleach before setting out fresh papers, and the pungent smell had provoked a cacophony of yelping from their brood that was giving her a splitting headache. She waved her hand at Bob, trailing grayish swirls of cigarette smoke through the air. "Don't you worry. I sold three dogs yesterday. The ad's workin', and now that it's spring, they'll go like hotcakes."

Barbara pointed a gnarled finger at her husband. "But I won't let just anyone have 'em. If I don't like their looks, or the babies don't like 'em, then I don't care how much money they have...the babies are stayin' with me."

"I found two new puppies in the yard today," Bob told her. "Someone just dropped 'em off...to stay with the other doggies, I guess." He shrugged.

Barbara beamed. "Well, none of 'em'll go hungry. I'll feed them before I feed myself."

The ad had run its course. For over a week, the pay phone at Coleman Service had remained silent as Barbara sat in her car, smoking cigarette after cigarette. She hadn't minded so much. It was quiet, and the heat of summer hadn't yet made it to eastern Oregon. In a few weeks, the car would be an oven, and she'd have to find shade or a new spot. Sitting in the car gave her time to think, and after the long week without a single call, Barbara drove home and ordered Bob to find a clean scrap of cardboard and a grease pen. The next morning, she crafted a sign. She culled the best pups from their *most recent litters and gently placed the wiggling puppies in a box. The determined woman toted her brood out to the station wagon and headed for Ontario, Oregon. Once there, Barbara traveled the familiar roads that took her to Wal-Mart.*

Ontario was right on the Oregon-Idaho border at the center of a rural area that extends for many miles in all directions. This was farm and ranch country, and Ontario was the financial hub, the place where one could find aromatic fast food restaurants, bungalow-style motels, and cavernous discount stores like Wal-Mart. Wal-Mart, with its mantra of "one-stop shopping," was particularly attractive to farmers and ranchers who often traveled long distances to stock up on food for themselves and their animals.

Evan Chronister, the Wal-Mart store manager in Ontario, recognized Barbara as he watched her slowly make her way into the store, clearly favoring her hip. She was a regular customer, a bizarre woman who occasionally engaged one of his clerks in a somewhat loony and distinctly one-sided conversation. He didn't know her name.

"Hi, Evan," Barbara said, her eyes flitting from his name tag to his face.

"Good morning," Evan said from his side of the service counter. His station was near the front of the store, a sort of "command central" from where he could watch customers go in and out and still be available to the checkout clerks.

"I have a question for you," Barbara said, going on before Evan had a chance to say more. She seemed to know exactly what she wanted. "Tell me, what kind of credit plan do you have?" Barbara leaned against the counter and grinned.

Evan smiled, reaching for a glossy, colored application from its countertop display. "We have the Wal-Mart credit card," he told her. "You need to fill out this application."

Barbara shook her head, ignoring the brochure in Evan's outstretched hand. "No," she said. "I don't want no credit cards. Can't I just open an account for credit and pay at the beginning of each month?"

Evan suppressed a laugh, knowing what his district supervisor would say if he ever tried such a thing. "I'm sorry, Ma'am. We only accept credit cards."

Barbara smiled back. She liked this man with his clean shirt and tie, his quiet voice, and his manners. "Well okay," she said, "thank you, anyway."

She eyed him for a moment, making Evan Chronister feel as if he'd not seen the last of her. Her gray hair was sprayed in all directions, and her clothes looked as if she'd slept in them. A very faint, somewhat foul odor was about her, wafting across the counter to challenge the crisp scent of his aftershave. She was an unsettling person with a disheveled appearance and a cloudy personality, only her eyes clear and penetrating. A hint of a smile traced the corners of her mouth, and Evan took a step backward.

"Is there something else I can help you with, Ma'am," he said, trying to keep his voice steady. The woman was unnerving him.

Barbara let him squirm for a moment. Finally, she spoke. "Can you help me load up some dog food?"

Back home in Harper that afternoon, Bob greeted Barbara at the back door. Dogs scurried about at his feet. "We don't have no water," he announced, "so I checked the pipe that comes out of the ground next to the laundry room." He held up a filthy blanket. "And they had this old, rotten blanket stuffed down it. Boy, it smelled bad when I pulled it out."

Barbara followed her husband to the laundry room at the back of their cluttered house. Bob flipped on the light switch as they walked in, and the loud, metallic click startled several mice who scampered across the shelves, disappearing behind the washer.

"That's comin' up from the well," Bob said, pointing at a two-inch pipe that jutted out from the floor. Barbara leaned toward it, then stepped back, wrinkling her nose.

"Pee-yooey!" she exclaimed. She looked at Bob. "I bet there's mice down there, too. We better pour some bleach down it, and I'll see if Verda'll get someone out here to check it."

"What we gonna do for water in the meantime?" Bob whined. He ran his tongue across his lips. The thought of having no running water made him thirsty.

Barbara glared at him. "Go into town and get some jugs of water," she ordered. "Brian'll let us refill 'em at Coleman Service." She laughed and pointed. Bob followed her finger to where a fat, black snake lay curled in the corner.

"Well, looky there," Bob said. "An old bull snake. He must've snuck up through a crack in the foundation." He stooped to get a better look.

"He's just a little guy," Barbara said. "Hi, there bull snake...hi there ol' Billy-the-bull-snake."

She reached out as if to touch it. The snake didn't move. "There's plenty around here for you to eat," Barbara said, eyeing an adventurous mouse that had suddenly reappeared on the shelf over the washer. "You won't go hungry in this house."

"Old Verda tried to tell me there was a cap on that pipe," Barbara complained a few days later. She'd just returned from Verda's. There had been no coffee and conversation today. Barbara had come loaded to hunt bear.

"She said we have to fix it ourselves," Barbara said, her voice frustrated and loud. "Then she said, 'There's probably frogs down there, but a little frog shit never hurt no one.' I'd like to see her drink frog shit."

"Did you tell her about the fire in the attic?" Bob asked. A week before, the Ericksons had looked up from their couch in the living room to see sparks flying from the overhead light fixture.

Barbara snorted with disgust. "I told her. She said it's gonna cost ten thousand dollars to fix it, and she don't have that kind of money. She blames us 'cause the thing caught fire."

"What about her insurance?" Bob asked.

Barbara was pacing back and forth, shuddering with anger. "She claims her insurance got cancelled 'cause of our babies."

She stopped and took a deep breath, then tossed a dismissive hand at the air.

"She wants me to get rid of some of 'em—like that'll happen!" Saying this seemed to calm Barbara, and she laughed. Bob wasn't amused.

"So, I guess we'll have to get a new well pump ourselves," he said, his shoulders slumping.

Barbara nodded. "Yeah, and she says I told her we only had three dogs when we moved in, and I told her thirty and..."

The pack grew with each passing month, but the Ericksons' income didn't. Bob's retirement and Social Security checks were immediately gobbled up. As the weather grew colder, puppy sales waned, and Barbara brought the smaller dogs into the house where Bob had cordoned off sections with plywood. Bob tried to keep the males in one pen and the females in another, but the litters kept coming. Winter passed followed by spring and another summer. The furniture was again placed in storage, this time in the old shed behind the house.

"Somethin's gotta change," Bob complained during their second winter in Harper. "Maybe we should stop takin' in more dogs...or get some of 'em fixed."

"No," Barbara insisted. "It costs more to spay and neuter 'em than to let 'em have their litters and sell the puppies."

"But we're not sellin' enough of 'em."

Two years later, with the Harper rescue just six months away, Barbara moved into her van with about forty of the dogs, driven there, she said, by the mice.

"I had my little heater in the van," she later told me during one of our weekly talks, "and a bed and a hot plate, so I could heat me up some food whenever I wanted. It was real nice. I'd take my doggies with me—the ones I've had for years and years—and we'd go to town to sell puppies." She paused, and I heard her breathing quicken. "That *Wolfe*...he let them destroy my van when they took it with my babies. And I had just got done cleaning it at the Texaco."

Chapter Nineteen

Wednesday, January 8, 2003—two weeks before the rescue.
"Verda didn't ask about the rent, did she?" Bob asked.

Barbara hobbled out the back door and headed for the van as if Bob's question had sailed past. "'Course not," she answered after pausing to catch her breath. It had been three years since any rent was paid, and Verda had stopped asking. "She knows this house ain't worth nothin'...and she's not gonna spend a penny of her own money to fix it. She'll just let it run down and down and down." Barbara had spent the morning at Coleman Service, telling Verda about her years in the U.S. Navy, but she'd left feeling more than a little annoyed. Verda seemed to wear a mask of perpetual disbelief.

"We're outta doggie food again," Bob said. "You wanna pick some up in town?"

Barbara was blank-faced. "Why would I be goin' to town?" she snapped at him.

"You said..."

"I just got back from town. Why would I go again?"

Bob remained silent, letting his experience win out. A moment later, Barbara held out her hand expectantly, and he helped her climb into the driver's seat of the van. He closed the door behind her.

"I better take some of these new little ones with me," she shouted out the window. "See if I can sell 'em before I go to Wal-Mart."

"Okay," Bob said. He went into the house and returned with one of the few cardboard boxes at their Harper home that had not been ripped to shreds by the dogs. Trotting about the yard, he grabbed as many scrawny, squirming puppies as he could catch, afterward shoving the box just inside the passenger door of the van. Almost immediately, Barbara put the van in gear and lurched off, a spray of gravel from her spinning tires sending dogs running in all directions. An hour later, she arrived in Ontario, Oregon, and pulled into the parking lot of the vacant store next to Wal-Mart. There were plenty of cars in the lot and an even flow of people streamed in and out, a favorable sign for puppy sales.

Barbara got out and immediately posted her usual cardboard sign, "Chawawas for sale."

She gently took one of the puppies from the box and cuddled it as she walked toward the blackened entrance to a huge building that had once housed the Akins Variety Store.

Barbara smiled as two girls dashed over. Without a word, she handed over the Chihuahua to one of the girls, a sandy-haired beauty with long arms and legs and a mouth full of braces with pink elastics.

"I have the whole litter in my van," Barbara said. "You wanna come see 'em?"

"Okay," the sandy-haired girl said. The other girl frowned. She was shorter and lacked braces, but was otherwise a mirror image of the taller girl.

"Lissa..." she said quietly, averting her eyes from Barbara's.

"Oh *come on*, Darcy," Lissa pleaded. We're just gonna, like, *look*, okay? It's not like we're getting in her *car* or anything, right?" She looked to Barbara for support. Barbara smiled warmly, but Darcy's look of skepticism was unwavering.

Lissa's face darkened. "Gaw, Darcy, we're not gonna end up on the side of, like, a *milk carton* or something. We're just gonna look at her puppies."

"Okay," the younger girl said quietly, "but we're just, like, looking, right?"

The two girls followed Barbara as she slowly shuffled back to the van. Stopping near the rear bumper, Barbara turned and smiled. "You girls stay here," she said. "Your mama would want you to stay where other people can see you." She smiled at Darcy who shyly lifted her eyes but didn't answer.

With the girls waiting, Barbara retrieved a second puppy from the van and brought it back, handing it directly to Darcy.

"Ohhh," Darcy said, "he has tears in his eyes."

"It's just a little cold," Barbara reassured her. "I had a pup many years ago who had the measles. He broke out in a really red rash, so I took him to the vet. The vet checked him out, and then he started laughin' up a storm."

Barbara studied the two girls. They seemed interested in her story. Their eyes were bright and clear and directly on her. They were hooked.

"And I said 'What's so funny?' and he said, 'He's got the measles!' Then he said, 'Keep him out of the sun and give him some antibiotics.'"

"I never heard of a dog having measles," Lissa said. For the first time, her face registered skepticism.

"Oh, yeah. It was measles all right," Barbara said, nodding her head vigorously. "Before then, that little dog caught double pneumonia, and I took him to the vet, and they wanted to put him to sleep, and I had a fit. His temperature was ninety-eight-point-six like ours, and I said, 'Can't you give him some antibiotics?' And they did, so I took him home and rubbed his little chest with Ben Gay. Then I put holes for his legs in a towel and wrapped him in it. I put him on a heatin' pad and gave him liquid vitamins...human liquid vitamins."

Barbara paused to catch her breath. Lissa and Darcy were cooing over the puppies. They'd stopped listening.

"And in three days that puppy was up and runnin' all over the place. I took him to the vet and said, 'This is the one you wanted to put to sleep.' And he looked at me real funny and said, 'Tell me what you done.' And I told him and he said, 'I got to keep that in mind.'"

Barbara spent the afternoon telling her stories and selling puppies until the sun hung low in the sky. Only two Chihuahuas were left when she climbed into the van, one of them the unfortunate little dog with the runny eye. Barbara settled back into the seat and counted her money. She'd earned enough to pay for ten bags of dog food. It had been a good day.

In the seat next to her, the two puppies were fast asleep, exhausted by their afternoon of being manhandled by potential buyers and their young children. Curled up next to each other, they hardly moved; their breathing was so soft that Barbara panicked. She reached out to touch them, keeping her hand in place until the gentle rise and fall of their tiny chests was certain. They were okay. Just sleeping.

Barbara leaned over and kissed each one. They felt warm and safe, and her eyes became watery. She'd sold her puppies to perfect strangers.

Barbara covered the two remaining dogs with her coat, grabbed her cardboard sign, and threw it out the window.

She wiped her cheeks dry and smiled at the two puppies who chose that moment to stretch and yawn as adorably as possible before settling back into each other.

Barbara started the engine and laboriously ground it into gear, afterward easing out of the parking lot and onto the road for home, forgetting that her unfilled Wal-Mart shopping list was tucked into the pocket of her coat.

Chapter Twenty

11:00 a.m., Thursday, January 23, 2003—the morning of the Harper rescue.
Kammy Rios was hard at work when the phone rang. A long-time animal advocate in Nyssa, Oregon, she was about to open an animal shelter just across the border in nearby Fruitland, Idaho. Kammy had been taking in stray dogs and cats for most of her life and the shelter—to be called "New Beginnings"—was not only an extension of her mission but a necessity. After her foster-care brood of animals swelled to include fifteen dogs and thirty cats, husband Guadalupe had issued an ultimatum. "Get a building or quit this!" He didn't have to tell her twice. A vacant store on a busy thoroughfare in Fruitland was available, and Kammy snapped it up. Once revamped, New Beginnings was to be a "no kill" animal shelter.

Like all good ideas, this one had been easy to conceive, nearly impossible to carry off. Nonetheless, this morning, Kammy had taken possession of the building and was beginning to remove debris left by the previous tenant. Afterward, Guadalupe would help her begin the construction of kennels. Almost grateful for the interruption, Kammy answered the phone, hearing the voice of her friend Sara Sharette.

"Remember that woman I told you about?" Sara's words came in a rush. "The one selling puppies at the Wal-Mart in Ontario?"

When Kammy didn't answer, Sara went on. "Barbara Erickson," she said, "the dog woman. She's got three puppies she wants to give up. She wants to meet me at the old Atkins store. I guess Wal-Mart won't let her on the lot anymore, so she's hanging out next door. "

Kammy remembered Sara's stories of the frizzy-haired woman with the funny "Chawawas" sign who had claimed to be both a vet and a lawyer.

"I wonder what the deal is," she said to Sara. "From what you told me, she seemed reluctant to give up any of her dogs...even to sell them. Did she say why?"

"I didn't get to talk to her," Sara answered. "She left a message on my machine. She said, 'Just be at the Akins parking lot at noon today.' Listen, Kammy, I know it's short notice, but could you house some puppies at your new shelter?"

Sara heard a rush of air as Kammy caught her breath, followed by a few seconds of silence.

"We're really not ready here, Sara," Kammy said slowly. "We have another week of work to do. Maybe I could keep them at home until..."

Sara didn't wait for her to finish. "Could you...could you come with me?" she pleaded, her voice trailing off. "Her dogs were in such sad shape the last time I saw them. I'd really like to get her to hand over some of the others, as well."

Sara hesitated.

"Please, Kammy," she said.

Kammy had work to do, a deadline to meet. Sara's plan would take her off course. Still, the urgency in her friend's voice was hard to ignore. She looked at her watch.

"Okay," she said. "I'll meet you at noon."

After Sara hung up, she immediately phoned the Malheur County Sheriff. After two rings, a steady, serious voice came on the line.

"Undersheriff Wolfe...may I help you?"

"This is Sara Sharette from Second Chance." She paused, but went on when Wolfe remained silent. "Is there a law that limits the number of animals a person can own?" she asked.

She heard the squeak of Wolfe's chair as he shifted his weight. "Oregon law states that a person can have as many animals as they can reasonably care for," he said. His answer seemed rehearsed, as if he'd used it before. "If the animals have food and water and appear to be healthy, there's no restriction regarding the actual number of pets."

"What if someone has thirty dogs in a van?" Sara pressed him. "What if the animals aren't doing well?" She heard the pitch of her voice rising along with her heart rate and took a deep breath. A moment later, she heard the words she'd hoped for.

"Are you calling about the Ericksons?"

Sara let her breath out in a rush. "Yes," she said gratefully, "it's Barbara Erickson."

"I thought so," Wolfe answered. Sara heard a rustle of papers, then Wolfe's voice again. "Where did you see her van?" he asked.

Sara spoke slowly, giving Wolfe ample time to scribble notes. She told him about her first meeting in the Wal-Mart parking lot, the subsequent follow-ups, and Barbara's request to place three pups with Second Chance.

"This morning, I called Kammy Rios from New Beginnings. Have you heard of them?" Sara asked. When Wolfe didn't respond, she continued. "They're starting a new shelter for animals. She's agreed to accept the dogs until alternative placement can be found." Sara plunged ahead. "*All* the dogs... not just the three Barb called about. I'm not sure if I was clear about that."

"Okay," Wolfe answered.

"They'll take *all* the dogs. None have to be left behind."

"I understand," Wolfe said. He hesitated, the tap of his pencil on the desk echoing through the phone. At last, he spoke. "We're going to need a search warrant," he said.

Chapter Twenty-One

1:00 p.m., Thursday, January 23, 2003.

Hundreds of barking dogs, the Ericksons' canine doorbell, announced the arrival of intruders. Before Undersheriff Wolfe and Deputy Oscar Martinez could open the gate, Bob Erickson appeared at the front door in soiled blue coveralls, an unlit cigarette in one hand.

"What are you guys doin'?" Bob stepped onto the porch, his slicked-back hair shining like obsidian. He gestured at the dogs that milled about the porch. "They're gettin' upset. Look at 'em. You're makin' 'em fight." Several barking dogs scurried forward in a small pack, yapping furiously at the officers before scattering.

Wolfe looked at Deputy Martinez and nodded. More dogs appeared from behind the house, some curious, others barking frenetically. Martinez peered through the eyepiece of his small video camera, aimed, and pressed the "record" button.

"What the hell are you doin'?" Bob demanded, his face red.

"We're videotaping." Wolfe kept his eyes leveled on Bob's. After a moment, the old man wilted. He looked away.

"How many dogs are in the house?" Wolfe asked him.

"Who knows? I don't count 'em."

"When will Mrs. Erickson be home?"

Bob wedged the cigarette between his teeth and flicked the lighter, producing a small yellow flame. Taking a deep drag, he shook his head. "To-day...sometime," he said, exhaling a cloud of smoke. "She's gettin' food for her babies."

Wolfe pointed at an empty dish just as one of the dogs upset it, trying to dig at the ground beneath. Martinez dutifully aimed his camera at the spot.

"Do you have any food right now?" Wolfe asked.

"You mean right *now*?" Bob's jaw jutted out for a second as he regained some courage, but one glance at Undersheriff Wolfe was enough to deflate him. He looked down at his shoes. "At the moment? No."

"When was the last time they were fed?"

"Yesterday."

Martinez aimed his camera at a pair of dogs who rutted near one corner of the house. Just behind them, a scrawny dog sat in the mud, shivering as he licked feebly at one paw. Bob followed their eyes.

"Ain't nothin' I can do 'bout that one," he muttered. Without another word, he turned and went back into the house.

The officers quickly made their way through the property, following the muddy path beneath the spruce trees at the side of the house. The odor was overwhelming. In the back, they videotaped pens filled with hysterically barking dogs. The larger dogs seemed relatively active and healthy, but most of the animals were listless and dirty, the coats of the long-hairs matted with mud and feces, the short-hair breeds shivering uncontrollably. More than a few dogs lay dead, scattered among the broken-down washers and dryers. As Wolfe and Deputy Martinez walked, more and more dogs surrounded them, jumping into and over one another, desperate for attention.

Icy winter wind kicked up, whipping and snapping the tarps that roofed the pens, funneling through the maze of shelters to produce a low howl. Wolfe stopped and bowed his head, pulling his broad-brimmed hat on tighter. Martinez kept going, slowly scanning the yard with his camera. Wolfe watched him for a moment. He was surrounded by dogs, their faces frantic and lost, the plaintive sound of their cries coalescing into a single thing, a wail that filled Wolfe's ears and brought tears to his eyes.

Suddenly, Deputy Martinez was next to him, the sound of his voice low and distant. Wolfe stared at him, trying to read his lips. Martinez's mouth continued to move, but his words were unintelligible, lost in the wind or the moans of the desperate animals. When Wolfe looked away, his deputy stopped talking. Wood waited, eyes narrowed against a brief sliver of sun that had momentarily pierced the overcast. After a moment, Wolfe took a deep breath and released it. Then, he looked at Deputy Martinez and nodded.

"You were saying?"

Martinez studied his boss for a moment, openly curious. "I was saying," he said, holding up his video camera and nodding grimly, "that this should be enough to get us a search warrant."

Chapter Twenty-Two

"What triggered the rescue?" I asked Undersheriff Wolfe during a phone call. I was following up on some details.

"We saw dogs in her van with health problems," he said. "They had open sores, and one had an injured eye, plus the complaints from neighbors. We took a camera to the Erickson house in Harper and videotaped the dogs in the mud and feces."

After Barbara asked Sara Sharette to take three of her pups, a plan had been hatched. Sara and Kammy Rios went together to meet Barbara in the parking lot near the Wal-Mart where she typically set up shop. Sara had often been there, checking on the condition of Barbara's animals. This time, however, Wolfe was there, too, and a confrontation ensued. Wolfe challenged the care the Ericksons were providing and was met by Barbara's standard response—anger, a flurry of lies, pleading, and excuses. She was a vet, he had no right to persecute her, her animals were well cared for, she would "sue his ass," and so on. But Wolfe persisted, informing Barbara that he and a deputy would be out that afternoon to gather evidence.

"The dogs she handed over to Sara and Kammy were in sad shape," Wolfe finished up. "Cherry eye, mange, you name it."

I asked Wolfe for a copy of the video, and he directed me to the Malheur County Clerk's Office. Another quick phone conversation with the court clerk, and a copy of the tape Wolfe and Wood had used to obtain a search warrant was on the way.

The video arrived in the mail within a week. I slid it into the VCR and pressed the "start" button, and the television screen was filled with frantic, barking dogs.

Watching the video, I was transported. Once again, I bounced along Coleman Road and turned down the rutted driveway, saw the deserted yard and the falling-down house. I reflexively covered my nose and mouth as I remembered the sound of my boots and the overwhelming stench as I'd slogged through the foul mud. It was otherworldly to see living creatures on my television screen, tattooing the sides of Verda Palmer's once cute, little house and pockmarking the yard with their footprints. They were apparitions, doppelgangers that seemed to exist, not as flesh-and-blood, but as images trapped inside the camera. I felt ashamed, realizing that after all my months of work on the story, I had yet to see a single real-life survivor from the Ericksons' pack, only video footage.

I rewound the video and reviewed it several more times, taking notes. Bob Erickson was on the tape, occasionally peering out the front door of the dilapidated house as if he were the neighborhood curmudgeon, ready to yell, "Get off the lawn." I tried to get a sense of him. For years, he had been the man in the shadow of Barbara's bold spirit. In the video, the legs of Bob's blue coveralls were covered with muddy paw prints. His movements were slow and indecisive. Barbara had often claimed that Bob had Alzheimer's disease, although I'd found no confirmation of the diagnosis. Yet, he did seem dependent, incapable of making his own decisions. "Ain't nothin' I can do about it," he'd told Wolfe. Apparently, the court agreed, because Bob was never ordered to pay restitution or undergo counseling. He was released from jail after less than a day, while Barbara was incarcerated for several weeks. Yet, other than Barbara, he was the one person who witnessed the full extent of the dogs' suffering. And he did nothing. Perhaps because he couldn't. Perhaps because he didn't care. Even now, as I write this, Bob Erickson remains a mystery to me.

Near the end of my fifth viewing, I stretched my back and stood in front of the TV. The barking dogs turned into static, and I reached for the remote. Suddenly, the static stopped. When I looked up, my hand went to my mouth, and I sat down on the floor again as video taken *inside* the house flickered across the television screen. The chorus of outside barking faded as the videographer moved slowly through the house, replaced by frantic yelping from the dogs living inside. Erratic light showed several inches of feces on the floor. As the camera panned the room, dogs could be seen everywhere, vying for positions on the furniture, their movement producing furry, undulating waves. I recognized the brown Formica-topped table that I'd shuffled past in the darkness just days after the rescue. Seeing it recalled the putrid odors of the Erickson farm, and I shivered, again covering my nose and mouth with one hand. As I watched, the picture swayed and jerked as wide-eyed, confused dogs rammed into the cameraman. Lean, muscular animals leapt about the furniture while smaller, bone-thin dogs lay on the floor, too weak to lift their heads. The sound was overwhelming—snarling, gnashing teeth, and howling interrupted by sudden shrieks—a blast wave of noise that seemed to bounce off the walls, gaining energy, and becoming louder still. I watched, horrified all over again, until static mercifully replaced the images.

Brian Wolfe had told me that the rescuers found an additional three hundred dogs living inside the Erickson's small, two-bedroom house. His voice had been distant and sad. I'd written the number down—just another fact—and filed it away. Now, watching the maddened, pleading eyes, I finally understood Brian Wolfe and Sara Sharette and Kammy Rios and Pat Vance and the other eyewitnesses I'd interviewed. They'd all displayed an initial reticence, and I'd chalked that up to distrust of a stranger. But, watching this brief video segment, lasting only thirty seconds, I began to understand. These were good, small town people to whom trust came naturally. Their reticence was not distrust, not at all. They were trying to understand what had happened and what they'd seen. Probably, they were trying to forget.

I shut off the VCR and TV, lay back on the floor, and stared at the ceiling. How much love and attention could each dog expect? The stronger, healthier dogs could push to the front, but what about the weaker ones who couldn't hold their spots? And the puppies—how easy to be trampled and injured, even eaten. What about the rest—those not strong enough to compete, but not weak enough to die? What about them? What about them all? I remembered what Barbara had repeatedly told me. "Hell no!" she'd claim indignantly. "There weren't five hundred dogs in all of the town of Harper. *They* just said that. They tried to make it sound worse to...you know...to raise donations. That Barbara Hutchinson...the one with Second Chance...she bought a new house. I wonder where she got all that money. And there wasn't a damn thing wrong with my animals. *They* just used a piece of tin...a badge...to steal. They..."

I shut off Barbara's cigarette-coarsened voice in my mind. There was nothing equivocal about what I was thinking. *I was mad.* Despite my understanding of animal hoarding through the reading I'd done and the many conversations with Barbara, despite my investigation and interviews, tweaking out the story of the little girl she'd been and the life she'd endured, despite it all, I was mad.

Chapter Twenty-Three

Thursday, January 23, 2003—the rescue begins.

Sara Sharette called Barbara Hutchinson, president of Second Chance, immediately after she, Kammy Rios, and Undersheriff Wolfe had confronted Barbara in the parking lot near Wal-Mart. She quickly detailed the plan to rescue the dogs on the Erickson farm. Kammy Rios, despite not yet having power or water at the New Beginnings building, was prepared to rush things along in order to take fifty to one hundred dogs.

"You know, we don't have funds for this right now," Hutchinson told Sara. She seemed hesitant.

Sara had her answer ready. "I'll call the media. Maybe we can get volunteers and donations that way. I can also call some local vets...see if they'll help out."

There was urgency in Sara's voice and Hutchinson responded to it. "Okay," she said. "I'll call the humane societies in Oregon and Idaho. They'll get veterinarians lined up, so you don't need to worry about that. They can work on placement of the dogs, too.

Sara breathed a sigh of relief. "Believe me, Barbara, I wish we had more time to plan, but..." She didn't finish. Hutchinson understood. Their window of opportunity had opened. If they were to save the dogs, they needed to act now.

Later that day, with a search warrant secured, the rescue operation began to organize. By that time, a group had formed that included Brian Wolfe, Oscar Martinez, a sheriff's deputy with arms the size of tree trunks, Sara Sharette, and Barbara Hutchinson. Wolfe brought along an additional half dozen sheriff's deputies and some Vale, Oregon, firefighters, while Hutchinson had recruited additional volunteers, including Don Coleman. One television reporter was there, joined by a reporter and photographer from *The Idaho Statesman*. In all, nearly two dozen men and women were gathering when Sara Sharette maneuvered the truck she'd wangled from Ryder Rentals into the vacant lot next to the Wal-Mart in Ontario. It was just before 4:00 p.m. on January 23, 2003.

Supplies were low as was the outside temperature, which would continue to fall as the ghostly gloom of a typical January day in eastern Oregon descended upon the expedition. Although given only a few hours, Sara had managed to collect about twenty-one portable kennels and dog crates, a box of rubber gloves, and a handful of disposable facemasks. It wasn't enough, but she knew it would have to do.

"Sara!"

The muffled voice coming from the other side of the truck cab startled her. Sara looked over and saw Barbara Hutchinson's face on the other side of the glass. She leaned across the seat and unlocked the passenger door.

"Wolfe just pulled up behind me, and the news people are here, too," Hutchinson said, after pulling open the door and poking her head inside the warm compartment.

Sara climbed down from the truck and followed Hutchinson to the rear where Wolfe and Deputy Martinez waited next to their patrol car. A Channel Six van was there along with two more cruisers. Before Sara could introduce herself to Martinez, a reporter approached, stretching a hand toward Wolfe.

"I'm Kathryn May with Channel Six News," she said. Her voice was confident, but not pushy. "Is this the dog rescue team?"

Wolfe nodded in reply and faced the group that had gathered around him in a semicircle. "Listen up, everyone," he said in a loud voice, waiting a few seconds before going on. "Okay, here's the deal. Deputy Martinez and I were at the Erickson house a couple of hours ago, and there looked to be at least a hundred dogs running around outside and we're not sure how many more in the house. Once we're there, everyone will stay on the road except for Deputy Martinez, Ms. Hutchinson, and myself. We'll have to read the search warrant to the Ericksons before anyone can catch any dogs. Afterward, we'll start gathering them up."

He indicated his square-shouldered deputy with a nod. "Deputy Martinez will hand out catchpoles and masks. It's a mess out there and the smell will overwhelm you if you don't have a mask."

Wolfe offered the group a weary smile, holding up a handful of masks.

"Believe me," he said, shaking his head, "you'll need the mask. It's a mess out there, and if the dogs don't get you, the smell will."

Sara Sharette raised her hand. "I have about twenty dog crates in the truck and a box of gloves."

Wolfe nodded. "Good," he said. "Listen, I don't want to scare anyone off—God knows we need all the help we can get—but the truth is that no one's been inside the house, and we really don't know what we'll find." He paused, looking down at the cracked pavement. When he looked up, his face was grim. "You can bet it will be worse than anything we saw on the grounds."

"You saw about two hundred dogs outside," Kathryn, the reporter, said. "How many do you expect to take in all?" Her pen was poised over a notepad, eyes firmly fixed on Wolfe's.

Wolfe lifted his eyebrows and shrugged. "I don't know," he said, afterward offering a humorless laugh. "More than two hundred...enough to occupy a few hours."

"What if there are more?" one of the volunteers asked.

Wolfe squared his shoulders. "We'll stay until we get every, last one."

Throughout the small group, heads nodded. They all knew the story, and Wolfe's answer reassured them that the right thing would be done. These were people used to serving the public; most of them pet owners, more than a few of them hunters whose dogs were an extension of their own personalities. The question had been asked, but they already knew the answer. You'd have to fight off these men and women to keep them from saving every dog they could. *Every last one.*

Hutchinson spoke up. "I'd like to add something," she said. "The dogs may very well have any number of diseases." She nodded at Sara. "The gloves will help some, but we all need to be very cautious about dog bites. I have a first aid kit if we need it."

"That's a good point," Wolfe said. "As far as we know, none of these dogs has been immunized or even tested for rabies. So be careful."

One of the reporters raised a hand, but Wolfe went on without waiting for the question. "The news media will not be allowed on the property until after the rescue," he said. Groans and objections were immediately hurled at him, but Wolfe was undeterred, letting the reporters' protests bounce off like ping-pong balls. "You guys can set up across the street," he told them.

With no other questions forthcoming, Wolfe nodded at Martinez, and they climbed into their squad car. Less than a minute later, a small train of cars was on Highway 20, headed for Harper, Oregon, led by Undersheriff Wolfe.

About forty minutes later, the caravan's arrival at the Erickson house triggered a frenzy of high-pitched barking from the pack of dogs that scrambled about the yard. Wolfe slowed his patrol car to a stop across the street, then slowly climbed out. Sara, with Barbara Hutchinson riding along, pulled her truck in behind him. The somewhat disgruntled reporters parked their cars across the street and gathered to watch.

"The smell is just unbelievable," Sara warned Hutchinson. She glanced across the street at the reporters, some of whom had pulled up their jackets or sweaters over their noses. With the overpowering odor coming from the property, they now seemed content to be barred from the site. Sara offered up a crooked grin. "Thank God we brought some masks," she said, opening her door.

Hutchinson slid out from the passenger's seat and joined Sara at the rear of the truck. Undersheriff Wolfe was waiting there.

"Ready for this?" he said to the two women.

Sara's stomach had already begun to jump and roll. She took a few steps, letting the truck block her from the view of the reporters, fearing that she might become very sick on television. She pinched her nose shut and took a deep breath through her mouth. "How about if I stay here to unload stuff," she said, a statement, not a request.

Wolfe nodded. "Okay," he said, glancing at Hutchinson and Deputy Martinez. "Let's go."

Clutching a video camera, Wolfe approached the front gate with Hutchinson behind him, their boots sinking ankle-deep into the cold mud. The howling escalated as they neared the house. A group of six or seven dogs rushed at them. These were larger and more aggressive than the Chihuahuas and terriers that Sara Sharette had previously seen, their teeth bared, growls low and ominous. The leader came at them barking furiously, but quickly turned tail when Martinez fended him off with the plastic dog crate he was carrying. The others followed at a safe distance, yelping their displeasure, pacing about and peeing to mark their territory.

Wolfe reached the house first and climbed the porch steps two at a time. He waited for Hutchinson and Martinez to catch up before rapping on the door with his fist.

"Malheur County Sheriff's Office," Wolfe yelled. "Barbara and Bob Erickson, open the door."

After half a minute with no answer, Wolfe was about to bang on the door again when it creaked open just enough to expose Bob Erickson's grizzled face.

"Open up, Mr. Erickson," Wolfe ordered. "I have a search warrant." He reached out and pushed on the door, at the same time hitting the "record" button on his video camera. Bob stepped back, allowing the door to swing open, and Wolfe caught his breath.

Hundreds of barking dogs swarmed the room.

"We're in trouble now," Wolfe said from the corner of his mouth. He leveled grim eyes at Bob. "Is Mrs. Erickson here?" he shouted, barely able to make himself heard over the clamor inside the house.

Bob slowly shook his head, keeping his eyes on the ground.

"Mr. Erickson, I want you to listen as I read this," Wolfe yelled. He read the court-ordered search warrant to a befuddled looking Bob Erickson with Barbara Hutchinson and Deputy Martinez steadily inching into the house. What they saw was utter chaos. Mostly small-breed dogs were packed nearly shoulder-to-shoulder inside the front room. The intruders seemed to excite them even more. They leapt about as if maddened, scrambling over furniture and slipping on the excrement-covered floor. A single golden retriever lay on a chair, surveying the pandemonium around him as if it didn't involve him. He studied Wolfe for a moment as the tall undersheriff finished reading the warrant, then lowered his head and closed his eyes.

"We'll never get them all in one trip," Hutchinson whispered.

Wolfe nodded. "I'll call Vale Search and Rescue. They should be able to round up some stock trailers. Otherwise, we'll be here all night." He backed out of the house and headed for his patrol car. Hutchinson stayed, pushing through the sea of fur to a table filled with barking dogs. After setting the wire cages she'd brought from the truck on the floor, she extended a hand for the dogs to sniff. The movement seemed to agitate several of the already frenzied animals. One ducked as if expecting to be hit, while others reared and lurched backward, knocking several dogs off the table. One of the smallest—a brown-and-white terrier snarled at her, its bared teeth a tongue-length from her hand.

"Watch that one." Bob warned her. "That's Bingo. He might nip you." The old man seemed amused.

Hutchinson pulled back her hand, glaring at Bob. "They know you better than me," she said, putting as much authority in her voice as possible. "Pick them up, and hand them to me." She said it as if giving an order, and Bob caved in just as she suspected he would. He shuffled over to the table.

"Aw...I ain't gonna hurt you, little guy," he said. His hand shot out like a frog's tongue, snatching Bingo by the scruff of his neck. Bingo writhed and snapped, his eyes bugging wildly.

"It's okay, baby," Bob cooed.

Hutchinson picked up one of the cages and opened the door, letting Bob set the crazed dog inside.

"Better close it qui..."

Before Bob could finish speaking, Bingo had sprung from the cage, darting across the floor and disappearing into the next room. Hutchinson watched him go. She glanced at Martinez and shook her head. "Let's try another one," she said.

With Hutchinson giving orders and Bob capturing, they gathered the dogs from the table one-by-one and put them in cages. Most of the inside dogs were small, fitting several to a cage. Within a few minutes, Martinez had hauled two full crates with about six dogs each out to the truck. Deputy Timothy McMenamin came from outside to help out.

"Found this on the porch," he said, heaving a kennel onto the table. The red-haired deputy wasn't wearing a mask, and within a few minutes, his face was pea-green.

"I'll be outside," he said, rushing for the door.

After McMenamin left, Deputy Richard Harriman, a young, blond bull of a man, replaced him. He came in with a plastic kennel in one hand and a catchpole in the other.

"We're running out of crates," Hutchinson told him, "so only the weakest dogs get kennel space. The others we'll load one at a time at the end of a catchpole."

"Yes, Ma'am," Harriman said. If the smell bothered him, he didn't show it. Hutchison looked him over—stern brow, rugged jaw, probably a strong stomach.

You'll do, she thought.

They labored on. Although not physically demanding, it was emotionally exhausting work. Just when Hutchinson thought she'd seen the worst of it, an even thinner, more pathetic dog would be discovered. After a while, only anger protected her from bursting into tears.

"There's a little one without any fur, and he's shivering," she said to Bob Erickson, making no effort to hide her contempt. "Let's get him in a cage." Bob settled the trembling pup into the brawny arms of Deputy Harriman who swaddled it in a blanket and gently slid him into one of the cages. "He looks like a little burrito, all wrapped up," the deputy said to Hutchinson. Afterward, he covered the cage with another blanket. "Better chance of keeping warm while he's away from his pack," he explained. His eyes were wet.

Hutchinson looked away, her throat full. "There's a mom and her babies in the corner," she said, fighting back tears. "Let's get them in a cage, too, before we run out." Together, the deputy and Hutchinson carefully plucked each tiny suckling from their skinny, listless mother, placing them in a crate that had been padded with a towel. Afterward, Hutchinson gently slid the mother in with her pups. She stood back, watching as local dairyman Joel Ward, a wriggling dog dangling from his catchpole, lurched into Harriman, nearly knocking him over.

"Trying to get the hang of this," he said, making no attempt to hide the frustration in his voice.

By now, Hutchinson had been inside the airless, foul home longer than any of the others, save Bob Erickson, who seemed not to notice the stench. She picked up the crate holding the mother and pups, looking at Deputy Harriman. He nodded, and she shuffled out of the house followed by Ward, a black mop of a dog hanging on the end of his catchpole. Together, they slogged back across the yard to the Ryder truck.

Out in the driveway, Sara stood in the back of the truck where she'd formed a makeshift barrier with a row of filled kennels. About twenty dogs roamed about behind her, trying to sniff a way out.

"What's it like in there?" Sara asked Hutchinson.

Hutchinson didn't answer right away. She'd spotted the brown-and-white terrier that had escaped. His bravado had evaporated, and he cowered at the center of his cage.

"The house is packed with dogs," Hutchinson said, her breath visible in the wintry air. She shook her head, studying the ground. "It's just...just... swarming. I cannot *even begin* to describe it. It's absolutely....we were swimming in barking dogs."

Wolfe soon joined them, tugging at his soiled gloves. "We have stock trailers coming with the Vale volunteers," he told the two women, "but they may not be here for another hour or so."

"It's gonna take us that long just to fill this truck," Hutchinson said, gesturing at the Ryder rental with her shoulder.

One of the firefighters appeared from around the corner of the truck, his muffler wrapped around his nose and mouth, tears running down his cheeks. "The ammonia's burning my eyes," he complained, blinking furiously. He picked up a pair of empty cages from the ground and headed back. Wolfe watched him go. "In my entire career in law enforcement," he said, "I have never, *ever* smelled anything so bad." Sara and Hutchinson nodded, as Wolfe went on. "I once took a call on a dead body left under an electric blanket for several weeks...and it wasn't as bad as the stench in that house." He exhaled forcefully. "It's unbearable."

"We'll pretty much have to destroy our clothes when we're done," said Hutchinson. "Shoes, boots, clothes...everything into the dumpster."

Wolfe and Hutchinson slogged back to the house where growling, nipping dogs darted about, trying to evade capture. Hutchinson didn't have a catchpole, but with Bob Erickson's help, she continued to fill the cages. After a while, Bob got into it, almost as if he were one of the volunteers, not a co-conspirator.

"Watch out...this one might getcha," he said, picking up a feisty Chihuahua. Then he kissed it, before edging it through the door of the cage Hutchinson held. "Bye-bye, Baby," he said cheerfully.

He picked up another dog. "This is Angel...she's a nice 'un." He kissed her good-bye and handed her over.

"You really seem to know each one," Hutchinson said.

Bob grinned at her. "They're our babies," he announced over the earsplitting yelps. "We named 'em all."

When he saw the skeptical look on Hutchinson's face, he drained the grin.

"I told my wife we was gettin' too many dogs," he said. Bob cuddled a pup. "I told her somethin' was gonna happen." He looked at Hutchinson, his face filled with innocence. "How long you 'spect this is gonna go on?"

The Second Chance President was speechless. For a moment, she stared at the old man, as if waiting for the punch line to a bad joke. Finally, she spoke. "We're going to take them all," she said.

Bob slumped like a rag doll. "That could take all night," he said. He remained quiet for a moment, then brightened as another skinny, mixed-breed dog nuzzled the back of his leg. He picked her up. "Bye-bye, Sheila," he said, "see you later."

Hutchinson and Bob Erickson continued to load up dogs taken off the single table in the room. As soon as Bob grabbed one dog, another leapt up and took his place, prancing about proudly on the newly claimed territory. It was like a magician pulling rabbit after rabbit from his top hat—no end in sight. After a while, Hutchinson stopped looking at the floor, knowing that a seemingly inexhaustible supply of dogs was waiting. Her patience—already strained—began to wear thin, and she stopped waiting for Bob's annoying, cutesy goodbyes to "Bootsy" or "Brownie," snatching the dogs herself and putting them in cages.

After what seemed a very long time, Hutchinson chanced a look about. The room was beginning to clear a bit. At the entry to the hallway, a gnarled sheet of plywood gated the opening, and furry, little heads bobbed up and down, illuminated by a single, bare light bulb.

Hutchinson sighed deeply. "I need a break," she said, although none of the other rescuers chasing dogs about the house paid the least attention. She grabbed a cage containing only two, small dogs and headed for the front door.

Once outside, Hutchinson stood on the porch for a moment, taking deep breaths. Compared to the rancid environment inside the house, the air seemed almost fresh. In the yard, uniformed deputies and civilian volunteers dashed about, shouting and cursing as they waved their catchpoles in the fading light. The easy catches had already been made, and the remaining animals were fast and elusive. Worse yet, the whole thing was a game to most of the dogs, a game of dog tag, one they were winning. It was almost comical, and Hutchinson might have found it funny had she not just escaped from the bedlam inside the house.

Over two hours later, Vale Search and Rescue arrived at the Erickson house, hauling two oversized horse trailers. The drivers parked alongside the forlorn house on Coleman Road, and by the time they'd climbed out of their trucks, volunteers had pulled open the trailer doors and were loading them up. Using catchpoles, they lowered dog after squirming dog into the trailers. Ernie Jones, a trapper from the nearby town of Nyssa and a volunteer for Vale Search and Rescue, watched with his nose in a perpetual wrinkle.

"How could they stand to live with this smell?" he said, directing his eyes toward a woman with two emptied cages.

"I'm Barbara Hutchinson," the woman said, handing him a cage.

"Ernie," he nodded.

"Wait 'til you go inside the house," she added. "It's a whole new level of stink."

With Ernie following, she tromped through the mud back to the house. The front door had been propped open and a hip-high section of plywood placed across the opening as a temporary barrier. This way, the dogcatchers could go in and out, while all but the larger dogs were trapped within. Hutchinson stepped over the plywood, motioning for Ernie to do the same. Tall and lanky, he easily cleared the barrier and stopped. Framed in the doorway, the T-shirt under his all-weather jacket pulled up to cover his nose and mouth, he quickly scanned the room.

Harriman, still working inside the house, moved toward him, a cage in each hand and the dogs cowering inside.

"You've been working in this for three hours?" Ernie asked him.

The deputy nodded, but didn't slow. He seemed exhausted.

Ernie let the T-shirt fall away from his nose and mouth, then immediately pulled it back into place, coughing. He looked at Hutchinson and shivered. He snorted and pointed with his free hand. Hutchinson followed his finger. In the next room, a small TV glowed, its screen dappled with paw prints, the audio drowned out by the barking dogs. "Always a TV," Ernie said, shaking his head. "No heat, but there's always a TV."

He moved forward into the room, his boots squishing with each step.

"There's dog poop in every room," Hutchinson said. "There's no place you can go without stepping in it, including the kitchen. In the hall, it's several inches deep." She paused and sighed, "and that's where we need your help."

She led Ernie through the house to the darkened hallway, which was cordoned off by another sheet of plywood. Behind it were dozens of dogs who milled about, yelping and yowling. Ernie's ears began to ring. He looked at Hutchinson who gestured at the pack with one shoulder.

"You're kiddin' me, right?" he said.

Her response was graveyard silence.

Ernie hadn't known what to expect as he'd driven to the Erickson farm. Certainly, he'd not expected what he'd found. He'd volunteered without thinking, for the excitement maybe, but this place with the barking that echoed through the house and the overwhelming stench, this wasn't what he'd bargained for. It wasn't in the playbook. For a moment, he considered heading back to his truck, settling in with some music on the radio until no one was watching. Then, he could bolt. He started to turn, but caught a glimpse of Hutchinson's face in the dim light. He stopped and studied her. She was exhausted, no, more than that. She was drained. A vacuum. She'd checked her emotions at the door, probably a couple of hours before. Yet, she was still here. Still pressing on.

"Okay," Ernie said, nodding at her. He leaned against the plywood and reached down to grab a dog with mange-infested ears, immediately jerking back and shaking his hand, his own yelp joining the chorus around him.

"Damn dog bit me," he grumbled to Hutchinson, although she never heard him. She had disappeared out the front door. A minute later, she was back, carrying a catchpole. She handed it to Ernie with a nod, then went back to work.

Ernie had never used a catchpole before but was able to figure it out quickly. Using it successfully was another matter. After nearly thirty minutes of failed attempts, he finally noosed a dog that cowered in a corner, his scabs of mange open and weeping. "Gotcha," Ernie said under his breath, lifting the runt over the plywood barrier. He headed outside, followed by Hutchinson who labored with the weight of two, wobbly, dog-filled cages. She watched Ernie carefully lower the pup into the trailer, seeing, too, the tears in his eyes.

"At least now they'll get the help they need," Hutchinson reassured him. Ernie stared at her and dropped his catchpole. He walked down the road to his car, climbed in, and drove off.

Hutchinson remained motionless, watching until his car had disappeared beyond a slight rise. She stumbled across the half-frozen mud and bent to retrieve his castoff catchpole, nearly collapsing when she straightened. For a moment, the world seemed to spin around her. She staggered drunkenly before regaining her balance. Ahead, she saw Oscar Martinez on his way back from the house with two, full cages. He seemed to be tilted sideways, and Hutchinson wondered how he managed to stay upright. Martinez dropped the cages he was carrying, bent over, and heaved. At the same time, Hutchinson sensed someone behind her.

"I think we have a full load," Sara said quietly.

Hutchinson stared at her, eyes glazed, sobbing.

"I don't think we can handle any more," Sara said. She gently moved Hutchinson, allowing the Deputy, who had retrieved his load, to pass.

The Deputy hoisted his cages, one-by-one, into the Ryder truck, then closed and latched its rear door.

"Let's head to Fruitland," Sara said, guiding Hutchinson toward the truck cab. With Sara's help, Hutchinson climbed into the passenger seat. By then, she was dry-eyed.

"I hope Kammy's ready for this," Hutchinson said, as the Ryder truck roared down Highway 20. She watched tiny ice particles hit the windshield. It was getting dark, and the lights of the other cars illuminated the crystals, making it seem as if the air around them were sparkling. Forty miles of road passed under the two women before either spoke.

"How could anyone live like that?" Sara said.

Hutchinson thought for a moment before answering. "You get there by inches," she said.

Dusk settled in, making it easier for the dogs to elude their captors. Don Coleman, one of the volunteers, suggested mounting the Search and Rescue team's spotlights on the roof of the house. While this was being accomplished, Don left, returning with a stretch of plastic fence, typically used to protect haystacks from hungry deer. Using it, the volunteers herded the dogs into one corner of the Erickson farmstead, where they could be snared without a chase.

Frenzied, the dogs crowded against the fence, piling up on one another. The lucky ones scrambled to the top of the pile, leaping over the fence to freedom. Others hid in burrows they'd dug beneath giant tree roots. Most were out-maneuvered and snared.

Chapter Twenty-Four

2:00 p.m., Thursday, January 23, 2003—Ontario, Oregon.
Barbara drove about Ontario aimlessly, fuming about her confrontation with Wolfe, Sara Sharette, and Kammy Rios. Nearly four hours had passed, but she was still too angry to think straight, carrying on one imagined conversation after another in her head. Although Wolfe was taking the brunt of her fury, she was equally angry with Sara Sharette.

She glanced at the gas gauge, which was hovering on empty, perhaps wondering how Wolfe knew to show up and who was the other woman. Her thoughts turned to her husband back home in Harper, certain that if Undersheriff Wolfe showed up, Bob would hand over the dogs without a fight. She vowed to let Bob have it when she returned home, never to leave him in charge again.

Barbara eased her brown Ford van to a stop at the edge of a vacant field behind the Texaco station, one of her usual stops in Ontario. The dogs barked crazily, leaping at the windows, trying to scratch the doors open.

"That's okay, babies," she told the dogs. "Mama's gonna let you play-play."

Careful not to aggravate her aching hip, Barbara got out of the van followed by a floodwater of excited dogs. They darted into the field, chasing after one another. Barbara watched them with a smile until the thought of Brian Wolfe drained it from her face. "That old Wolfe wouldn't make a good pimple on a bad cop's ass," she grumbled to herself.

As the dogs played, Barbara emptied the van of its soiled newspapers and carpet samples, filling the dumpster behind the gas station. She opened a small, built-in cupboard behind the front seat and retrieved fresh newspapers and carpet samples, using them to cover the floor of the van, afterward refilling several water bowls. It was a simple set of tasks, but with her hip and smoker's lungs, she was soon out of breath, barely able to blow the whistle that called the dogs back.

"Come on, babies it's bye-bye…" Barbara's sentence ended in an eruption of coughing that left her bent over and blue-faced. The ground reeled about her and flat, wormlike floaters filled her vision. Barbara tried to raise the whistle to her lips but was interrupted by another round of coughing, while out in the field, her dogs played on. Minutes passed. Barbara remained bent, hands on her knees, the lifeless whistle hanging loosely from a string around her neck. Finally, the ground stopped moving, and her head began to clear. A few minutes more, and she was able to straighten and put the whistle to her lips. Cautiously taking a deep breath, she wheezed into it, producing an anemic toot. Nonetheless, in a flash, the dogs scurried around her, and she began to lift them into the van.

"Smooch, smooch," she baby-talked, kissing each one until the entire pack had been settled in.

Afternoon became evening. Her errands were done, and Barbara knew she should head back to Harper. She was worried about her dogs, about Bob's ability to manage things without her. Yet, she remained in Ontario, driving about the quieting city as it settled in for the night, a distant voice telling her that she shouldn't go home. Just after dusk, sleet and icy rain began to fall, sending Barbara back to the Texaco station where she used the filthy, graffiti-covered phone booth in front to call Brian Coleman. As she waited for him to answer, her foggy breath foretold the cold night ahead. When she heard Brian's voice, she jumped in, not bothering to say "Hello."

"What's goin' on up at my place?" she demanded.

There was static mixed with Brian Coleman's gentle voice. "The TV stations come up," he said, "and they've been asking questions." There was a pause before Brian went on. "And the Sheriff's there trying to take the dogs."

The glass of the phone booth rattled as Barbara slammed her fist into it. "I'LL SUE 'EM IF THEY TOUCH MY BABIES," she yelled. A pair of customers at the gas pumps, their backs curled against the building wind, looked to the sound of her voice, but Barbara glared at them until they looked away. When she continued, her voice was lower. "Wolfe said we wasn't takin' care of 'em, but those babies are fine. You know that, Brian. It's just muddy right now."

"There are a lot of police over there…and some local people are helping them."

"They better not take my babies. Wolfe is behind this, and he's a damn liar."

"He's got the badge, Barbara."

"That don't mean nothin'! It's just a piece of tin. I'm gonna get down there, and when I do, I'm liable to hurt someone."

Barbara's voice had again risen to a shout, and the Texaco station manager appeared behind the half-open, front door. He scowled and stepped outside, still eyeing her.

"Just stay where you are," Brian said. "The roads are slick, and fog is coming in."

"But my babies…"

"Stay in Ontario for the night," Brian pleaded with her, but Barbara had already hung up as the Texaco station manager approached, his face grim and impatient.

Barbara hobbled back to the van, the gouging pain in her hip worse than ever. She hit the ignition and the engine roared to life, followed by the grinding of gears, a sound that masked the groan she was unable to keep inside. Tires screeching, she lurched out of the Texaco station onto the slick streets of Ontario, the van's headlights glowing in the misty air. A few miles farther on, she turned south onto Highway 20, heading for Harper and home. Tears welled at the thought of losing her "babies."

A vehicle using its fog lights approached, making Barbara blink hard against the glare. For a moment, she was blinded. Then, the blast of a horn sent her foot slamming into the brake pedal. Her van shuddered, sliding sideways, and she frantically wrestled with the steering wheel as her dogs careened about the interior, yelping as they thudded into the doors and windows. For the second time that day, the earth spun around her, this time for real. As quickly as it had begun, the road was dark again, and she was facing north, her heart pounding in her ears, the red tail-lights of the massive semi-trailer truck she'd nearly hit head-on slowly disappearing into the ghostly fog that now hung low over the icy road.

Barbara remained there, for how long she would later not remember. Around her, the fog settled in, blanketing the countryside as if it had swallowed the van with Barbara and her babies inside. It remained still and thick nearly all night, until the thin rays of first light began to burn it away. By then, Barbara had been nestled under a blanket of her dogs for hours, parked behind the Texaco station in Ontario where towering halogen lights glared through the frosted windows of the van, producing no warmth, their light as brilliant as noonday sun.

Chapter Twenty-Five

10:00 p.m., Thursday, January 23, 2003—the first dogs arrive at New Beginnings.

Darlene Gladson, Kammy's mother, stood at the front door of New Beginnings. "Brace yourself, dear," she said, looking crestfallen. "Sara Sharette called. They're on their way with over two hundred dogs."

Kammy gasped. She looked at her husband, Guadalupe. Blank-faced, his shoulders sagged, the hammer he'd been using to construct pens hanging loosely at his side. For a moment, Kammy was close to tears. Two days before, New Beginnings had no power, no heat, only a building filled with the previous owner's cast-off trash. She was exhausted. They all were. The three of them—Kammy, Guadalupe, and Darlene had worked nearly around the clock to get ready for as many as one hundred dogs. But now...

Mrs. Gladson crossed to her daughter and took her hand. "And they have to go back for more," she said. Her words came reluctantly, as if a tooth were attached to each one.

Kammy's mouth dropped open, followed by the clatter of Guadalupe's hammer hitting the floor. The sound of it cleared her tears. She jerked her hand away. "What?" she nearly shouted. "We can't handle that many dogs."

For a moment, Kammy wanted to strangle her friend, Sara Sharette.

Kammy eyed her husband's hammer, still lying on the floor, then the tempting plate glass window fronting the store.

The sound of her mother's voice interrupted her private tirade. Darlene Gladson's voice was quiet and familiar, a voice that had calmed and consoled Kammy since infancy. It had worked on her then, and it worked this time, too.

"I'll help you, dear," Kammy's mother said.

Guadalupe picked up his hammer and took a tight grip on it. He'd seen the look in his wife's eye, too. "There's no choice, Kammy," he said, smiling grimly. "We'll just find a way."

Guadalupe moved toward one of the open doorways near the back of the store. "We can block off each room with plywood and let the dogs run free inside," he said. He glanced at the already-built kennels, their lines true and solid. "There won't be time to build more kennels. We'll use the ones we have for special-needs dogs."

Guadalupe looked at his wife. "What about Dr. Ashton?" he asked.

Kammy studied her husband's face. He was utterly calm. Guadalupe had already shifted into his "fix-it" gear. Like many men, he wasn't interested in what had caused the problem, only in what could resolve it. At a time like this, Guadalupe was a good man to have around.

Kammy thought about Dr. Ashton, a veterinarian from Fruitland, Idaho that she'd enlisted to help care for the dogs. Kammy and Guadalupe's family vet for years, he'd agreed without hesitation. "I didn't ask him to be here 'til morning," she replied. "We'll just feed and water them for tonight."

For the next couple of hours, Guadalupe worked quickly, hammering together plywood chutes and room dividers to use in routing the dogs from the trucks to the four large holding rooms at the rear of the building. In the meantime, the story hit the television evening news, bringing several volunteers with bags of dog food and supplies to the doors of New Beginnings. By the time the first truckload of dogs backed up to the front door, they were as ready as they'd ever be.

The appearance of Sara and Barbara Hutchinson's Ryder truck launched Kammy and her crew into action. They aligned themselves on either side of Guadalupe's newly-built chute, counting the dogs that scrambled past. It was an impossible task, with frantic dogs backtracking and jumping over one another. Some escaped by wriggling through cracks in the flimsy plywood or jumping over it. It would be another day before these animals were recovered, hiding under a building next door where they were lured out with tasty treats. When the truck was empty, totals were compared with as many different figures as people counting.

Hutchinson and Kammy unloaded the cages that held dogs too sick to tolerate the frenzy of the pack. They were separated from the main group of dogs, some offered food and water in their cages, while others, too weak to eat on their own, were fed by hand or intravenously. Hot water bottles were placed next to the weakest dogs, their cold, frail bodies seemingly near death.

Meanwhile, a stream of new volunteers began crowding into the small lobby, asking what they could do. Hutchinson gave them a terse, but consistent, response. "Grab a dog and cuddle."

Kammy Rios kept things as organized as possible. "We've had our share of bites," she warned a pair of new recruits, a slender teenager named Pam and her mother, a clear-eyed woman with an unapologetic mane of gray hair and a length of masking tape she'd stuck on her shirt as a makeshift name tag. It said "Stephanie."

"Go slow when you approach them," Kammy continued. "There are lots of dogs with old injuries or abscesses and lots of sick dogs. We just want to get them warmed and fed for now. The vets will be here in the morning to treat them."

"Look at this little scroungy pup," Stephanie said. "With his calico coloring, he could almost pass for a cat." She picked up the dog by the scruff of his neck and settled him into her arms, unable to keep the horror from her face. "My God, his skin just sticks together." She pointed at a tent of nearly hairless skin where she'd grasped the puppy on its neck.

"That's a sign of dehydration," Kammy said, nodding. "We'll get him on IV fluids."

Stephanie gently lay the terrier on the examining table as Kammy rummaged through her supplies, looking for an IV needle. His listless eyes drooped. "How long do they go without water before this happens?" Stephanie asked, her voice trembling.

"It varies," Kammy answered. "Lots of things affect it—stress, size of the dog, outside temperature, fever." She expertly inserted the IV needle into the front leg of the dog who remained motionless, almost as if he didn't feel it. He slid the catheter off the needle and into the vein. "With the amount of dehydration I've seen in these dogs, I suspect they've been several days without water."

Kammy connected the IV catheter to clear tubing that snaked up to a bag of fluid she'd set on the roof of the animal's crate. Stephanie immediately picked the dog up and cradled him in her arms.

"I suspect the bigger, stronger dogs got most of the food and water," Kammy said, watching the woman as she rocked the tiny animal like a baby. "By the time the alpha dogs were done eating, it's likely there was nothing left." Kammy shrugged. "Same deal for the injured dogs; they just couldn't compete. By the way, keep that IV bag above his heart or blood will back up into the tubing."

Kammy left Stephanie and crossed the room to retrieve another animal, this one a furry, black bundle. Pam trailed her, so far having shown a greater mastery of baby-talk than work. By the time Kammy transferred her new patient to the examining table, a reporter had joined them.

"What happened to him?" asked the reporter, a small, ferret-nosed fellow with searching eyes whose pencil seemed to be as much a part of him as one of his fingers.

Kammy looked at him, immediately pegging him as a newspaperman. He lacked the smooth looks and eighty-dollar haircut of a TV reporter. "It's hard to say at this point," she answered as she cautiously extended the pup's twisted leg. "This could have been caused by inbreeding or a broken bone left untreated. Little Furball here definitely had a hard time getting to the food bowl. He's just skin and bones." Kammy passed the dog to Pam. The girl's eyes widened, but she quickly recovered, cooing and baby-talking to the puppy as she wandered off. Kammy watched her go as she reached deep into a cage for another one. She rummaged around as if searching for a specific animal, which was, in fact, exactly what she was doing. When she lifted out the dog she'd been looking for, the reporter turned ashen and looked away.

"This is Storm Born." Kammy said, remembering another of Barbara's preposterous tales, this one about how she'd miraculously saved Storm Born after a salesman had kicked him and broken his jaw. Like all of Barbara's stories, she'd outsmarted the vets and saved her *baby*. Kammy held up the little dog. His jaw seemed to be missing, but was actually still attached, dislocated and hanging uselessly to one side.

"Oh my God," the reporter groaned. "How could he eat?"

"I don't know," Kammy replied grimly, trying to control her anger. She was working up a healthy hatred for Barbara Erickson and her big mouth. "Barbara...Mrs. Erickson...said she took him to a vet but it cost too much money to fix his jaw, and she didn't want him to be euthanized, so she left it broken." She looked at the reporter whose horrified face reflected his disbelief.

"She would rather let him suffer than put him to sleep peacefully," he said, a statement, not a question.

Kammy didn't answer right away, instead scooping some canned food onto her finger. She held it to Storm Born's mouth, and the dog tentatively lapped at it. "Maybe she just told herself it didn't hurt him anymore," Kammy said, shaking her head sadly. She looked at the reporter with darkening eyes. "Dogs don't react to pain the way that humans do. But that doesn't mean they aren't feeling it."

The reporter didn't speak for a few moments as he scribbled angrily in his notebook. It was almost as if he were expending his fury on the paper so that when he asked another question, his voice could be suitably detached and professional.

"Will the vet be able to fix it?'

Kammy shook her head. "Probably not," she said. "He'll probably just stop the suffering."

The reporter remained silent, then, "You mean euthanize him?"

Kammy nodded.

A small television on the counter aired news reports throughout the evening. The rescue was being called the largest and worst case of animal hoarding in recent memory. An expert on the subject—Dr. Gary Patronek from Tufts University School of Veterinary Medicine in Massachusetts—was liberally quoted. He described the phenomenon of animal hoarding as a public health problem characterized by the accumulation of a large number of animals concomitant with the failure to meet minimal standards of nutrition, sanitation, veterinary medical care, and a lack of response to the deteriorating condition of the animals, their environment, and the animal hoarder's own health.

"In some cases, the hoarders simply disappear and resurface months or years later in a neighboring jurisdiction, with the same or newer animals," a sonorous news anchor droned, his voice filled with fake interest. "One woman reportedly purchased a new home every few years as each successive residence became uninhabitable."

Local reporters swarmed the area, their cameras scanning the shelter where masked-and-gloved volunteers handled dogs matted with feces, others having no coats at all—only mangy scabs. The images they captured told much of the story: a pup with gnarled and withered back legs; a tiny Chihuahua who vomited and whimpered before dying in the arms of a silently weeping woman; the frenetic, crazed dogs attacking food and water dishes. In all, the animals rescued from the Erickson farm consumed two hundred pounds of dog food within the first hour along with gallons of water. The reporters dutifully gathered their facts, broadcasting the call for more food, supplies, and volunteers. They speculated that the number of dogs would top three hundred, a woeful underestimation as it turned out.

Midnight came and went, and exhaustion crept up Kammy Rios's spine. She sought refuge in the restroom when she could, sitting on the toilet with her aching feet propped up on the stall door. The barking went on unabated. She'd lost count of how many dogs had been unloaded at New Beginnings. One unanticipated problem had arisen when people began walking out of the facility with dogs under their arms. Kammy had witnessed one such dog nap-ping—an older woman who tunneled through the crowd of dogs and people—vanishing into the winter night before Kammy could follow.

"Sara, we've got to watch the door," she told her friend. "No one can leave with *any* of these dogs until they've been tested for diseases."

Not all that was unanticipated turned out badly. A professional groomer showed up with a tub filled with her tools and supplies. She'd seen the report of the rescue on the ten o'clock news and had decided to brave the icy roads to lend a hand. A grateful Kammy Rios set her up in one corner of the facility, where she immediately went to work on a long-haired fellow whose growling mop of black, feces-matted tangles hung over his face in dreadlocks, making it hard to tell one end from the other. Within seconds, as the dog anxiously tap-danced on the table, the groomer had expertly clipped the hair from his face, revealing shiny, inquisitive eyes.

By 3:00 a.m., the last trailer had arrived. Blurry with fatigue, a skeleton crew along with Kammy Rios and Sara Sharette unloaded and checked them in. Although stronger and healthier than the earlier dogs, this last group had eluded capture for hours, working hard to outfox their pursuers. Now, empty of will, they folded.

With the volunteer crew dwindling, Kammy and Sara sat down to develop a system for tagging and counting the dogs. Paper collars, donated along with the other supplies, were numbered and listed on a ledger. Each dog would be examined, collared, described, and listed next to a matching number. The two women worked on into the early morning hours as New Beginnings finally began to quiet. The dogs were settling into their new home, albeit a temporary one.

"It's very traumatic," Barbara Hutchinson had told a reporter hours earlier, talking about the process of transferring the animals from one home to another. "It's traumatic for the people doing the rescue as well as the Ericksons." At that point, she'd paused to level clear eyes on the reporter who stopped writing long enough to look back. "But it's *really* hard on the animals," she told him. "You're ripping them out of the only home they've ever known. It may have been bad, but it was still their home."

She'd looked about slowly and said, "I know this shelter looks awful right now, but I'll tell you what...this is *paradise* compared to where they came from."

Chapter Twenty-Six

8:00 a.m., Friday, January 24, 2003—the morning after.

It was Friday morning, and volunteers bustled about New Beginnings like ants in an ant farm. The unexpected and somewhat overwhelming community support had produced chaos initially, but with a refreshed Barbara Hutchinson in command, each helper soon queued up for an assignment: feeding, watering, cuddling. When the volunteers began to outnumber the chores, Hutchinson gratefully developed a schedule that eventually extended into the following week. By the end of the morning, a giant semi-trailer filled with dog food and pet supplies had been donated and was parked outside. Volunteer groomers showed up with shampoo and expertise. Thorough examination of many dogs had been impossible because their fur was matted with feces and mud. The groomers shaved and cleaned these dogs for the first time in the animals' lives. Dogs with mange were given medicated baths. With the knowledge that no more dogs were coming, the mood grew hopeful.

Dr. Wayne Ashton arrived early in the morning. A veterinarian in western Idaho for nearly thirty years, he was known by nearly everyone within fifty miles. Even the Ericksons had enlisted his services in the past. "Barbara came in with one or two dogs to be treated, then wanted to buy medication for the rest without having them seen," he told Hutchinson when she called to recruit him.

Kammy was glad to see Dr. Ashton. His calm demeanor and experience were reassuring. He made her feel as if they could face anything and handle it. "These are the worst," Kammy said after she and Sara led Ashton to the room where the sickest animals had been housed. She waved at the cages with one arm. Unlike the dogs in the rest of the facility, these animals were virtually silent. "There are dogs with missing teeth, old cuts, and swelling over their extremities," she said, motioning at a wall of cages across the room. She waited for questions, but Dr. Ashton still hadn't recovered from his initial shock. He was slightly slack-jawed, his eyes wide and round, an expression Kammy was becoming accustomed to, given the numbers of new volunteers. "There are lots of abscesses," she went on, "and some *very* skinny, *very* emaciated dogs. Especially this one." Kammy opened the door and reached into a cage holding a scabby, blond Chihuahua, his jaw lax, eyes drooping. She took him out, holding him up for the vet to see. "He has paddles for back feet...see how flattened and webbed his toes are?"

Ashton nodded. "Paddle-feet" were a classic sign of inbreeding.

"He's covered with mange, too," Kammy added, shaking her head sadly. She handed the dog to Dr. Ashton. He cradled the tiny, limp animal in his hands and spoke for the first time since arriving at the shelter.

"Has Barbara Erickson signed a release allowing us to make decisions regarding these dogs?" His face had changed, his jaw set, eyes narrowed. The *decisions* he referred to were clear. Some of these animals—including the one he was holding—needed to be mercifully put down. Soon.

Kammy looked to Sara for an answer.

"The sheriff is working on it," Sara said. She went on, saying what they all were thinking. "I knew we'd have to euthanize some. We can't keep every sick dog, every deformed dog, every mean and vicious wanting-to-kill-us dog. I come from a no-kill shelter, but this is reality. Some of these dogs don't even want to live. There is no quality of life for them, whatsoever."

Dr. Ashton looked down at the pup and shook his head. His pursed lips held back the sigh that escaped through his nose. "Let me know when you get the release," he said, quietly.

"I'll call Undersheriff Wolfe," Sara said, adding, "I don't think they have Barbara in custody yet."

Chapter Twenty-Seven

8:50 a.m., Friday, January 24, 2003—the home of Cathy Cook, Ontario, Oregon.

Cathy Cook wasn't surprised to wake up with Barbara Erickson banging on the front door. The weather had been nasty last night, and Barbara often slept in town with her dogs rather than test the roads back to Harper. As usual, Cathy had invited her in, listening politely to Barbara's ramblings, while putting on a pot of coffee. She'd met Barbara a few months before, selling dogs outside the Wal-Mart. Cathy had wanted one of the puppies, but a previous head injury from a car accident had combined with diabetes and old age to make it impossible. Taking care of herself was about all she could handle. Still, she loved animals, and Barbara's van was like a traveling petting zoo. After a while, she and Barbara had become friends. Cathy enjoyed the company. Barbara did most of the talking so that Cathy didn't have to sort out her thoughts, something that was becoming increasingly more difficult.

Outside Cathy's house, Barbara's brown van sat next to the curb, swaying slightly with the movement of the dogs inside. Barbara seemed upset, her eyes flitting about. Unable to stay in one spot, she paced from the tiny window over the sink to the battered kitchen table, muttering to herself. Cathy had seen this before. Barbara often became agitated over nothing. At times like that, she didn't welcome conversation. She needed a listener.

When the coffee was done, Cathy poured two cups and brought them to the table.

Barbara sat and took a sip. She set the cup down and looked at her friend, expectantly.

"Sugar," Cathy said, nodding. She retraced her steps to a cupboard next

141

to the sink but stopped before opening the cabinet door, her eyes drawn to the window. Outside, two police cars had bracketed Barbara's van. A pair of officers was approaching the house. Cathy motioned to Barbara who joined her at the window after arising with some difficulty from her chair.

"What are they doing here?" Cathy asked.

Barbara hissed when she saw the officers, cursing under her breath.

"They got my dogs last night, Cathy," she said, her words razor-sharp. "Now they think they can get me."

Before Cathy could protest, Barbara limped to the front door and opened it.

"What the damn hell do you think you're doin'?" she yelled at the cops.

Both men were startled, crouching defensively, their hands touching their sidearms. With eyes firmly fixed on the two women, the lead officer nodded, and the other took a position where he could cover his partner.

"Are you Barbara Erickson?" the lead officer said. It was Deputy Oscar Martinez, his eyes bloodshot with dark bags hanging beneath them.

Barbara scowled defiantly but remained inside the house, one hand on the door ready to slam it shut. "Yeah, and what business is it of yours?" she said, pointing her chin at him. She stepped onto the porch followed by Cathy Cook. Seeing that the two women were unarmed, Martinez approached, his watchful buddy remaining in the background.

"Barbara Erickson, we have a warrant for your arrest," Martinez said. He reached the porch and climbed the steps in two strides. "You need to come with us." He held open the screen door and peered inside the house, while the other officer approached from behind.

"A warrant for what?" Barbara demanded, glaring.

"Animal abuse, Ma'am."

Barbara snorted. "I never hurt no dogs. Fact is...I protect them. I won't turn them out on the highway to be killed."

By now, two Ontario police officers had rolled up along with another Malheur County sheriff's deputy. With the backup and satisfied that no one else was in the house, Martinez turned his full attention to Barbara. "Mrs. Erickson, I want you to turn around and put your hands behind your back." He reached out and took firm hold of her arm. Barbara tried to jerk away, but his grip was like a vice.

"You act so important, but I have no respect for you," she snapped at him.

"You have the right to remain silent."

"I respect the law, but I don't respect you. Respect has to be earned, and you haven't earned it."

"Anything you say can and will be used against you."

"You sit on your butts drinkin' coffee and eatin' donuts."

"You have the right to an attorney..."

Cathy Cook watched from the door as a pair of patrolmen led Barbara down the walkway and past the brown van, the dogs inside yapping hysterically. Barbara squirmed, firing epithets at the officers as she struggled to maintain eye contact with the dogs plastered against the van's smeared windows for as long as possible. Meanwhile, a crowd of neighbors was building, maintaining a safe distance from Cathy Cook's house.

"My babies are barkin', 'cause they don't like uniforms either," a handcuffed Barbara snarled at the onlookers as she was eased into the back seat of a patrol car.

Cathy, still in her bathrobe, had made it to the front yard where she waved as the cruiser carrying Barbara quietly pulled away from the curb, gathering speed before disappearing around the corner. The sheriff's deputies remained. Cathy looked at them, wondering if she was about to be arrested.

"What now?" she asked.

"We wait," Martinez replied. "Some folks from the Second Chance Animal Shelter are on the way to pick up the dogs."

"Barbara'll sue anyone who hurts those dogs, ya know," Cathy said, suddenly brave.

Martinez ignored her, watching as one of the deputies staggered backward from the rear of Barbara's van. He'd opened the door, releasing a blast of foul-smelling air. Martinez snorted. "You shoulda been there last night," he told the officer who was bent over, trying not to vomit.

A few minutes later, Sara Sharette arrived, and with the help of Cathy Cook who seemed to know many of the dogs, the officers and Sara emptied the van. During the process, one of the animals bit Cathy's hand.

"That's Rascal," Cathy said, looking at a fierce, bug-eyed little Chihuahua. "He's the papa of them all."

The last dog was easy to catch. Martinez slid his lifeless body into an evidence bag and carried it to the car.

"That's her Jocko," Cathy said. "He must have died last night."

Chapter Twenty-Eight

9:15 a.m., Friday, January 24, 2003—at New Beginnings, Fruitland, Idaho.

"I have a release prepared, but I doubt that Mrs. Erickson will sign it," Under-sheriff Wolfe said to Sara. Sara sighed, holding the phone between her shoulder and her ear as she scanned the long list of veterinarians yet to be called.

"I was hoping she'd just sign the darn thing," Sara said. I'm up to my ears in alligators over here."

She waited for Wolfe to jump in with an offer. He remained silent, and Sara sighed again.

"Well," she said, "Barbara trusted me enough to hand over three dogs. I think I can convince her to let me help with the others."

If Wolfe was skeptical, his voice didn't reveal it. "Okay," he said.

Less than an hour later, Sara arrived at the Malheur County Jail and was greeted by a deputy who shot her a cracked-egg grin as he escorted her back to the cellblock. The jail was standard issue construction: a hallway with three cells to a side, cinderblock walls painted a startling white that reflected the glare of the merciless, artificial light, heavy iron bars, and utilitarian furniture bolted to the floor. Barbara's cell was at the end and, as they approached, Sara could see the top of her head bobbing as she talked to a woman in the adjoining unit. As usual, her voice was loud and adamant. She didn't seem to hear them although the sound of their footsteps against the cold, stamped concrete floor reverberated throughout the cellblock.

"First time?"

Sara was startled and blinked. The deputy had slowed and was studying her, the same goofy grin on his face.

"First time?" he repeated, adding, "in a jail?"

Sara laughed nervously, recalling every prison movie she'd ever seen. "Yeah," she said.

They stopped in front of Barbara's cell. Inside the thick bars, a half wall around the toilet offered the only privacy. No sink was in sight. Sara shivered.

"Home sweet home," the deputy joked. He clanked a heavy key into place and turned it, the metallic sounds echoing in Sara's ears. "Visitor for you, Barb," the deputy said, his voice loud but friendly.

He opened the heavy door, waited until Sara had stepped in, then clanged it shut and locked it behind her. The place was scary enough, Sara thought, but with the door locked, it had gone from scary to downright creepy. She shivered again, clenching her teeth. Looking around, the walls seemed to be closing in; damp, moldy walls that bore the fingerprints of thousands of desperate men and women, thousands of shattered dreams, and poorly chosen roads. Thousands of lost souls.

"How are my babies?" Barbara was peering at Sara. If surprised to see Sara, she didn't show it. Barbara motioned for her to sit on the metal cot, which occupied most of the space in the small cell. "How are my babies?" she repeated, after Sara was seated next to her on the doughy mattress. Barbara wore a faded green jail smock and hospital slippers.

"They're okay," Sara replied, trying to keep her voice even and matter-of-fact. "I have a release form I need you to sign so that we can take care of them. It will..."

"I'm not givin' up my dogs!" Barbara interrupted, although her voice was tired, lacking its typical ferocity.

Sara continued, ignoring Barbara's blustering. "Your dogs need this signed so I can take care of them," she explained patiently. "They need medical care, Barbara. Don't you want them to get the best care possible?"

Barbara stared at the gray bars opposite her bunk, tears streaming down her cheeks. "What's that Wolfe tryin' to do to me? He wants to kill all my babies."

She looked at Sara, her eyes swollen and red. "And Bob just handed 'em over 'cause of his Alzheimer's."

She shook her head, her breath coming in fits.

"His damned Alzheimer's."

Sara began again. "Barbara...?"

She was interrupted when the older woman reached out and snatched the release form from Sara's hand. She read a sentence or two, her lips moving with the words. Barbara shook the paper so hard, Sara was afraid it might be torn to bits in mid-air.

"I'm not signing this," Barbara said. "If I do, I'll *never* get my dogs back."

Sara stood up. The woeful Barbara of a minute earlier had quickly become the flinty-eyed, combative Barbara she'd seen before. Sara spoke, suffusing her voice with as much authority as possible.

"You'll have to sign these dogs over, Barbara. You're sitting in jail. How can you take care of them? I need to help them, and I can't until you sign this." Sara finished with her hands on her hips. She didn't like being a bully, but it was the only thing that seemed to work with this crazy, old woman.

Barbara's eyes again welled with tears.

"What about when I get out of jail?" she pleaded, looking up at Sara. "I'll want my babies back."

"Let's deal with that when it happens," Sara replied. "Right now, we need to get these dogs taken care of."

Barbara wiped tears from her cheeks with the back of one hand, sniffing dramatically. "I never hurt none'a my babies," she cried, her voice weak, eyes on the floor. She almost seemed to be talking to herself. "I did it for *them*," she continued. "I couldn't take 'em to the shelter and pay twenty dollars for each dog to be killed. I needed the twenty dollars for dog food."

Barbara's life was crumbling around her, but Sara pressed on. She'd worked through the night at New Beginnings, had seen the suffering. She held out a pen and pointed at the release form.

"I don't have time to argue, Barbara," she said. "I have to get back to the shelter."

Barbara looked up at her. "I couldn't just turn them out on the highway to be killed," she said, crying. "And what about little Storm Born? He needs soft food 'cause his jaw is broken, and little Sheila has to eat vegetables only... and Baby...I nursed Baby when she was a puppy, and they said she would die. Now, she'll die of loneliness."

Barbara stared at the paper, her hand so limp she could barely hold the pen. Sara was unmoved. In the past two years, she had seen too much to be sympathetic—too many tricks, too many stories, too many sick and dying dogs. Too much Barbara Erickson.

"Just sign it, Barbara," she said.

Chapter Twenty-Nine

11:00 a.m., Friday, January 24, 2003—the rescue ends.

Sara bounded into the lobby of New Beginnings, waving her copy of the release Barbara had signed. The room was filled with reporters and their omnipresent cameras and notepads, as well as volunteers snuggling pups in their arms. Across the room, Dr. Ashton looked up from the puppy he and Kammy were examining. The dog was too weak to lift its head.

"I got the release," Sara said, unable to contain her exuberance. She crossed the room to the kindly veterinarian who had already gone back to his examination.

"Good," he said grimly. He looked at Sara with tired eyes. "Some of these animals are in such bad shape, they need to be put down, now."

Sara looked at the pup, then at Dr. Ashton. His face was drawn and gray. He seemed to have aged twenty years in a day. "How can I help?" she said softly.

Dr. Ashton straightened. "We need a quiet area," he said, indicating the swarm of reporters with a lift of his chin. "These exams will be easier if we can keep the dogs away from the lights and interruptions."

He arched his back and winced.

"And I need a chair. This table's so low, it's killing my back."

Sara nodded solemnly. "Okay," she said. She glanced around the room, stopping when her eyes found a corner. "We can hang a cover over there," she said, pointing. "You'll have just enough space for the examining table." With the aid of one of the volunteers, a balding bull of a man with a sun-crinkled face, Sara found a tarp and suspended it from the ceiling, partitioning off one corner of the facility to make a small, private room. She stood at the opening

149

between the tarp and the wall with a clipboard as a line of volunteers holding dogs began to form. The sickest dogs that had been sequestered in the shelter's back room were the first in line. Some were too sick to move, while others squirmed and nipped their holders. As she waited, Sara reviewed their list. She was frustrated. So much time had been spent attending the dogs' basic needs, only fifty had been properly catalogued in preparation for the court case. She thought about the night before when she and Kammy finished up their day in the wee hours, devising a system to identify and describe each animal. Sara sighed.

At the shelter entrance, Kammy appeared, lugging a cracked plastic lawn chair she'd scrounged from the trash heap behind the building. She weaved her way through the crowded lobby, nodding at Sara before slipping behind the makeshift barrier they'd made with the tarp. With Dr. Ashton now seated, Kammy continued to assist with the examinations, tagging each dog with a labeled collar, while Sara matched a description of the dog to a number on her list. It was an arduous process, made harder by poorly socialized animals.

"We'll have to muzzle this little guy," Sara said, lifting a cage onto the examining table. Inside was Bingo, the wild-eyed terrier/Chihuahua mix that had nearly bitten Barbara Hutchinson on the day of the rescue. He growled and snapped at the air ferociously, his patchy coat seeming to stand on end. Kammy opened the door and tried to coax Bingo out with a treat. When he refused to budge, she cautiously reached in and grabbed him by the scruff of his neck, but not before he'd sunk his teeth into her hand.

"Ouch!" she cried as she pulled him out.

Kammy held the dog's nape tightly while Sara and Dr. Ashton muzzled him, shaking her hand before wiping it on her apron. "Dang," she muttered over and over.

"We've got him, Kammy. Go wash out that bite," Dr. Ashton said. When she didn't go, he spoke again, adding a smile of reassurance. "I don't think this little guy's rabid...just pissed."

Kammy sighed with relief and headed for the restroom near the back of the shelter. Ashton and Sara stayed, holding the dog firmly, trying to gentle him with their voices. It was no use. Bingo seemed mad with fury, squirming and fighting, his eyes reddening as he tried to get the muzzle in his teeth. Ashton looked at Sara and shook his head. This dog was like a few they'd seen—inconsolable, irretrievably enraged. Nothing was going to work with him, and Dr. Ashton and Sara both knew it. This dog could not be socialized. There would be no new owner, no new home. He was lost.

Kammy returned with a napkin taped over her hand. "How's he doing?" she asked, although the terrier's maniacal growling made the question superfluous.

Ashton looked at her, his faced haggard with guilt. "We'll have to put him down," he said. Kammy's lips parted with surprise, but Ashton went on before she could speak. "I know, I know...he's not sick. But he can't be socialized to humans, and I'm not sure how he'd do away from the jungle environment he's been in." He settled the dog back into its cage, pulling his hands out and quickly closing the door. The terrier immediately threw himself into the wire door and began to cry, a high-pitched, primordial sound that sent chills down Kammy's spine.

"It's not my favorite thing either," Dr. Ashton said, sighing. "I hate to do it, but there are times when it has to be done." He looked at the two women, his face solemn as the winter day outside. "And this is clearly one of those times."

With Kammy keeping firm hold of the dog, Dr. Ashton filled a syringe with clear liquid from a vial he'd retrieved from his bag. Sara stepped away from the table and stood guard at the makeshift opening to their examining room. Dr. Ashton patted the dog gently on its back as Kammy stroked its neck. An instant later, the easy-going veterinarian had slipped the needle into a vein and injected the solution. Within seconds, the dog fell limp. After a couple of minutes, Ashton pressed his stethoscope to the dog's thin, ribby chest, listening. Finally, he nodded, and Kammy reached for a plastic bag.

"He's calm for the first time," she said.

Ashton looked at her, puzzled.

"He's at peace, maybe for the first time in his life," Kammy added.

Ashton looked down. He didn't answer. Sara poked her head outside the tarp and motioned for the next dog.

It was a long afternoon. For every four treatable dogs, one had to be euthanized. They saw things they hoped they'd never see again: mange-encrusted animals with scabs replacing their coats of fur; toothless pups so starved they looked like walking skeletons; other dogs like the fiery, deranged Bingo who were too un-socialized to survive in a new environment. They injected the poor dogs, trying to console them in their last minutes, trying to believe that the animals somehow understood and accepted their fate. They watched as peacefulness fell over them. After a long moment, they placed them in plastic bags, feeling guilty that so desperate a life should endure so unceremonious a departure.

Sara and Ashton shared the despair that washed over Kammy as their afternoon dragged on, darkening their small, curtained corner of the shelter. When it was over and Kammy had disposed of the last dog, placing it in a truck that would transport it to a landfill, Sara gave in to the pain of so much suffering. She began to cry, reaching out to Kammy. The two women embraced, murmuring comforts to one another.

"We have to face facts..."

"I know."

"They suffered like this day after day."

"I know."

"They're at peace now. They can rest."

"Yes, I know."

Pat Vance, Director of Operations for the Idaho Humane Society (IHS) arrived several hours later to assist in removing healthier dogs that were ready for transport. Other offers of help continued to pour in. Dr. James LaRue of Filer, Idaho agreed to come over that evening, freeing up Dr. Ashton, who headed back to his own clinic. The Idaho Veterinary Medical Association sent a mass e-mail to area vets, asking for help. The Atherton Shelter in Ontario offered to take adoptable dogs once released. The IHS made their facility available for spaying and neutering, as well as to administer immunizations.

Sara showed Vance around the shelter. "Overall, these dogs seem to be in better shape than the ones we took during the Midvale rescue," Vance commented. She studied Sara's drawn face. "I'm sorry. I know it doesn't help to hear that right now."

As they walked, Sara looked to Vance for answers, searching for an explanation, no doubt wondering how this could have happened even once, let alone several times. "With many dog hoarders, it's a monetary issue...breeding and selling," Vance explained. "Some owners let their dogs breed freely in order to maintain a continuous supply of puppies. Puppies are easier to sell."

Late Friday night, Dr. LaRue arrived with his Vet Tech, Justin Ash. Unlike Ashton, they weren't locals and had come from nearly two hundred miles away to help out. When Barbara Hutchinson called, LaRue hadn't hesitated. She hardly knew him. They'd only met once—at a conference on animal planning—but Hutchinson had been immediately impressed. In addition to his veterinary practice, Jim LaRue had established a non-profit animal shelter in Filer and worked to educate residents about responsible pet ownership, humane treatment, and prevention of overpopulation.

Sara and Kammy showed LaRue and Ash around the facility as a handful of volunteers continued to fill water dishes and organize supplies. The tour was a quick one: the tarp-enclosed triage area, its examining table empty for the moment, the "sick room" where Kammy had first sequestered the worst of the dogs; the female room; the male room; the hallway where about fifty dogs had been cordoned off.

"Some of the dogs have recently given birth," Kammy told LaRue and Ash, "but there are few puppies to be found. They must've been eaten by the others." She said it with virtually no emotion, surprising even herself. When LaRue stopped, his mouth open in disbelief, Kammy went on. "I'm not talking about one or two," she said. "Maybe thirty dogs recently whelped...and their puppies are gone."

Dr. LaRue didn't answer, lifting his chin and staring at the ceiling. Ash, just out of high school and anxious to learn, seemed nearly as lost and confused as the rescued dogs. All around, the tide of barking and yapping was rising, probably in response to the newcomers. LaRue seemed deaf to it. Finally, the Filer veterinarian spoke, turning and heading back to the reception area as he did. "The ventilation in this building is inadequate for so many dogs," he said, "and the dogs won't be able to stay crowded like this for long. Let's get the most adoptable animals tagged and ready for transport to other shelters." He stopped and looked at the others. The color had returned to his face. "We'll send the critical cases to animal hospitals in the area," he finished up.

Sara retrieved her logbook and began placing stars next to the dogs that were ready to be moved. As she wrote, LaRue looked over her shoulder and grimaced.

"I've never been involved in anything like this," he admitted.

Sara nodded in response.

"The state humane societies usually handle things."

"They've been helping," Sara told him.

A hard knot had been forming in Dr. LaRue's jaw, and he began to talk, not containing his anger. "I'm amazed that *not one* governmental agency stepped up to the plate until now," he said, waving at the air with one hand, "especially when the Ericksons had a history of this behavior."

Sara nodded. She thought about how Undersheriff Wolfe had been quick to respond when she'd first called, wishing she'd made the call sooner.

"I have dealt with county commissioners before," Dr. LaRue fumed. "It's all about *money* for them. They sing the same tune: 'If we confiscate the animals, who will take care of them?'"

He was on his soapbox now, and the others listened.

"They say, 'We're just a small, rural community. We don't have the money.'"

He exhaled hard through his nose.

"So, they close their eyes. It makes rural communities attractive to animal hoarders because they're less likely to get caught."

Justin Ash, LaRue's tech, cringed. "There are unwrapped sandwiches on the counter over there," he said in a horrified whisper. He shuddered. "How can anyone stand to eat in here anyway?"

Dr. LaRue followed Justin's eyes to the counter.

"I'd toss those if I were you," he said to Sara and Kammy, "and you better tell everyone to clean their shoes with bleach before going home. We don't know *what* diseases these dogs have."

Within two weeks the rescue had come to a close. Lotteries were conducted for the hundreds of people who wanted to provide homes for one or more of the rescued dogs. The prospective owners filled out applications and were given reading material to educate them on the process of helping pets adjust to new environments. Newscast footage of the desolate Erickson yard and the frantic, starving dogs was gradually replaced by videos of newly-groomed dogs being cuddled by happy owners.

The list of euthanized dogs grew to 134, but most of the survivors recovered from their ailments and found new homes. Over four hundred dogs were saved, most with behavioral problems of one sort or another. One veterinarian reported that an owner complained that her dog insisted on defecating on the coffee table and asked what could be done to discourage the behavior. The veterinarian suggested she move the coffee table outdoors. She complied and the dog gradually adjusted to using the grass.

Kammy Rios estimated that only twenty people returned their pets, all within the first month. In each return case, the new owners described entrenched behavior problems and sullen, lonely dogs that could not be housetrained. It was not a surprise to animal experts. The dogs' social system and hierarchy had been dismantled. A new master had replaced the old alpha dog. Once displaced from the hundreds of dogs who had been their family, they were lost and unable to make the transition to a conventional home life.

For several days after the rescue, Sheriff's deputies from Malheur County returned to the Erickson farmstead in Harper after receiving reports of dogs roaming the hills behind the house. In all, seven dogs had managed to escape, but the deputies ultimately recaptured only three, using food traps. The rest found freedom more enticing than food.

Chapter Thirty

Barbara and Bob Erickson were charged with felony criminal mischief in the first degree with regard to the damage done to Verda Palmer's home, as well as 134 counts of misdemeanor animal abuse (the euthanized dogs) and 418 counts of misdemeanor animal neglect (the survivors). Bob pled guilty and was quickly released, but a recalcitrant Barbara remained in jail for several weeks. After her release, she and Bob stayed in Ontario, Oregon while awaiting trial, taking a room at the Colonial Inn, a temporary residence, Barbara hoped, until they could rent a house with a yard. She still expected to be given custody of her dogs following the trial. A few days after moving into their new residence, a police report was filed by Paula Haines, a resident of Ontario, Oregon. In it, she claimed that Barbara had stolen her pregnant cat. When the police investigated, Haines's cat was found with its brand new litter of kittens in Barbara's rented room, neatly tucked into a cardboard box lined with scratchy hotel towels.

"I tried to tell her, but she don't listen to me," Bob whined to the officer who quickly ascertained that Barbara called all the shots in the Erickson family. She was arrested and jailed for contempt of court.

Barbara denied everything, as usual, later complaining to me during a phone conversation that the police had refused to check out her side of the story. Shortly thereafter, her attorney negotiated an agreement with the Malheur County prosecutor to drop the contempt of court charge if Barbara agreed to plead guilty to the previous indictments. A pre-sentence hearing was set, and Barbara walked out of jail.

Kammy Rios later reported that Barbara had attempted to place Paula Haines's cat and its kittens with New Beginnings until after her trial. She likened harboring cats for Barbara to offering a drink to an alcoholic.

A few weeks later, with a deal nearly hammered into place, Barbara Erickson met her court-appointed attorney, Manuel Perez, just a few minutes before the sentencing hearing. This was their first face-to-face meeting, and she liked him immediately. He reviewed her case, maintaining eye contact and speaking respectfully. He was accompanied by Kim Gomez, his case investigator, an attentive woman whose willing ear had already endeared her to Barbara. At the hearing, the likeable and persistent Malheur County pre-sentence investigator, Casey Kline, put into evidence police reports, statements from the defendant and the victim—the Idaho Humane Society—and photographs of the Erickson home and surrounding property. Included with Undersheriff Brian Wolfe's report was Gary Partonrek's 1999 study that defined animal hoarding and characterized animal hoarders.

Malheur County Lead Prosecutor, Dan Norris, sought $25,000 in damages on the criminal mischief charge and five years supervised probation on the abuse and neglect charges, with the additional provisions that Barbara Erickson would reside in the state of Oregon within the incorporated city limits of Nyssa, Vale, or Ontario and submit to a psychological evaluation, adhering to all subsequent treatment plans. In addition, Barbara could keep no more than two spayed or neutered dogs who would be implanted with tracking microchips. As a corollary to the third provision, Barbara was to waive her fourth amendment rights to search and seizure with regard to the monitoring of her home by police or probation officers.

Manuel Perez challenged the monetary damages, citing the Ericksons' limited financial resources and Verda Palmer's alleged failure to make needed repairs. He also quoted a report submitted by Dr. Michael Mallory, a local psychologist who had evaluated Barbara.

"Dr. Mallory indicates that the only reliable source of support and love in Mrs. Erickson's entire life has been animals," Perez read. "Since she was a very young person, animals have been a source of comfort, love, and even protection for her, and that is what compels her to have dogs around. I don't think she intended to have 539 dogs."

Judge Patricia Sullivan presided, bringing along a reputation well-known to the lawyers who argued before her. She expected preparation and no attempts to muddy the waters with psychobabble. The law was the law. When Perez and Norris were done presenting their arguments, the judge studied the documents on her bench. She looked up and fixed steely, unsympathetic eyes on Barbara.

"I've read your statement, Mrs. Erickson," she began, "and frankly, you can take the statement and the actual photographs of what happened here and put it in a psychology textbook for students to learn about what an animal hoarding disorder is. I'm not going to argue with you about the many things in your statement that are preposterous, because I just don't think that you recognize how disturbed you are with this disorder. You don't see that what happened to these animals was totally out of control and really tragic. I think at this point maybe a treatment professional can address it with you."

With that, Judge Sullivan ordered Barbara to pay $15,000 in restitution, sentenced her to sixty months supervised probation, and limited her to no more than two dogs in accordance with the pre-sentencing agreement between the attorneys.

"Mrs. Erickson, you may appeal this sentence if done so within thirty days," the judge concluded.

Barbara did.

Chapter Thirty-One

While awaiting sentencing, being out of jail had created a predictable problem for Barbara. It had been a treat to have a shower and a warm bed at night, but day after day, staring out the window of her hotel room at the steady, gray drizzle, she missed her dogs. She missed cuddling with them at night and taking meals together. She especially missed being needed...and accepted. Unable to contain herself, Barbara had convinced Bob, who had gotten off with probation only, to drive her to New Beginnings in Fruitland, Idaho. Once there, the familiar barking, the smell of the kennels, and the wagging tails lifted her spirits. Kammy Rios remembers Barbara's visit. She'd seemed to harbor no animosity toward Kammy, although she remained unrelentingly furious with Brian Wolfe and Sara Sharette. At that point, Barbara was certain the court would return her animals and took the opportunity of her visit to offer a barrelfull of unsolicited advice, later telling people Kammy had offered her a job.

Over the years, Barbara had maintained the notion of strength, and, yes, even humor. Yet beneath that shield was a different woman—vulnerable, with a naked, forsaken, me-against-the-world loneliness. All this in a person who was never alone. Her story has often reminded me of another. Years ago, a friend—Karen Swank—told me about one of her aunts who had been an animal hoarder:

> "When I was six years old, my dad told me we were going to visit Aunt Esther and her puppies. My excitement and anticipation turned to horror as we walked up to the front door. The house was in the middle of a forest, and there was a lot of barking. We were surrounded by dogs as we entered the house and the smell was unbearable. Magazines and junk were piled up everywhere. Newspapers covered the floor and were soaked in urine. Everything was dirty. There were dirty dishes piled everywhere and

constant barking. I just remember being frozen with fear and wanting to go home. That night I wrote in my journal, 'Today we visited a witch.'"

Karen's aunt had refused help, even after she'd come to the end of her financial means. In 1958, two years after Karen's visit, her aunt was found dead in her bed. The old woman's animals were taken to a local shelter and euthanized. Just like that, all traces of their little family were wiped off the face of the Earth. Without each other, they'd been alone. Nonexistent. From my reading, I'd learned that isolation from friends and relatives was common in hoarding cases. At first, I'd assumed that isolation and loneliness triggered the hoarding, but the more I read, the more I realized that the opposite was true. Animal hoarding results in isolation and loneliness as the hoarder retreats from interactions with others to hide the squalor and chaos.

Recalling my friend's story reminded me that, after many months on the story and many conversations with Barbara Erickson, I knew her only as a voice on the telephone. I wanted to meet her in person.

Chapter Thirty-Two

With her sentencing complete, Sherry "Barbara" Erickson finally agreed to meet with me. Our first face-to-face meeting after months of phone conversations took place in a small, two-bedroom cottage located on a large, bare corner lot that dwarfed the house. The home sat on a main thoroughfare in Ontario, Oregon, and nearly continuous traffic buzzed about behind me as I grabbed the black, iron handrail and climbed the steps to the porch.

Barbara looked altogether different than her newspaper photos. She beamed at me in greeting, painted eyebrows arched, cheeks rouge-rosy. She introduced me to Bob who offered me a twisted, gargoyle-like grin as his wife led me through their rental home. Two pugs, determined to make their own introductions, bounced and barked at our feet. Glass trinkets filled every shelf, and teddy bears were scattered about the living room. The Queen Anne coffee table I'd first seen in the splintered, ramshackle shed behind the Harper house was polished to a shine and laden with doilies.

We settled at the kitchen table, my tape recorder and notepad and her ashtray and cigarettes between us. The yapping stopped and our eyes locked. Barbara tapped a cigarette against the table, beginning the smoking ritual of an old pro. She pulled a lighter from her purse and flicked it to life, taking a deep drag and exhaling thick smoke.

"Well," she said, smiling, "we finally meet."

"Yes," I answered, "finally."

"And you're a pretty, little gal," Barbara added.

I pressed the "record" button on my tape recorder, watching for signs of discomfort. There were none. We began talking, and our first face-to-face meeting stretched into the afternoon. After a while, I felt as if I were spending my day with a not-so-distant relative. She rambled on as Barbara is wont to do, her stories a mixture of pathos and bravado. She is an entertaining storyteller for the most part, having well honed her skills at charming people with wit and anecdotes. At times, she had me laughing. At others, I fought back my tears. Through it all, one thing stood out. Like 418 of her beloved babies, Sherry "Barbara" Erickson was a survivor. She had built and rebuilt her family many times over, nurturing and loving them as best she could, just as they had nurtured and loved her. With cunning and drive and a refusal to bow to the norms of society, she had survived.

It was hard to use the name "Sherry." I'd known her for so long as "Barbara." But after a while, it became easier, more natural. "Sherry" was a name that seemed to suit her. We talked on, or rather, Sherry talked, and I listened. I'd come to meet a woman named Barbara Erickson, someone who had always seemed likeable and friendly over the phone, yet the same person who'd lived in that rundown house in Harper, who had allowed a hell to exist on Earth— a person some called a monster, a criminal, an animal hoarder.

But the label—like all labels—was an imperfect fit.

The afternoon lazily tumbled toward dusk, and I knew I should take my leave. But I stayed, listening, watching. Grasping the fragments of a shattered past and trying to put them together again. As her stories fell further back into the years, the labels that had been cruelly applied gradually started to curl and peel away. The bone-cold, dark house in Harper, Oregon faded, and, instead, I began to feel the warmth of her love and the sting of her pain. I stopped seeing anyone other than a little girl named Sherry Hawkes, laughing and running in the autumn sun of Kittitas County at harvest-time.

And last of all, as Sherry smiled and leaned down to kiss each of her pugs, I saw running next to the little girl—chasing joyously after their truest friend—a collie named Lady and a German shepherd named Buddy, a stick in his mouth, both their tails wagging.

Epilogue

It took several rings of the doorbell to awaken Bob Erickson from his nap in front of the blaring television. At the front door, he greeted Janice Thompson, Barbara's probation officer, with a gaping yawn. Without a word, he pivoted and returned to the sofa, lying down and staring at the TV. On the back of the sofa, a gray cat lounged, his eyes half open. On the floor, the two dogs allowed the Ericksons' home in accordance with Barbara's sentencing were a tangle of legs, dead asleep. Before Officer Thompson could say a word, a wide-eyed Barbara Erickson appeared in a side doorway. The edge of an unmade bed was visible just behind her. Barbara didn't offer a greeting, instead crossing quickly to the sofa. She scooped up the cat and scuddled to the back door. The two dogs briefly awakened, lifted their heads, and appraised the situation with complete disinterest, then settled back into sleep. The cat, for his part, seemed entirely at home with the little family.

A convoluted series of excuses followed—the cat wasn't really theirs, Barbara explained. He belonged to a neighbor or he was a stray or she didn't know how he'd gotten in. Thompson accepted Barbara's explanation but had noticed how familiar the animals seemed to be with one another. She reviewed the conditions of their parole with the Ericksons and left them with a stern warning.

A month later, Thompson showed up on the Ericksons' doorstep and found two cats sitting on the porch. When Bob opened the door, the cats pranced in and made themselves at home next to a third tabby who slept on the sofa. Thompson had the Ericksons arrested. By this time, Barbara had taken back her childhood name, "Sherry," and it was as Sherry Erickson that she again appeared before Judge Sullivan who determined that the inconvenience of the arrest and subsequent appearance in court were punishment enough. She could hardly be blamed. Sherry Erickson had added heart problems and diabetes to her emphysema and arthritic hip. What was the judge to do with a defiant, but ailing, elderly woman? The jails were already bulging with serious criminals.

There was a second violation of Sherry's parole about six months later. She had been skipping the court-ordered counseling sessions, although she seemed to genuinely like her counselor, Sandy Abegg. She claimed that Abegg had given her a "clearance paper," another tall tale. When I asked about it, Sherry was unrepentant. "They're just harassing me," she complained. "I got a notice posted on my door from Washington, D.C., that says it's against federal law to harass senior citizens." She sputtered on a bit more. "It's *my* damn life," she said. Her voice was edged with bitterness. "Ain't nobody gonna tell me how to live it." A month later, Sherry was in front of the judge again, facing yet another violation. She now attends her counseling sessions regularly.

When I next talked to Sherry, she was a patient at Saint Alphonsus Hospital in Boise. Emphysema and an irregular heart rhythm had combined to steal her breath away. She was sitting up in bed as I entered her tidy hospital room, her breathing so labored she'd not slept lying down for weeks. Her legs dangled over the side of the bed, ankles swollen and blue. Sherry greeted me with a wet cough that forced her head down.

She looked up with tired eyes. "How you doin', Honey?" She managed a thin smile before another wave of coughing engulfed her.

Bob sat in a chair next to the window, nicotine-stained fingers held in a V-shape, as if his usually present cigarette were actually there. He looked at me dull-faced, and I nodded in greeting.

"She couldn't breathe," he said, "and her heart wasn't beatin' right."

Sherry adjusted the thin, flexible prongs that disappeared into her nose. The prongs were connected by a long, transparent green tube to a bubbling bottle attached to the wall behind her bed.

"Oxygen," she said, following my eyes. "They gave me some stuff—medicines—but now they think I'm gonna need a pacemaker." She fingered the green oxygen tube between her fingers. "I'll have to be on oxygen all the time, and I can't smoke no more."

She glanced at her husband, who was staring out the window, following the monotonous movement of the hospital groundskeeper as he zipped about on a lawn tractor, mowing. "I don't mind not smokin', but Bob's not gonna like it. He'll have to go outside."

Bob didn't respond. He didn't appear to be listening.

I sat next to Sherry on the bed. "Have you been able to sleep since you were admitted?" I asked, putting my hand on hers. Curiously, her face lit up, and she launched into a speech that went on for several minutes.

"Oh, I can't sleep with all this stress. It's a horrible mess, and I got papers off the Internet about the Legal Abuse Syndrome and how the courts harass the elderly and make them sick and..."

Sherry Erickson's doctor implanted a pacemaker the following day. Afterward, the color returned to her cheeks. Her eyes brightened, and her smile returned. I continued to visit her regularly, talking less about the rescue than the growing of tomatoes and flowers.

Sherry "Barbara" Erickson is now eighty-two years old. She continues to battle emphysema and heart disease, along with chronic bronchitis, sinus infections, and the complications of diabetes. She lives with Bob in an old, well-tended house owned by a landlord who stops by monthly to collect the rent and keep an eye on the place. Pets are allowed, she tells me, so her two pugs, Angel and Rudy, are fixtures on the back of the couch, yapping through the window at passers-by. Other visitors are rare, but Barbara Hutchinson occasionally pops in bringing a bag of dog food or toys. Sherry remains mostly upbeat, despite her health problems.

"The doctor gave me a prescription for a Chihuahua," she told me one day after seeing her physician. Her cheeks seemed rosier, and her eyes were soft and warm. "And you know," she said as if imparting a great secret, "they are good for asthma and everything."

PART TWO

Inside Animal Hoarding

Arnold Arluke

PROFILE

Celeste Killeen's vivid and moving account of the Erickson case is but one instance of animal hoarding. While not every case of hoarding is the same, there are some noticeable patterns that provide a context for the thinking and behavior of the Ericksons.

Animal hoarding exists in virtually every community. Based on the estimated national animal shelter population of six million, there are about twelve hundred to sixteen hundred cases per year, and based on the human population served, six hundred to two thousand cases per year in America with 60% being repeat offenders (Patronek 1999). Cats and dogs are the most commonly hoarded species, but wildlife, dangerous exotic animals, and farm animals have been involved, even in urban situations. Although the number of cases climbs each year, this trend is most likely the result of increased public awareness and reporting of the problem.

Animal hoarders come from varied backgrounds, despite the stereotype of the neighborhood "cat lady" who is an older, single female, living alone. As with many stereotypes, there is an element of truth to this image. In one study (Worth and Beck 1981), just 70% of the sample were unmarried women who had cats, while in another study (Patronek 1999), 76% of the sample were women, 46% were over sixty years of age, most were single, divorced, widowed, and cats were most commonly involved. Barbara Erickson partially fits this profile–she was an older female, although she did not hoard cats and did not live alone. However, it is not uncommon for hoarders to be living with dependents–children, the disabled, the elderly–and Barbara, too, lived with a dependent–her husband, whom she claimed had Alzheimer's disease. In reality, this behavior cuts across all demographic and socioeconomic boundaries. As most hoarders are very secretive, many can lead a double life with a successful professional career; hoarding behavior has been discovered among doctors, nurses, public officials, college professors, and veterinarians, as well as among a broad spectrum of socioeconomically disadvantaged individuals.

There also is not one type of animal hoarder (Patronek et al. 2006). Although not full-fledged hoarders, some people with many animals seem headed in that direction. These *incipient* hoarders try to meet minimum standards of animal care as proscribed by law and are likely to be aware of problems that develop. However, their ability to provide proper animal care deteriorates, unless their situations change markedly. A second type of hoarder, the *breeder-hoarder*, at first breeds animals for show or sale, but the animals are not kept in the home, and human living conditions are good compared to other types of hoarders. Eventually, it becomes increasingly difficult to provide proper care, but despite deteriorating conditions, they continue to breed because they have little insight into the animals' condition and their ability to care for them. The *overwhelmed caregiver* minimizes rather than denies animal care problems that result from economic, social, medical, or domestic changes, such as loss of job or health, but cannot remedy these problems. Despite their strong attachment to animals, the overwhelmed caregiver's compromised situation gradually leads to a deterioration of animal care. Although socially isolated, they are less secretive and more cooperative with authorities than are most hoarders. The fourth type of hoarder, the *rescuer*, has a missionary zeal to save all animals. Not too socially isolated, they may be part of a network of enablers whose offers to take animals are never declined. They also actively seek to acquire animals because they feel that only they can provide adequate care and because they oppose their euthanasia. Barbara Erickson's behavior, as detailed by Celeste Killeen, would most likely qualify her as a rescuer hoarder who tried to save dogs rather than relinquish them to shelters and risk their euthanasia. Finally, the *exploiter* hoarder is the most challenging type to manage. Considered to be sociopaths and/or to have personality disorders, their lack of empathy for people or animals means they are indifferent to the harm they cause. Somewhat charismatic and articulate, they present an appearance that suggests competence to the public, officials, and the media.

ETIOLOGY

Why hoarders like the Ericksons amassed hundreds of animals is the first question asked by the public and professionals alike. Understanding why people hoard animals is complex, and any explanation must be tentative. It is complex because it is likely that a number of different psychological, social, and even cultural factors are behind the emergence and recognition of this behavior. It is tentative because the current state of research knowledge about animal hoarding is somewhat limited and still evolving; social science explanations of this behavior are relatively recent, replacing the antiquated, but still expressed, view that it is mere eccentricity.

Eccentricity

For much of the twentieth century, unconventional ownership of large numbers of animals was considered to be an eccentricity. As part of American folklore, neighborhood "cat ladies" were largely tolerated, although not understood, for their excesses. Considered "strange" or "odd," the collection of animals, although not fully revealed to outsiders, was ignored or tolerated but not seen as an expression of serious mental illness.

Eccentricity continues to this day as an explanation for owning large numbers of animals but with a social class spin. Although not technically hoarding, because there is no neglect, people with enough money can afford to keep and care for many animals. Michael Jackson, for example, was known to keep a menagerie of animals–many difficult to manage–without their abuse because he could pay others to do all the work of feeding and cleaning their cages while providing all the necessary housing and veterinary care. After child molestation charges, legal expenses strapped Jackson for money, and he lived elsewhere, causing his Neverland estate to suffer along with his animals, which, according to the Neverland zoo veterinarian, starved and lived in squalor. Later, after a complaint filed by PETA, Department of Agriculture inspectors found no evidence of violations of the Animal Welfare Act at Neverland.

Views of animal hoarding as an eccentric behavior appear in news reports of this behavior.[1] Some articles paint a picture of hoarders as strange or "wacky," arguing that the difference between "sensible" pet owners and hoarders is that the latter "don't stop at a few dogs or even a dozen." One article, for example, portrays a hoarder of dogs, birds, foxes, guinea pigs, iguanas, and a baboon as bizarre but well meaning, calling her "a nice woman who needs a little help." The major thrust of another article is that the hoarder is an eccentric, cantankerous fake—a real "character." The article suggests that she falsified her college attendance, used a phony English accent, lied about her age, used many aliases in court, wore fake animal clothing, and earned a living as a psychic. Moreover, the article lightheartedly questions the seriousness of her neglect, asking, "Her alleged crime?" and answering, "Owning Bugsy, Vampira and their kittens." In the same light spirit, the article notes that this hoarder had been "playing cat and mouse with animal control officers for thirteen years." Similarly, a reporter asked a humane official, "What drives people to take in more animals than they can handle and how [can] people spot hoarders in their neighborhoods?" to which the official replied, they have an "illness" but "they're average, normal people."

A variation of the eccentricity model sees hoarders as plagued by a "blind spot"—not a serious mental disorder—that prevents them from seeing the ill effects of their basically good intentions. Many news articles, for example, characterize the impulse to "save" animals as a matter of having "too much love" or "compassion." These popular, lay theories often provide sympathetic portrayals of hoarders as people who simply "loved animals too much," images supported by hoarders and their friends and lawyers who, when permitted, defend their actions as well meaning although excessive. Hoarders were animal "lovers" and headlines such as "Compassion Unleashed" or "Animal Passions" emphasize this point. Many articles elaborate this theme. One, for example, notes, "This woman loved animals so much she could not turn them away." Another cites the hoarder's lawyer, who claimed, "This is not an animal abuse case. It's an animal loving case that went too far." Other articles claim that hoarders love their animals too much to give them up, even though they cannot care for them.

Sometimes hoarders' presumed strong love for animals is not specifically stated but implied as though a mysterious force drove them to amass animals. One hoarder explained that he had eighty-eight dogs because "it was impossible to give them away." In another case involving sixty-eight dogs and cats discovered in squalid conditions, the officers conducting the investigation said that the hoarder appeared to be unable to turn away a stray because of her feelings for animals. And in a case involving two hundred cats, a humane society representative said that the hoarder "can't seem to get rid of" the animals.

A few hoarders showed some awareness of the problem, acknowledging that their love for animals had "gotten a little out of hand." One hoarder, charged with animal neglect for failing to sufficiently feed and water eighty horses, ponies, donkeys, and dogs, said that her intentions were to "save animals," but she had "acquired more animals than she could handle." "Between sobs," the article reports, the hoarder "said she was sorry she had not cared for the animals properly. 'I would go hungry myself before my animals would go without.'" Similarly, a hoarder in another case said, "I have loved animals all my life and would never set out to make them suffer. But because of my stupidity and arrogance in thinking I could cope, I made these gentle creatures suffer. It is something I will never forgive myself for." And yet another hoarder admitted, "I just got a little overwhelmed. I'm just a good person whose heart was bigger than my abilities."

Because they had so much "love" for their animals along with the enormous responsibility of caring for their charges, hoarders retreated from human contact. This retreat furthered an image of eccentricity more than mental illness. Hoarders' animals were their "only family and friends," "babies," or "children." The title of one article reads, "Dog Owner Is Told to Curtail His Collie Clan" and elsewhere refers to the hoarder's "pack." Another article points out that because the hoarder has so many animals, she does not take trips or use television or radio. A number of articles, somewhat pathetically, note that hoarders feel as though their entire purpose in life was taken away from them if their animals were seized and destroyed. "What else do I have anymore?" one hoarder said.

This blind spot casts animal hoarding as a minor psychological problem rather than as a serious pathology. Saying that hoarders suffer from "too much love" assumes strong positive feelings toward animals that might include nurturing and other socially sanctioned behaviors. That these feelings for animals simply went astray reduces this behavior to an inability to control impulses that is almost admirable and certainly not criminal. As one hoarder said, "These people act as if you have a psychological problem if you want to help animals. I did nothing illegal, yet they treat me like a common criminal." In recent years, animal hoarders are less often dismissed as eccentric "animal lovers" whose quirkiness falls short of full-blown mental illness.

Psychological Disorder

Animal hoarding is not yet recognized as indicative of any specific psychological disorder. Indeed, there is no specific mention of it in the latest version of the *Diagnostic and Statistical Manual* (*DSM*), used by mental health workers to diagnose various disorders. However, evidence from case reports indicates that many hoarders are eventually placed under guardianship or other supervised living situations, suggesting their incapacity to make rational decisions and manage personal affairs. This may well indicate a strong mental health component. And the trend over the past two decades has been to more readily label hoarding as a disease, although attempts to do so have been disappointing because many hoarders do not fit so neatly into various diagnostic labels that have been offered up, only to then lose popularity over time.

Experts have suggested several possible psychological models for animal hoarders, generally falling short of overtly psychotic behavior (Worth and Beck 1981), but including the claim that hoarders suffer from delusions, dementia, addiction, attachment disorder, borderline personality disorder, obsessive compulsiveness, or compulsive care-giving. Each model is consistent with at least some of what we know about animal hoarders and certainly some of Barbara Erickson's behavior.

However, each model also has its limitations, suggesting that animal hoarding, as a psychological pathology, defies conventional diagnostic labeling. This diagnostic confusion is due to several factors, including the likelihood that some animal hoarders suffer from multiple pathologies, that a novel pathology underlies their acts, and that too few hoarders have been studied to properly determine their true pathology. Given this imprecision, each of the following models appears to have some diagnostic validity.

For example, there is an argument for the delusional disorder model (HARC 2000). Like people who hoard inanimate objects (Frost 2000), animal hoarders lack insight into the problematic nature of their behavior. Most have a persistent and powerful belief that they are providing proper animal care, despite obvious and overwhelming contradictory evidence. And most are equally unable to grasp the extent to which their home environments have become unfit for any living creature, sometimes to the point of needing to be torn down. Further suggestion of delusional disorder in hoarders is evidenced by their paranoia about officials and their belief that they have a special ability to communicate with animals.

The addictions model also seems to fit the thinking and behavior of many hoarders (Lockwood 1994). As with substance abusers, hoarders are preoccupied with animals, are in denial over their problems, have many excuses for their situation, are socially isolated, claim to be persecuted, and neglect themselves and their surroundings. Other evidence consistent with the addictions model is the similarity of hoarders with people suffering from impulse control problems, such as compulsive shopping (Frost et al. 1998) and compulsive gambling (Meagher et al. 1999). Some hoarders report to compulsively collect strays and shelter animals.

Animal hoarding is also consistent with dementia (Patronek 1999). This is suggested by the number of hoarders who are placed in a residential facility or under guardianship (26%), and that show no insight into the irrationality of their behavior. Indirect evidence for dementia's role comes from Hwang and others' (1998) finding that 20% of inanimate hoarding cases involved this illness. However, as Frost (2000) points out, there is no direct evidence for this model; institutional placement may be due to conditions other than dementia and many other conditions manifest lack of insight.

Attachment disorder is another explanation that has been suggested for animal hoarding. These individuals are deprived in childhood of close relationships with parents because they are absent, neglectful, or abusive. This developmental failure makes them unable to establish close human relationships in adulthood. Relationships with animals are preferred because they are safer and less threatening than relationships with people. Evidence for this explanation comes from reports that animal hoarders desire unconditional love from animals (Worth and Beck 1981) and are raised in chaotic homes with inconsistent parenting (HARC 2000).

Some have argued that animal hoarders suffer from borderline personality disorder (Poses and Weishaupt, n.d.). People having this disorder experience unstable and intense interpersonal relationships due to their fear of abandonment, feelings of emptiness, difficulty with anger, and occasional paranoia. Those with this disorder often come from families where they had a history of unresolved grief due to tragic, untimely deaths or losses and emotional or physical abuse. Absence of nurturing relationships in childhood cause these people to have a deep sense of aloneness in adulthood that can never be filled. This leads them to seek a "perfect love" to repair their wounded self and make them feel worthy, only to be constantly disappointed, given the nature of human relationships. Animals may provide this perfect, unconditional love, as reported by Worth and Beck (1981). However, just as their own need to be loved was not met by their parents, so, too, do they neglect the needs of their animals who are dependent on them. As some animals die from lack of care, the hoarder's sense of unworthiness is only confirmed as is their fear of being abandoned, in this case by the dying animals.

The most parsimonious explanation of animal hoarding, according to Frost (2000), is obsessive-compulsive disorder (OCD). Many have argued for this model (Ball, Baer, and Otto, 1996; Lockwood, 1994; Rasmussen and Eisen, 1992; Strubbe, 2000; Winsberg et al. 1999), although with little if any research data to support their claim. Hoarding of inanimate objects is seen in a variety of psychological disorders but is most commonly observed in OCD (Frost et al. 1995). OCD affects 2%-3% of the human population, and 15%-30% of those have hoarding as a primary symptom. It is unknown what proportion of these individuals hoard animals. One expert (Nathanson 2009) questions whether obsessive compulsiveness is the correct explanation for animal hoarding, arguing that amassing material objects versus sentient beings are reflections of different psychological pathologies. While it is true that a subgroup of hoarders views their animals as objects and therefore could have OCD according to Nathanson, most are involved in a "dynamic relation" with them, despite their numbers and neglect.

The most recent psychological explanation (Nathanson 2007) claims that animal hoarders suffer from a particular kind of attachment disorder known as insistent caregiving (Bowlby 1980) or the compulsion to devote as much time as possible to giving rather than receiving care. Adult compulsive caregiving has its roots in traumatic losses that leave children feeling like they need care and help, which parents fail to provide. As these children reach adulthood, they have learned to reverse parenting roles but have lost ability to express needs or ask for care. They are always trying to help others when deep inside they want care and help. Although it can be argued that hoarders are notorious for not providing care, they adopt a caregiving role by claiming to rescue and save many animals from certain death.

Of course, caution must be exercised when applying these labels to anyone until individual hoarders are thoroughly examined and more is known about the psychological causes of this behavior. With this caution in mind, a number of these disorders seem to aptly capture Barbara Erickson's thinking and behavior, as well as their roots in a chaotic if not traumatic childhood, characterized by loss of significant others and abuse.

Most hoarders have psychological and social histories beginning in childhood that are chaotic and traumatic. Preliminary research (HARC) suggests that hoarders grew up in households with inconsistent parenting, in which animals may have been the only stable feature. The vast majority report feelings of insecurity and disruptive and experiences in early life, including frequent relocations, parental separation and divorce, and isolation from peers. Barbara Erickson's formative years, according to Celeste Killeen's report, were no different. Raped by her grandfather (and possibly by her father) it was Barbara's German shepherd, Buddy, that chased the old man away, and her collie, Lady, that comforted her during those terrifying moments. Barbara also experienced difficult losses as an adolescent. Her mother abandoned the family, and then her baby was lost after her father allegedly killed it.

Following suit, several psychological explanations of animal hoarding are consistent with what we know about Barbara Erickson's thinking and behavior. The delusional model, for one, easily fits what we know about Barbara Erickson's adult life. She claimed to speak with FBI agents, to have graduated with five degrees, and to be a lawyer and a veterinarian. When it came to her animals, she repeatedly turned down offers of help, including taking some of the dogs and relieving her responsibility, because help was not needed and the dogs' condition was fine. As Celeste Killeen observes, Barbara not only failed to see that her home and animals were deteriorating, she could not see how these conditions adversely affected her husband's and her own health.

Two other models, compulsive caregiving and the related attachment disorder model, also shed some light on Barbara Erickson's actions. According to Celeste Killeen's case study, Barbara appears to have experienced little if any consistent parental affection, or "love," during her childhood due to significant losses and abuse. To Killeen, these emotional traumas played out in Barbara's adult life as a "search for love" that could never be satisfied. Presumably, she displaced the need for these unfulfilled emotions into perpetual accumulation of dogs as both a source and object of love. Her reluctance to surrender their animals–even to responsible parties who promised to care for them—reflected how seriously and dearly she played the parental role with her animals. This role is also suggested by her emotionality when considering the loss of any one of her many dogs and by the fact that she allegedly lost her own baby and had been unsuccessfully searching for it throughout her life. Indeed, Barbara often referred to her dogs as her "children." Seeing the dogs this way meant that they could serve as objects of care and sources of nurturance, allowing her to simultaneously play parent and child roles.

Social Construction

A psychological approach to animal hoarding relies on a medical model of this problem that sees it as a symptom of a disordered personality and hoarders as "sick," irrational, or at least seriously "misguided" people. Medicalization of problem behavior occurs when various "experts" weigh in on what they think causes people to behave this way. Individual cases become symptomatic of a larger problem, as specialists or authorities offer their explanations of the problem's causes. Once particular behaviors are seen as symptoms of disease, health care institutions become identified with the proper management of these people (Best 1995; Mills 1959; Sacco 1995; Schneider and Conrad 1992).

Drawing on these expert opinions, the media helps to convert private troubles into medical problems by selectively gathering up the building blocks of individual experiences, investing them with broader meaning, and making them available for public consumption. Indeed, much of what people read in the news is a distillation of how social problems are made sense of by organizations that enforce laws, rescue survivors, and otherwise intervene in these situations (Fishman 1995). Although journalists do their best to present these ideas to readers of the news, they are sometimes very tentative, if not conflictive, because the behavior in question may not be fully understood by those experts weighing in on its nature, scope, and treatment.

Experts, often with the support of the media, are increasingly weighing in on the nature of animal hoarding, and are choosing to define it as a mental disorder. The problem of amassing and then neglecting large numbers of animals is seen as emanating from the individual, who presumably would profit from counseling or similar interventions, if an accurate clinical diagnosis can be made. Once portrayed this way, the health care profession becomes the designated social institution to rule on what constitutes hoarding, who is a hoarder, how hoarders should be treated, and which professionals should manage them.

In a relatively short period of time, the consensus in the animal welfare community has moved toward widespread agreement that animal hoarders are not only difficult and challenging to manage but are suffering from one of the mental disorders reviewed above. This consensus has evolved largely on the basis of unscientific reports. Only two research studies have been published on animal hoarding that report information directly collected from hoarders—the first on "multiple animal ownership" (Worth and Beck 1981) and the second on demographic and public health concerns (Patronek 1999). Otherwise, there is virtually no published research literature on this problem that presents and analyzes firsthand data from animal hoarders themselves—hardly enough to draw firm conclusions about the nature of this problem.

One group of experts, the Hoarding of Animals Research Consortium (HARC), has sought to remedy this research vacuum and, in so doing, has helped to transform the perception of animal hoarding from a human-interest story about eccentricity to a serious public health issue about mental disorder. Composed largely of social workers, psychologists, and psychiatrists,[2] this group has taken a psychiatric approach to the problem of animal hoarding, focusing largely on questions relating to individual pathology and its treatment. For example, the group has been particularly interested in the relationship between chaotic childhoods and later animal hoarding and the identification of an appropriate diagnostic label for hoarders.

Given the lack of research on this problem and the absence of an official diagnostic label, press and television stories frequently include the opinions of people untrained in psychology or social work who are quick to label animal hoarders as "crazy" or "far out of reality" (Arluke et al. 2002). These stories matter-of-factly refer to "animal hoarder syndrome" as though it were an established and proven diagnosis. Anyone is cited with an opinion about hoarding, including housing inspectors, firefighters, police, animal control officers, caseworkers, and humane officials, as well as unnamed "researchers" or "authorities." Typically, these comments lack much psychological depth, sophistication, or consistency. "Symptoms" of this "disorder" vary from article to article and are often vague and clinically questionable, such as the suggestion that a hoarder has "too much love" for animals. One article, for example, is heavily sprinkled with talk by a journalist and a humane official about "obsession" and "addiction" and, at one point, compares hoarders to "tobacco addicts or shopping addicts."

The effect of such popular psychologizing is to create a folk diagnosis of animal hoarding, in the absence of an official mental health category agreed upon by trained health care professionals. As a folk, or unscientific, label, people will assume that animal hoarding is a mental illness of some sort, locate the problem within the disordered individual, and begin to address the problem by treating the individual with counseling or another one-on-one approach. Although those who directly deal with animal hoarders are often convinced that some mental disorder is present and that some such psychological approach is warranted, it seems unreasonable to lump together all these cases. While some animal hoarders are no doubt plagued by very really pathologies, others may not. The latter subgroup of cases may represent an entirely different ilk of animal hoarding where the problem is due to social breakdown or highly compromised living situations that result from personal, familial, neighborhood, or community social problems.

Social Enabling

As research on animal hoarders picks up steam, most studies will undoubtedly take a psychological approach to the problem. However, doing so narrows our thinking as it sees mental disorder emanating from within the individual. While we must not dismiss animal hoarding's psychological roots, it is also facilitated by interpersonal and cultural factors that, if considered, will produce a more nuanced understanding of the nature and origin of this behavior. Family, friends, neighbors, the wider community, and society at large must be factored into our analysis of why and how hoarding starts and continues. By taking a broader and more complex view of the problem, interventions can address the contextual roots of the problem rather than only focusing on the individual's underlying mental disorder.

For example, some cases of animal hoarding are likely a product of, or at least facilitated by, a dysfunctional society (Poses and Weishaupt, n.d.) rather than being due solely to the acts of disturbed individuals. If the finger of blame is to be pointed, in such instances, it must be shared with the larger society. In many parts of America, abandoned and stray animals remain a big problem, in part due to irresponsible breeding of pets that produces millions of unwanted animals. Euthanasia practiced by "kill" shelters becomes a way to manage this overpopulation problem, since not all of these unwanted animals can be adopted or kept indefinitely in their cages.

Animal hoarders, and whatever family and emotional support system they have, become an expedient and injurious dysfunctional system that responds to this societal problem. People in the community, knowing the hoarder's reputation for apparently wanting so many animals, may drop off unwanted pets at the hoarder's home, thereby feeding their ever growing collection. In this way, the neighborhood "cat lady" or "dog lady" serve as a convenient, impromptu shelter where there will be no guilt imparted for dropping off unwanted animals (Frommer and Arluke 1999) and no risk of euthanasia. According to Barbara Erickson, she played this role in her community when people anonymously left animals at her door rather than abandoning or taking them to a shelter.

Animal hoarding also can be perpetuated—indeed even started—through social support that provides animals to hoarders as well as food, veterinary care, and other essentials for them. One type of support comes from networks of like-minded or sympathetic people. Friends who identify with the hoarder's feelings and approach to animals may deliberately acquire unwanted animals from various sources, such as veterinary offices or shelters, and to prevent their euthanasia, give them to the hoarder. In the Erickson case, after Barbara's dogs were seized in one intervention, her friends tried to get her animals from the shelter by claiming that they were their own, and then returning them to her.

Another type of support comes from misguided people who inadvertently enable hoarders to amass many animals. The latter can sometimes "pass" as normal people by concealing their private world with animals. One such hoarder, who masked herself as a legitimate breeder, was protected by friends in her community who did not understand the depth of her psychological problem or the way she treated her dogs (Stola Education Group 2006). She did not allow anyone to visit her home and was charming at public dog events.

Finally, there is an interpersonal component to animal hoarding when other people know about the problem but choose to ignore, if not tolerate, the problem. Neighbors, friends, and relatives can be aware that hoarding is taking place, but do nothing to intervene or even report it to authorities. Understandably, it is difficult to take such action for fear of alienating personal relationships with the hoarder and for lack of hard evidence to provide authorities. Nevertheless, such inaction allows hoarding to continue unchallenged.

MANAGEMENT

Keeping large numbers of animals in inappropriate, inadequate, and over-crowded conditions that cause starvation, disease, behavioral problems, or death seriously challenges relatives, friends, neighbors, and community agencies that want to help hoarders and their animals.

The complex nature of hoarding cases makes them difficult to investigate and to resolve. The jurisdiction for these cases cross many state and local agencies and departments, including mental health, police, zoning, sanitation, fish and wildlife, child welfare, animal control, public health, building safety, aging, and social services. So it is the rule rather than the exception that they are procedurally cumbersome, time consuming, and costly to resolve. Although common sense suggests that the accumulation of large numbers of animals in homes can have important public health implications, including placing neighborhoods at risk due to unsanitary living conditions, facilitating the spread of zoonotic diseases, and endangering the health of vulnerable household members, particularly children or dependent elderly, the potential for these consequences in animal hoarding cases is not widely appreciated by government agencies.

The absence of joint agreements between agencies over their missions and roles in these cases may create more conflict than cooperation. And to date, most communities have not discovered how to bring together available resources, expertise, and authorities to achieve comprehensive solutions. Celeste Killeen's description of the community's handling of the Erickson case is more the exception than the rule. According to Killeen, veterinarians, shelters, police, volunteers, and journalists worked together rather seamlessly when they intervened in this case without any formal agreements between county and state agencies. They accomplished this by focusing on the problem and how to solve it, rather than their own jurisdictional issues. This is exemplified in the Idaho Humane Society's offering resources to a case in Oregon and in the Second Chance Shelter in Fruitland, Idaho, which worked closely with an Oregon Sheriff's Office prior to the rescue by reporting the problem and organizing the rescue, then offering to house and care for over five hundred dogs.

Difficult issues of personal freedom, lifestyle choice, mental competency, and private property rights also confound intervening in these cases. For one, to protect people's civil rights, most laws restrict agencies from intervening unless others are being harmed. In many animal hoarding situations, other family members, like minor children, dependent elderly persons, or disabled adults, are present and are also victims of this behavior. Serious unmet human health needs are commonly observed, and the conditions often meet the criteria for adult self-neglect, child neglect, or elder abuse.

Options for intervention are also limited because few hoarders seem to meet the criteria for mental incompetence or immediate danger to the community. For most hoarders, living spaces are often compromised to the extent that they no longer serve the function for which they were intended. Appliances and basic utilities (heat, plumbing, and electricity) are frequently inoperative. Household functioning is often so impaired that both food preparation and maintaining basic sanitation are impossible. From a community health perspective, the clutter can pose a fire hazard. In some cases, fireplaces and kerosene heaters are used for heat. Rodent and insect infestations, as well as odors, can create a neighborhood nuisance. These are important public health aspects of animal hoarding that go largely unrecognized, and which may provide avenues for intervention. In one hoarding case, the air ammonia level after the house had been ventilated by the fire department was 152 parts per million; the National Institute for Occupational Safety and Health lists three hundred parts per million as a concentration immediately dangerous to life or health, and twenty-five parts per million as the maximum average occupational exposure during the workday.

Cases typically come to the attention of authorities because of complaints from neighbors. The primary problems reported about hoarders are unsanitary conditions, "strong," "obnoxious" odors or "stench," and occasionally nuisance problems such as "loud barking." Neglect is seldom the initial complaint because animals are usually concealed inside hoarders' homes. So, too, with the Erickson case. There, neighbors complained to the Oregon Health Department about smells coming from the farm, leading to an investigation, an order to remove the waste, and a threatened five hundred dollar fine that was dropped after the Ericksons removed the waste. Sanitary conditions often deteriorate to the extent that public health authorities condemn dwellings as unfit for human habitation. By the time these situations have deteriorated to the point they cannot be ignored, expenses for veterinary care and housing of animals, litigation, and clean-up or demolition of premises can run into the tens of thousands of dollars. Unfortunately, because of ill health, contagious diseases, and the large numbers involved, euthanasia is often the only option for many of the animals rescued from such situations.

Initial attempts to follow up complaints are usually unsuccessful. Often described as "uncomfortable around people" or as "quiet and somewhat reclusive," hoarders sometimes board up windows, erect tall fences, rarely appear outside, and do not answer phone calls or doorbells, making them notorious for their fortress mentality and hostility to and suspicion of outsiders. The Ericksons even had a sign posted on the door proclaiming, "This is private property. Stay to hell out!" If approached, outsiders are almost always turned away before they get into the hoarder's home. The Ericksons, for example, never allowed anyone inside their home; Barbara would intercept anyone before they got to the front door. On more than one occasion, she suffered health problems requiring an ambulance, but instead of inviting paramedics into the house to treat her, she met them at the street. This isolation makes it difficult, if not impossible, for neighbors to know much about them or their animals. Law enforcement authorities are eventually called to the scene, typically discovering many suffering or dead animals that are taken away from angry or grieved owners who potentially face charges of cruelty and possible conviction and sentencing.

As a result, systematic procedures for resolving these cases are lacking, as are effective preventive strategies. In one famous case, a woman living in a school bus with 115 dogs had been investigated in several jurisdictions in four states. In each case, she had essentially been given a tank of gas and been told to get out of town. When finally prosecuted in Oregon, she went through three prosecutors and six judges, finally serving as her own attorney. Her trial lasted five weeks.

Charging Hoarders

It is ironic that while the medico-legal framework for intervention to help people in these situations seems to be inadequate, there are comparatively effective and easily implemented laws in place to allow for the rescue of animal victims.

Every state has statutes that mandate that caretakers provide animals with sufficient food and water, a sanitary environment, and necessary veterinary care in case of illness or injury. Therefore, technically speaking, hoarding violates animal cruelty statutes in every state, making hoarders criminal under the law. Hoarding cases are often initially investigated and handled by representatives of the local animal shelter, humane society, or other animal protection group. In cases where an animal protection organization does not have jurisdiction, local police officers or municipal animal control officers may be the initial agents to investigate a case.

In some jurisdictions, violations of animal cruelty statutes may be summary offenses prosecuted by local humane agents or animal control officers in front of a magistrate, whereas in others, they may be misdemeanors, or in some cases, felonies, requiring prosecution by the district attorney's office. In the worst of abuse cases, humane law enforcement agents may prosecute someone who has harmed an animal in ways that cause suffering for a relatively brief period–if they are not killed instantly (Arluke 2004). Penalties in the event of a guilty finding can range from a nominal fine to forfeiture of the animals and jail time (Arluke and Luke 1997). Some state statutes provide for the recovery of the costs of boarding and medical care for animals in cruelty cases.

Although technically a violation of animal cruelty law, hoarders can be difficult to criminally charge. Cases involving many animals are often prosecuted as a single case because the expedience of judges discourages multiple counts of cruelty. And cruelty law focuses on the abuser's intent to harm and torture a comparatively small number of animals rather than the suffering of many. Hence, hoarders are legally viewed as chronically neglecting, rather than purposely abusing, a single animal. The absence of intent, then, can make it difficult to criminally intervene in hoarding cases, even though hoarders deliberately acquire and keep animals they cannot care for properly. Indeed, the recent attempt by many states to impose more serious penalties on abusers by classifying the intentional harm of animals as a felony crime has sidelined cases of neglect, even though the collective degree of suffering can be enormous in hoarding cases (Patronek et al. 2006).

Portraying the plight of animals as mere neglect seems to diminish the seriousness of their mistreatment, downgrading it from more serious abuse. Hoarding outcomes can be more disturbing than incidents of deliberate cruelty toward or torture of individual animals. Often, the former affects many animals kept for months or even years under conditions of horrendous deprivation and suffering (Lockwood and Cassidy 1988). Without apparent intent, hoarders cause an enormous amount of suffering and death, far surpassing the number of animals harmed or the duration of their suffering found in the vast majority of intentional animal abuse cases. They ignore basic animal care, failing to properly feed and water, if at all, their animals, and to treat veterinary problems that exist or develop. Consequently, these animals are victims of severe emaciation, they often have serious health and behavioral problems, or they even die. Those rescuing the Erickson's dogs in the 2003 case found many of those alive to be starved and dehydrated to the point of immobility. Those that could be rescued had many health problems such as roundworm, Demodectic mange, Cheyletiella mites, coccidiosis, Giardia, open sores, and old bodily injuries.[3]

In this vein, one article (Colin 2002), entitled "Loving Animals to Death," describes animal hoarders as "keeping a light foot in the serial killer camp: Like serial killers they are pathetic but obsessively thorough and are motivated by a perversion of something that could maybe almost make sense." Further on, the article contains an interview with a California resident. He stated: "I think that [hoarders] believe they are loving those animals...but animal cruelty is just as bad as cruelty to children" (Colin 2002, 2-3). Some (Poses and Weishaupt, n.d.) have noted the irony in the hoarders' belief that there is no fate worse than death, given that their treatment of animals creates a condition that is worse than death—a living death—or a life of suffering. Because of the scale and degree of suffering in these cases, some have preferred the term passive cruelty rather than neglect (Vaca-Guzman and Arluke 2005).

The role played by animals in criminal proceedings also encumbers prosecution. Because seized animals are treated as evidence, they must be held in shelters until cases are completed. In complicated cases, protective custody can last for years. According to one study (Berry 2005), to avoid re-victimizing animals through such extended stays, humane agents may negotiate dropping charges and restricting future ownership of animals in return for immediate custody.

Consequently, reports of cruelty charges actually being filed are uncommon. When charges are filed, they tend to be for other problems like child endangerment or assault and battery of an investigating police officer. Guilty verdicts or no contest pleas are rare. Most often, if any sentence is passed, hoarders are ordered to give up animals, not get any more either temporarily or permanently, or stop breeding them. Occasionally, they are modestly fined or made to reimburse shelters for the cost of food and veterinary care. Jail time is almost never imposed, despite frequent mention of maximum sentences, such as "Helen Miller [a hoarder] could face up to seventeen years in prison." In rare reports of hoarders receiving jail time, the sentence was usually for crimes having nothing to do with animals. For example, one hoarder, charged with "extreme" neglect of twenty-eight animals, was immediately jailed because of child neglect and charges of "felony child endangerment." In other cases, hoarders were sentenced to jail for contempt of court, fraud, and violation of probation.

There are many reasons for this leniency, although hoarders think it is stern to impose any limit on their animal ownership. Certainly, hoarding—despite the numbers of animals involved and the extent of their suffering—will be overshadowed in court by the many serious crimes against humans that officials see, and hoarding is classified under the law as neglect rather than abuse, calling forth more sympathetic than punitive responses. In addition, the prevailing view of hoarders as eccentric, if not mentally ill, makes criminalization seem inappropriate.

The first time Barbara Erickson appeared in court for animal neglect, charges were dropped against her after she agreed to stop selling dogs, spay and neuter her animals, and allow a veterinarian to make unannounced visits. However, after the final rescue of 552 dogs, the Ericksons were charged with felony criminal mischief (for destruction of their rental house), 134 counts of misdemeanor animal abuse (the euthanized dogs), and 418 counts of misdemeanor animal neglect (the survivors). Barbara was jailed for several weeks, ordered to pay $15,000 in restitution and obtain psychological counseling, sentenced to sixty months supervised probation, and limited to no more than two dogs.

Although it is difficult to criminally prosecute animal hoarders, prosecution has an important role to play in how hoarding cases can be approached in the future. Taking a criminal justice approach to these cases may help encourage prosecutors, judges, police, and legislators take them more seriously than they have in the past. Also, mental health intervention or negotiation may not work with certain types of hoarders who are very irrational and uncooperative. Aggressive prosecution may be the only effective way to deal with hoarders who must be stringently monitored and strictly sanctioned to prevent recidivism. As noted by Patronek, Loar, and Nathanson (2006), the "broken window approach" to crime (Wilson and Kelling 1982) may apply to cases of hoarding as well; in other words, the progression to major offenses can be prevented by aggressively intervening when there are early warning signs of social breakdown, whether they are small crimes in the neighborhood or the first stages of animal hoarding.

Some states mandate psychological counseling of offenders, whereas others make it an option for the court. However, at least as reflected in press reports of judges' actions, courts have not always viewed hoarders as seriously disturbed. Judges rarely suggest or require counseling. Indeed, even when they allude to possible mental health problems in hoarders, they may not order or recommend therapy. In one such case, the judge simply commented, "I think it's clear you are fixated on animals. In your obsession, you really are misguided." This reticence to recommend psychological help is surprising for three reasons. First, a number of hoarders' behaviors seem symptomatic of serious psychological disorder based on how badly they neglect their animals, homes, and themselves. Second, sometimes hoarders' own attorneys cite their clients' histories with mental illness, suggesting chronic and serious problems. And third, sometimes investigators specifically ask judges to approach hoarders as irrational or disturbed individuals.

Even with court-ordered counseling, there can be several problems implementing it. Many hoarders are on fixed incomes or are unemployed. Even if they have health insurance, they may only qualify for a limited number of visits to mental health providers and reimbursement rates to these providers can be low. If providers are seen on a fee-for-service basis, it is likely that hoarders will pay them slowly or not all, given their resistance to treatment. Monitoring required counseling, when it comes to matters such as attendance and responsiveness to a counselor's recommendations, will fall in the hands of a probation officer who, in all likelihood, will already be overwhelmed with a very large caseload.

Occasionally, there may be prohibitions on future pet ownership or limitations imposed on the number of animals, along with a requirement of periodic monitoring of the situation by authorities. Supervised probation has been recommended over court probation as a better way to ensure compliance. Prohibitions against future pet ownership are effective only to the extent that monitoring is practical.

Some communities attempt to either prevent or remedy hoarding situations by passing ordinances that limit the number of pets a person can own. There were no laws in Oregon that restricted the number of dogs one could have, although some states do have such regulations in place. There is no data to indicate whether these measures are effective, but what is known is that they are wildly unpopular, difficult to enforce, and likely to be opposed by a broad coalition of pet fanciers, breeders, rescue groups, and animal protection organizations. This is a harsh and probably ineffective remedy that needlessly penalizes responsible pet owners.

The worst situations may be avoided through regulations that stipulate housing densities, sanitation requirements, veterinary care, and which provide for regular inspections of licensed facilities. For example, Colorado has developed licensing requirements and comprehensive standards for the operation of an animal shelter or pet rescue organization. Such criteria also could help the media and the public, as well as the courts, distinguish between legitimate sheltering efforts and hoarding. Because of the Erickson case, Malheur County enacted a law requiring a shelter license for anyone with ten or more pets. The license allows for periodic inspections inside the home by an official who could then report neglect or abuse.

Managing these cases is complicated by the fact that hoarders not only have a high recidivism rate, often continuing their behavior after seizures leave them without animals, they move to different towns or states where they are unknown and under the radar screen of local humane and law enforcement authorities. In a typical example, two fifty-year-old women and their seventy-three-year-old mother were discovered living with eighty-two live, and 108 dead, cats. They fled from the investigation, rented a new apartment nearby, and had seven cats and a dog two days later. A hoarder can escape enforcement, even when monitoring is practical, by moving to a new jurisdiction, often only across town or county lines. Indeed, Barbara Erickson abandoned many dogs at her prior rental house in Midvale, Idaho when moving to another home in Council, Idaho, although she returned to feed them after her eviction. After a complaint was filed against Erickson for fifty dogs kept in her Council, Idaho home, she moved to Oregon.

Seizing Animals

Because of the severity of animal suffering and need for expediency, a common scenario is for the hoarder's animals to be removed for their own protection through use of a search warrant, with the hoarder subsequently prosecuted under state anti-cruelty laws. (Unless relinquishment can be negotiated, the animals must be held as evidence until the case is concluded.) However, seizing animals in hoarding cases is a complicated, expensive, labor intensive, and emotionally upsetting process. The entire financial cost of managing these cases, including the seizure itself, can easily run into the tens of thousands of dollars to cover expenses from veterinary care, animal sheltering, staff salaries at different agencies, and legal fees. Seizing animals typically requires the coordination of many agencies and organizations, let alone friends and family. The last and largest "rescue" of the Erickson's dogs required coordination among humane societies in Idaho and Oregon, some of which lacked sufficient funds to pay for all the animal care and staff salaries required in such cases, local veterinarians and animal shelters, law enforcement officials, firefighters, reporters, and volunteers.

Emotional costs are high as people venture into disturbingly chaotic homes, deal with hoarders who can be extremely sad or very angry, see animals that are dead, emaciated, very sick, and often living in cramped, inhumane conditions, and end up euthanizing many. Those who intervene often find the experience of carrying out the "rescue" (less often called a "seizure" or even "raid") to be very dramatic and disturbing as they try to help animals or people put in danger by hoarders. A law enforcement presence is usually necessary to manage hoarders and take aggressive steps needed on behalf of animal victims who need to be "taken away" with some urgency. Rescuers often paint each case as the "worst" or "most horrifying" incident, describing animal neglect in superlative terms. One news article cites a humane official who said, "'You can't imagine people accumulating that sort of filth and garbage.' ....Frazier said that it was the most foul scene he had encountered in his six years on the job." Another official maintained that a different case involved the "largest number of neglected animals ever seen."

In the Erickson case, humane society staff and volunteers tirelessly worked to clean, feed, and water the many dogs, while burying others. In this case, the rescue was deemed a success because dogs were seized and the Ericksons were taken to court and briefly jailed. Often, however, many seized animals are so sick they must be euthanized. For example, when shelter workers seized Erickson's over five hundred dogs in Midvale, Oregon, over one hundred had to be euthanized because they were too ill to survive, though none of them tested positive for parvovirus. Several of the dogs that were adopted had such entrenched behavioral problems they were returned to local shelters within weeks of the rescue.

Hoarders predictably protest and resist rescues, claiming unlawful and unnecessary seizure of their "children." One is described in a news article as "so belligerent the police were called to help," at which point the hoarder wrestled with police, who sprayed him with pepper spray and finally arrested him. Others have histories of being uncooperative or hostile. It is common for news reports to describe repeated attempts, sometimes spanning years, to take animals away from hoarders who resist these efforts by authorities. In one case, an article features the headline, "Notorious Cat Hoarder Jailed" and details the exploits of a "wily and elusive foe." Another article notes that "as is true of most animal hoarders, Becker had a track record," listing her history of being deceptive and difficult with authorities as she chronically acquired animals.

Rescuers also will be confounded by hoarders' paradoxical accounts of their own behavior, sometimes professing great love for animals. Indeed, Celeste Killeen's take on Barbara Erickson is that she saw herself as one with a "limitless need to love" that was turned on dogs. Certainly, the thought of losing her dogs seriously disturbed Barbara Erickson and made her cry. It is not clear, however, whether this "love" is a genuine motivation or a dishonest way to appear socially acceptable, if not praiseworthy. Others may claim to be pet rescuers or "no-kill" shelters attempting to help unwanted pets, and some may be professional or hobby animal breeders. All too frequently, these excuses may be used as effective ploys for the media or as defenses in court. Despite these claims of professionalism and good intentions, hoarders are usually oblivious to the extreme suffering, obvious to the casual observer, of their animals.

When animals are rescued from these situations, euthanasia is often the only practical recourse because of the extent of the animals' illnesses, poor condition, and lack of socialization. These are cases no one wants to handle, and it is not uncommon for them to be sidestepped until the situation has deteriorated to the point it cannot be ignored. By that time, the cost of veterinary care, housing of animals, litigation, and clean-up or demolition of premises have usually become extremely expensive. Procrastination also may increase the likelihood that the resolution will garner media attention. Greater recognition of this syndrome, as well as improved understanding of standards for responsible animal sheltering and rescue are needed.

Indeed, humane organizations are sometimes criticized in the news for intervening in hoarding cases, adding another layer of complexity to these cases. Some readers question the legitimacy of shelter workers who seize and euthanize these animals. They argue that the real "criminals" in these cases are humane law enforcement agents and shelter workers who are seen as insensitive and cruel to victimize hoarders by seizing their animals. Rather than eliciting public indignation toward hoarders for putting animals in this position, readers can be inflamed by the actions of agents and workers who can appear in newspaper reports to be in a rush to dispose of these animals. Many news articles reporteded that humane workers kill hoarders' animals because they are considered unadoptable in their current condition. Animals are "euthanized," "destroyed," or "put to sleep." At other times, this outcome is suggested as a possibility. For example, a few articles note that "making room" in shelters for hoarders' animals means that humane workers "might" have to euthanize healthy shelter animals. Other articles are blunter and could easily make humane officials appear to bear total responsibility for killing these animals, even though hoarders create the problem in the first place. One headline, for example, notes "55 Cats Given Death Penalty: Owner to Pay Up to $5000 to Try to Save 10 Other Felines."

Other elements of news reporting make it easy to blame these workers and think of them as cruel. While some articles describe the ill health of animals that apparently justified their killing, not all provide such detail and some only briefly mention animals' veterinary condition. To the uninformed reader, it may not be clear why these conditions warrant killing animals rather than having veterinary personnel treat them. For example, in one case, an animal control officer confiscated 143 dogs, "many of which were in such bad shape they had to be put to sleep right away…[and] many of the dogs had severe mange." It was unclear, however, exactly how many dogs were killed, whether mange was their only problem, and why mange was such a difficult problem to treat. In another case, a hoarder's 205 dogs were seized, twenty-five of whom were "in such bad condition that they were euthanized." The only ill health noted was that the dogs' problems ranged from "lack of food and shelter to oozing sores," conditions that would appear to be treatable. Interestingly, there is little discussion about the behavioral problems of these animals that would make their adoption unlikely, even if they were healthy, that might make the public more sympathetic to the plight of officers and shelter workers who must deal with these animals.

And finally, news articles never report humane staff members' feelings or reservations about euthanizing these animals. Without such reports, these workers might appear to be heartless or uncaring, despite the fact that they experience considerable distress over euthanasia (Arluke 1994b). In one story, a humane official acknowledged and bemoaned this unfavorable press image, noting, "When you go to court, you're the one who looks like the bastard." Indeed, their distress about the plight of hoarders' animals is rarely reported. While humane officials, in a few articles, acknowledge the sadness of hoarders when their animals are confiscated, very few articles report the feelings of animal control officers about the plight of hoarders' animals—feelings that might soften the media image of these officials. In one of the few articles to describe such feelings, the animal control officer said, regarding two hundred sick rabbits confined to small, unsanitary sheds, "It made me very, very sick. Because I'm an animal lover, it made me very, very sad because they couldn't get out. They were imprisoned in there." Less emphatic was one humane official who said that the hoarder's situation was "upsetting to anyone who cares at all about animals."

Media coverage can elicit public criticism of humane societies and their employees. In one case picked up by the media, a woman with eighty cats and two dogs moved to a motel with her animals because she claimed her water pipes had burst. Since the motel permitted only one pet per rented room, the collector surreptitiously smuggled her animals into the room. The motel staff had no idea that the animals were there because the woman declined maid service, and the animals were not inside the rooms long enough to create an odor. A motel spokesperson claimed that had the collector been there a full week they would have smelled the animals. Tipped off that there might be a problem, officers entered the motel room where they found "wall to wall cats." Although one newspaper article quoted an officer as saying the cats "were quiet and friendly. Most of them didn't seem sickly," they were seized by law enforcement officers from the local humane society and taken to shelters for evaluation. One person on the scene who was not a law enforcement officer said, "It will have to be determined which cats are healthy enough to keep alive. That's their call. I would hope that the decision would be made fairly quickly so that the cats won't have to suffer." However, all were found to be extremely sick (rotted-out eyes[4], leukemia, respiratory illnesses, and ringworm and other parasites) with very bad prognoses, and they were unsocialized. Despite humane society press statements noting that it was always their goal to save animals and make them available for adoption, all were "destroyed" because they had an extremely low possibility of adoption even if a lot of money and time were spent on making them healthy, and they would use much-needed cage space. Media coverage alerted concerned animal people, who read the story and became outraged that the humane society would kill all of these cats. Headlines in local newspapers included, "Animals Found in Motel Destroyed."

Press coverage of this bad case created a number of problems. In one letter to the editor, an irate citizen decried the destruction of the cats, writing, "It is unfortunate that the humane society, with its vast resources, felt it expedient to put these animals to death rather than treating those that might have been curable." Other people threatened to stop making donations to the society, and these threats continued for months after this news broke. Feeling the need to respond to this public outcry and criticism of the seizing of these cats and their subsequent destruction, supporters of the agents and the society wrote a number of letters to the editor and op-ed articles to defend their actions. These letters and articles reiterated the society's position that their destruction of the cats was not a cruel, heartless act but rather an act of mercy. "Our mission," a member of the society wrote, "is to help reduce animal suffering, and the cats were euthanized purely out of humaneness to them." In another response, the author tried to create some sympathy for the officers by making it clear that the hoarder victimized the animals: "It is not unusual for law enforcement officers…to wear protective gear to mask the stench caused by the accumulated mix of feces and urine of dozens, even hundreds of cats or dogs crammed into houses. Pathetic pictures of rescue raids show them crammed into spaces no larger than a phone booth or in stacked filthy cages often deprived of light and human companionship. Hoarders obtain their victims, for victims they are, by any means, often taking household pets that are 'let out' in the belief that they are being rescued."

Such defenses, however, may do little to allay the concern of some people that hoarders are being unfairly pressured to relinquish their animals. Indeed, in the wake of charges suggesting the culpability of agents and shelter workers, along with news that questions the extent to which animal suffering occurs in these cases, if at all, readers are likely to be confused about animal hoarding—how wrong it is and how hoarders should be seen. Further confusing readers are defenses by hoarders themselves.

EXCUSES AND JUSTIFICATIONS

Much of what the public learns about animal hoarders comes from reading news reports about them.[5] Although the news is a platform of communication, the hoarder's voice is permitted expression only within narrowly confined limits. The constraint to present "balanced" stories with many sides and viewpoints and to defer to the opinions of "experts" leaves scant room for this voice. So, in the end, the public and professionals alike learn little about the animal hoarder's perspective.

This certainly held true in the Erickson case. Despite journalists' efforts, they never interviewed Barbara Erickson herself. As Celeste Killeen astutely suggests, media reports tend to simplify the complicated, if not contradictory, reality of hoarding cases because they so rarely listen to hoarders themselves.

In the public arena, there is little room for the animal hoarder's voice because it is overshadowed by the opinions of various authorities whose presumed expertise trumps the occasional defense of hoarding. Nevertheless, as Barbara Erickson illustrates, hoarders are not passive actors who watch on the sidelines as the press constructs a confused and unflattering identity for them; instead, they confront it head on as they strive to refashion pity into praise, horror into honor. Hoarders resist professional knowledge, despite its widespread legitimacy, by reasserting who they think they are and why they believe that others "have it wrong." These presentations of self are not constructed in a social vacuum but are shaped by what hoarders learn through interaction with others. At least in a general way, they discover how society defines animal neglect and regards those accused of it.

When we listen to animal hoarders, it is clear that many are aware of and sensitive to being seen as reclusive and strange in their ways. Speculation about the nature of hoarding can easily shame hoarders when it is both public and negative. One hoarder claims that such thinking implicitly asks her, "How can you do it? How can you live like this? How can you live with animals, it's filthy, it's dirty, if nothing else, don't you care about other people? Don't you this? Don't you that? I never hear the end of it."

Animal hoarders learn culturally derived vocabularies of motive that diminish responsibility or deny wrongdoing (Mills 1940). Much like other groups who, when feeling maligned or threatened, use such "accounts" or "neutralizing techniques" to frame their behavior in a positive light or cast aspersions on law enforcement officials and others (Hewitt 2000; Lyman and Scott 1970; Snyder 1985; Sykes and Matza 2002). These accounts give hoarders some control over how they wish to be regarded by journalists, sociologists, therapists, law enforcement officials, neighbors, friends, family members, and others with whom they interact. They lessen the stigma of hoarding by either claiming that the behavior is reasonable or by denying responsibility for these "bad" acts. In other words, they either justify or excuse their acts. Justifications accept responsibility for the act in question (Scott and Lyman 1968) but deny that it is bad or claim that it is not "that bad" (Snyder, Higgins, and Stucky 1983). Alternatively, excuses admit that the act in question is wrong but deny full responsibility. Hoarders' justifications and excuses can sometimes seem as outlandish as their behavior toward animals and property, starkly contrasting the grim "reality" of these situations. Yet, that they have them is unsurprising.[6]

To say that these accounts merely counter criticism belies the potential protective benefits of neutralizing techniques. Hoarders' esteem would be threatened if they accepted the opinions of experts and others critical of their neglect of animals, home, family, and self. Because animals and their care are important bases for hoarders to create identities, seeing themselves as a failure in this regard would likely be devastating. In this sense, justifications and excuses are necessary illusions (Snyder and Higgins 1988) that shield or prop up their sense of self by helping them soften the blow of any critical voice or audience. That hoarders draw upon multiple excuses and justifications, then, may give them such added protection.

Neutralizing techniques also can provide secondary health benefits. At the same time that hoarders' behavior is very unhealthy for animals, their accounts may be physically healthy for them to create and use. Orbuch and others (1994), for example, note that failure to engage in account-making can lead to chronic problems, including psychosomatic illness. While certainly not an argument to encourage or allow hoarding to continue, if true, understanding such secondary gains provides insight into the many consequences that accounts have for those who create them.

Of course, some readers might find it unsavory to focus on the benefits of these accounts. It is important to recognize that they are harmless if this were their only consequence. Unfortunately for hoarders, their accounts stand in the way of future "recovery" by allowing them to overlook what is often extreme neglect of animals, people, and property. By justifying or excusing their behaviors whenever challenged, hoarders continue to avoid the problems they create. However, authorities and experts who seek to manage these problems would do well to understand hoarders' logic and thinking. By doing so, they can enhance their dialogue with hoarders and develop more sensitive treatments for them.

There also is a practical reason to be aware of these accounts, beyond capturing the hoarders' voice in and of itself. Detailed knowledge of how hoarders explain their behavior can help those who deal with them in a legal or mental health capacity to better anticipate and respond to their defenses. To intervene and remedy hoarding situations, animal welfare groups, veterinarians, animal control, public health and mental health agencies, child welfare and adult protective services, and housing authorities would do well to know how hoarders think about and defend their actions, instead of dismissing their talk as idle or defensive, if not an indication of delusion or mental disorder. Only then can these authorities engage in more effective dialogue with hoarders and their supporters than is now the case.

Justifications[7]

Denial is the simplest type of justification. By completely rejecting any incrimination, subjects deny that their actions are immoral, strange, or untoward. Animal hoarders use this technique in a variety of ways. At times, they deny all accusations without further explanation, while at other times, they contend that animals are well cared for, that they have profound love for them as though they were own children, or that their animals are happy and love them back.

Simple denial without elaboration by hoarders is rare. In one case, when fifty neglected animals were found in a filthy home, an animal control official stated that the owner truly believed she had done nothing wrong.[8] When arraigned in court, Barbara Erickson claimed to be innocent (although her husband pled guilty to the same charges of animal neglect and abuse and destruction of property). It is more common to find complete denial followed by a short explanation to support their point. In this manner, a man denied that it was filthy to live with twenty-seven dogs and forty-seven cats in a loft covered in animal waste. He claimed it was cleaned "every day, sometimes twice a day." When challenged by the reporter who asserted he could smell the filth, he answered "Well, do you know what dogs and cats do? They mark their territory."

Other hoarders describe how well they care for their animals and the benefits enjoyed by them. This was certainly asserted by Barbara Erickson who claimed to feed, water, and love all her dogs. In another case where thirty-eight dogs were found living in a single room, the owner of the animals said, "They got a room of their own. We got two windows in there, they get air and sunshine. They won't come outside because they are scared." Furthermore, the animal control officer intervening in the case described the owner as "a very sweet woman" and stated, "I have no doubt she absolutely loved her dogs. This is the most difficult kind of case." In another case, where thirty-seven starving dogs were found living in a home filled with disease, the owner stated that they all were well cared for. "This is heaven for them," he said. "They're playing ball...love it...and they don't have mange and they love it here. Did you see that dog there wag its tail?" he said, pointing at a dog. "That dog wants to play ball. It's the elephant man thing. Looks are deceiving. That's not what you judge suffering by." In both cases, hoarders supported their denial by providing details of the excellent care given to their animals. By asserting that the animals were happy and healthy, hoarders painted a picture of their animals' love for them. This assertion suggests that hoarders consider their animals' love as evidence that they received appropriate care.

Many hoarders claimed to love their animals as their children and stated that "they all had names," as evidence of proper care towards them. Thus, to justify their behavior, hoarders identify animals as family members and profess to love them. For example, Barbara and Bob Erickson spoke of "loving" and "protecting" their "babies." Another hoarder claimed, "My dogs are my children, to be quite honest. They are the things that give me the most joy." The subject also spoke of his roommate and business partner, saying, "He is very conscientious in his day to day care for animals. He is in love with the dogs. He knows every name, he knows their birth dates." The humane society intervening in the case claimed that the forty-four dogs discovered in the house lived in horrendous conditions. In another case, where one hundred animals, including eleven cats, rats, guinea pigs, a baboon, a potbellied pig, an iguana, a tarantula, and a skunk were seized from a filthy home, a neighbor of the hoarder described the woman by saying, "She truly loved her animals. She has names for each and every one of them."

A second type of justification is the Good Samaritan strategy. Snyder (1985) calls this process "exonerative moral reasoning." By considering an ill deed as a necessary part of a larger virtuous act, the wrongfulness of the performance is diluted by the honorable purpose. In other words, they lessen the negativity of their performance by grounding the act in something noble. By claiming to be animal rescuers or shelters, they frame what others might see as gross neglect as a kind-hearted, benevolent act to care for animals that no one else will help or save. In a Pennsylvania case in which eighteen emaciated dogs were seized from a home, the hoarder explained to authorities that she was starting her own humane society. Similarly, a hoarder of more than twenty-four dogs told reporters that she rescues the dogs and gives them shots. She explained, "They were so skinny when I got them out of the Warwick pound that the three kennels that I had them boarded with said they [the dogs] were totally emaciated. They put weight back on and have their shots and they're eating." In another case, when thirty-nine cats were discovered living in horrible conditions, the hoarder said she was trying to establish a no-kill shelter. She claimed, "I am not a hoarder, people said I was a hoarder because I refused to associate with shelters that euthanize." Finally, a hoarder of twelve pit bulls told reporters he took the animals after the original owners did not want them. He claimed that he saved them and tried to find homes for them. This type of account attempts to elevate the act by claiming some altruistic motive. By employing this tactic, hoarders claim their behavior is reasonable or, in some cases, even morally admirable.

Although some hoarders do not claim to be rescuers or no-kill shelters, they claim to be doing a good thing for the animals, thereby refuting the charge of animal neglect by defining their behavior as a virtue. Within this category, saving animals from death seems to be a recurrent theme used by hoarders to justify their behavior.[9] The frequency of this type of claim suggests that hoarders consider potential death to be a strong argument in favor of keeping animals in horrid conditions. The Ericksons believed they were saving many of their dogs from death in animal shelters or from getting killed on the highway. Another hoarder who was found living with sixty dogs and two cats claimed that only nine dogs were his, while the remainder belonged to people who had asked him to care for them. "It was a goodwill gesture. I want those animals to live. I'd rather be put to sleep myself," he said, choking back tears. And yet another hoarder, this one of thirty-one cats, said he refused to take the felines to a shelter because he did not want to see them euthanized. "I love animals and I don't feel any animal should be put to death," he said, citing religious reasons. The owner of sixty-four pit bulls and a Rottweiler claimed, "That was my family. I took care of dogs people were trying to kill." These claims reveal that hoarders consider death to be an unthinkable option, believing that any other possibility, no matter how horrific, is better for the animals.

A third way to justify behavior is to discredit the source of criticism. The individual shifts the focus of attention from his own deviant acts to the motives and behavior of those who disapprove of his actions. Thus, by changing the subject of the conversation from the bad performance to the reactions of others, the wrongfulness of the behavior is more easily repressed or lost to view (Sykes and Matza 2002).

Many hoarders used this type of justification, the most common way being to claim that officials and/or animal groups intervening in cases had personal vendettas against them. In other words, they believed that the whole "system" was against them. In a case where more than 150 dogs, fourteen cats, three monkeys, and a pregnant potbellied pig were discovered living in squalid conditions, the hoarder denied that the animals were improperly cared for and charged that the local humane society and police were harassing her family without reason. She claimed the police bruised her wrist and breasts and treated her elderly mother with no respect. "For 12 hours I sat in jail, treated like a criminal," she said. In addition, a hoarder of thirty-three dogs complained, "I'm sick and tired of this harangue. For doing something good I am getting nailed and being treated as a common criminal." Some of his acquaintances expressed similar sentiment. In fact, an anonymous donor posted the hoarder's bail from jail and expressed that "he loves animals and thinks what [the hoarder] does is wonderful. He feels he's been a victim of the system."

Another way to discredit critics is to plead victimization, which hoarders sometimes claimed. For instance, in a case in which almost two hundred emaciated dogs were confiscated from a Georgia home, the hoarder alleged the real reason for the seizure of her dogs was "bad blood" between the officer in charge of the county's animal services and her. The hoarder also accused officers of damaging her pens and costing her money because she had no other source of income than selling the seized dogs. In another case, after winning "conditional" approval to have two of her dogs back, the hoarder of nineteen seized dogs said, "They [animal control officers] want to come up once a month and tell me how to feed my dogs. I'm a United States citizen. They're treating me like a criminal. Don't you think that's horrible? I can't understand why the county is always after me." Additionally, in a case in which 465 neglected felines were found living in a six-room "no-kill shelter," the "rescue director" thought the investigation was a personal vendetta against her. "She [referring to the animal cruelty investigator] is challenging and attacking my shelter. We are not hoarders, we do adopt our cats out," she argued. And in a case where fifty-three diseased and neglected dogs were seized after being found kept in cages, the owner argued, "They had no right to take my dogs. It was a total setup. They just made up this thing, it's not true. They stole my property. They took my dogs away from their home. They are liars and thieves as far as I am concerned." In such instances, hoarders deny accusations against them and attribute the problem to personal spite against them.

Excuses

Excuses accept the negativity of a performance but deny or deflect full responsibility for the act (Alonso 1985; Scott and Lyman 1968). Claiming lack of responsibility for "bad" actions sharply reduces the effectiveness of disapproval

(Sykes and Matza 1957). This lack of responsibility is typically attributed to extenuating circumstances relevant to the bad performance. The excuse-maker admits the negative connotation of the performance, but continues with a series of "yes, but..." verbalizations to deflect responsibility (Snyder 1985).

Hoarders resort to a number of excuses.[10] They often point to the difficulty of the task they face with so many animals. If the task is sufficiently challenging, the excuse-maker reasons that anyone would do poorly in that situation. By demonstrating that most people would do the same thing in his situation, the individual's responsibility is lessened. Hoarders using this excuse recognize that it is unacceptable to own so many animals and that, as a result, they have neglected them, but claim that others would have behaved similarly because of the difficulty of the task.

More specifically, many hoarders claim that they became "overwhelmed" or that the number of animals "proves too much for them." For example, Bob Erickson claimed that they had so many dogs because they could not afford to spay them all. News reports often mentioned the number of animals initially owned by hoarders, as well as their good intentions and kindness towards them. The reports also may contain an explanation, from the hoarder, a friend, or relative, about how the collection "started snowballing" or "got out of hand." For instance, in a case in which twenty-seven cats were discovered in a squalid trailer, the hoarder explained that he started by rescuing three kittens and that they started breeding. After claiming he was not a hoarder, and that he only wanted to find the cats good homes, he noted, "It [the situation] just got a little out of hand. I'm just a good person whose heart was bigger than my abilities." In another case, where a woman was discovered living with ninety-six cats, nine dogs, six mice, a turtle, and a rat in filthy conditions, a neighbor commented that the hoarder seemed to be trying to do the right thing, but the situation got out of hand. "It is a shame. She was trying to make an effort. I think she wanted to do the right thing and maybe got overwhelmed." In addition, an article covering the case of a couple who hoarded ninety-six dogs and cats in a three-bedroom home reported that the hoarders provided a loving home for the animals, but that things had gotten "out of control" after breeding the dogs over a number of years. The woman explained that because they could not afford to spay or neuter them, their dogs began to multiply. She also said that friends gave them more dogs.

In some cases, hoarders claim that they become overwhelmed without providing details about how and when the situation got out of control. For example, in a case in which twenty-four live animals and five dead cats were found in a soiled home, the hoarder stated that he tried to take care of the animals, but their upkeep proved too much for him. Additionally, in a case where the police removed 105 cats and twenty-two dogs, neighbors maintained that the hoarder was a "kind person who just got overwhelmed." Also, a hoarder of seventy-two sick cats that were confined in a small barn was defended by her attorney by stating, "It was just too much with 72 cats for her to be in a strict time schedule, but she didn't do intentional acts based on the animal cruelty statute."

This type of excuse implies that hoarders who employ it are "sane" because they acknowledge that they have too many animals and that they are poorly kept. By claiming that they became overextended, hoarders recognize the inappropriateness of their behavior. For example, one cat hoarder said of herself, "The thought of giving up any of [the] cats…hurts. I got so close to the baby cats that I couldn't give any of them away.…I figured no one else could take care of them like I could." When officers entered her home they found about two hundred cats, floorboards soaked and warped by urine, and feral animals burrowed inside walls. Some of the cats were malnourished or sick. A few had already died. The hoarder told reporters that she was trying to find homes for her cats. Their numbers simply spiraled out of control. "I know this sounds bizarre," she said. "But I'm a rational person." This insight into the rationality of their behavior does not seem to be present in hoarders that utilize other types of accounts, especially those who totally deny wrongdoing, those who claim to be victims of the system, and those who employ some of the strategies described below.

Another excuse is for hoarders to claim that they are not fully informed or that their "will" is not completely "free." Thus an individual might excuse himself from responsibility by claiming that certain information, which would have altered his behavior, is not available, or that available information misrepresents the facts. Alternatively, an individual might excuse himself by claiming interference with his "free will," due to duress or undue influence. Finally both will and knowledge can be impaired under certain conditions that constitute a mitigation of responsibility, such as intoxication or temporary insanity (Scott and Lyman 1968). Hoarders lessen their responsibility by using this kind of excuse.

One way they do this is to invoke some restraint on their free will, although only a few cases did this. A hoarder of ninety cats, explained, "I got so close to my baby cats that I couldn't give any of them away." Another hoarder explained that he ended up having eighty-eight dogs because spaying and neutering them "didn't work out" and because after the puppies were born "it was impossible to give them away." He added, "They are not just animals, they have a soul." In another case, where sixty-eight cats and dogs were discovered living in squalid conditions, the officers involved in the case said that the hoarder appeared to be someone who loved animals and could not turn away a stray. Additionally, a hoarder of two hundred cats was excused by a local humane society representative and by the sheriff, who stated, "These things escalate over a period of time. Hoarders like [the hoarder in this case] are not trying to abuse the animals. Hoarders just keep collecting and can't seem to get rid of the cats and kittens." These examples suggest that hoarders' actions are driven by a mysterious force, often referred to by them or by the media as "extreme love." Thus, these hoarders recognize that what they have done is wrong, but they claim not to be fully responsible because their love for the animals obscured their free will.

Less frequently, hoarders make an appeal to defeasibility by citing a lack of knowledge. In one case, a woman found living in filth with sixteen non-vaccinated dogs alleged that she did not know that she needed a license to have that many animals in her house. She said that her dogs had no vaccinations because they were indoor dogs, and that county officials told her she only needed to have three of her dogs vaccinated for rabies. In another case, in which over one hundred emaciated and fifty dead cats were found in a home, the hoarder was described by animal advocates as a woman who often did not know where to draw the line when taking stray animals. An old friend said, "I know how much she loved animals. She is an animal lover through and through."

Scapegoating is another excuse used by hoarders. This one shifts blame and responsibility away from themselves to a target person or group. By scapegoating, hoarders allege that their questioned behavior is a response to the behavior or attitudes of another (Scott and Lyman 1968). They do this by blaming people that bring unsolicited animals to them, people that lose or abandon their pets, and the community in general for not helping homeless animals. Barbara Erickson maintained that strangers left many dogs at her house and never returned to take back their animals or help with their care. She believed that turning them away would be tantamount to killing the dogs, so she had to keep them. Similarly, another hoarder, whose eighteen animals were captured after being found living in filth, explained that many cats had been left at her place by acquaintances when they could not breed them. "What can I do when just born babies are left at your doors?" Moreover, a rabbit hoarder said she began with one animal and over the years wild rabbits began visiting through the fence. She added that unwanted pets started showing up in her yard as well, especially after Easter. Additionally, in a case where sixty-three live and thirty dead cats were found in a "shelter," a volunteer expressed, "There was no ill treatment of animals there [at the shelter]. Those animals were loved. They were fed and watered every day, not thrown out like the people who are the reason why they are there do." Furthermore, a hoarder of thirty-two cats and two dogs explained, "If only other people would take care of them [cats], I wouldn't have to." She added, "I felt I was doing the city a favor. Those were 32 cats who weren't getting pregnant and spreading disease in our area." Finally, a hoarder of about ninety dogs claimed to be doing the county a favor by taking in dogs because there was no animal control facility in the area.

Excuse-makers also engage in more concrete blaming tactics by pointing to a precise subject whom they consider responsible for the bad performance, instead of making a global accusation. Very few hoarders claimed that another person was actually responsible for the animals. For instance, the lawyer of a hoarder of thirty-nine sick cats explained that the animals were not hers, but her sister's, therefore claiming that the hoarder should not be held responsible for the neglect.

Another excuse of hoarders is to claim lack of intentionality. Research suggests that intended actions, if they have negative outcomes, are perceived as being worse than unintended actions (Rotenberg 1980). Similarly, people are held as being more accountable for negative actions that are foreseeable as compared to those actions that are unforeseeable (Shaw 1968). Hoarders also used this excuse to lessen their responsibility for charges of animal neglect by claiming there was no intention to do so.

Typically, hoarders claimed they did not mean to harm animals but were just trying to help them. One hoarder of exotic animals, who was living with crocodiles, turkeys, wolves, spiders, reptiles, a miniature horse, a lynx, a mountain lion, and an emu, and was surrounded by filthy bags of fecal matter, carcasses, and cockroaches, said he was a well-intentioned man with a broken dream. "I have nothing left," he said after his animals were seized. "I made some mistakes but I did what I thought was right at the time," he added. The hoarder claimed he was months away from opening his own living museum. In another case, thirty-four dead and sick cats were found in a home including seven kittens in the freezer. A friend of the cat hoarder remarked, "She taught me a lot about cat breeding, she loved those cats. I don't think she was intentionally cruel to those cats."

Although only a few hoarders explicitly claim a lack of intention, most excuse their behavior in the same manner, even if they do not say "I didn't mean it." Behind every other account hoarders use to defend their behavior, there is always the implicit assumption that they did not mean to harm the animals. Every type of excuse, as well as the Good Samaritan justification, contains the assumption that their behavior or its results were not intentional. In this sense, intentionality may be defined as a determination to act in a certain way with full consciousness of the nature of one's act and its consequences. Thus, every type of excuse used by hoarders contains the supposition that they were not determined to harm the animals, and that they were not fully aware of the consequences of their acts, but instead hoarders were trying to care for the animals. Similarly, the core idea of the Good Samaritan justification is that the hoarder is an animal rescuer; thus, the lack of intentionality to harm the animals is implicit in this type of account.

Another excuse used by individuals to lessen responsibility for a poor performance is "self-handicapping." According to Jones and Berglas (1978, 406), self-handicapping is "any action or choice of performance setting that enhances the opportunities to externalize (or excuse) failure and to internalize (reasonably accept credit for) success." In other words, their own limited abilities make them not fully responsible for their bad actions; if they were free of disabilities, they would have performed better.

Some hoarders employ this type of excuse. One way was to cite physical or mental problems that caused poor treatment and accumulation of animals. For instance, in a case in which two hoarders (mother and daughter) were found living with eighty dogs, sixty-five chickens and ducks, and fourteen rabbits in a trailer, the daughter explained she had obsessive-compulsive disorder (OCD), "but it is not as bad as hers," she claimed, referring to her mother. She also told reporters that she takes medication for her OCD, depression, and fear of people. In another case, a hoarder of thirty-six horses, thirty-two dogs and ten donkeys had a defense attorney who claimed, "My client is mentally ill. She is a homeless person, she was mentally ill at the time this took place." In another case, a brother of a horse hoarder explained that his sibling suffered from lupus and back problems that made it difficult for him to care for the horses. Similarly, a dog hoarder charged with animal cruelty after thirty dogs were found starving or dead at her home told investigators that she had been ill and did not have enough time to properly care for the animals.

Other self-handicaps include economic deprivation to excuse behavior, claiming that lack of money prevents them from properly caring for so many animals. In this way, a hoarder of 164 dogs claimed to be a dog breeder and to sell the dogs to supplement her low month disability income. She explained that she had been unable to sell many dogs over the past year because of poor health and the high cost of ads, although she maintained that she still took good care of the dogs. In a case in which fifty-three dogs and nine cats were discovered living in a broken down, feces-ridden home, the owner said she received disability payments and used most of them to clean and feed the pets. She explained that unsanitary conditions in her home came about over several years. "With what little bit I live on, of course, I take care of my babies first. And then I do whatever else I can with the help of the church." A friend of the hoarder defended her as well. "The only thing that lady is guilty of is just loving animals," he said. "It just got out of hand because she had breast cancer." He also claimed to often help the hoarder with repairs on her home, but his own personal problems kept him away for the past three months.

Another way to excuse a poor performance is to attribute it to external unforeseeable circumstances. This kind of account lessens the responsibility of the excuse-maker by attributing blame to an unpredictable event that causes horrendous conditions. Hoarders often claim to be victims of circumstances that cause their animals' poor conditions. By diverting attention from the bad performance, they lessen or even eliminate responsibility for their actions. The alleged accidents include personal jams, unanticipated logistic or administrative problems, weather conditions, or any other unforeseeable event.

For one, some hoarders point to problems with spouses or partners to excuse their behavior. For instance, a cat hoarder claimed that he had thirty-nine in his room because his girlfriend left him a couple of weeks before, and he had been unable to continue caring for the cats. He said, "I love the cats. I adore them. I've been with them their whole lives. I can trace them back to four females." Moreover, in a case in which four hundred dead or malnourished cats were discovered in an abandoned home, the hoarder explained he had tried his best to care for the cats after his wife died. "I felt she was more important than those animals, but I did go there and did feed them," he noted.

Other hoarders mentioned they had an ambiguous "problem" without engaging in specific details about how it resulted in the neglect of animals. For instance, a cat hoarder discovered living with sixty-seven dead cats and dozens of other neglected felines told authorities she had personal problems that kept her from attending to the animals. In another case, a woman charged with twenty-six counts of animal cruelty for neglecting her horses, dogs, cats, and birds maintained she had never abused her animals, and that her horses were naturally skinny. She acknowledged that some of the cages were dirty and attributed this to some "problems" she was going through.

Other "accidents" often alleged by hoarders, such as logistic and administrative problems or other unexpected events, are illustrated by the following cases. In one instance, when more than two dozen hungry and thirsty dogs were discovered alone in a home, the owner explained she had not intended to be gone for five days but was in jail for a traffic conviction. In another case, a ferret hoarder who was discovered living in filth with 235 ferrets insisted that the animals became ill in transport and that they were all healthy in her care. A similar case involved 171 dogs in a trailer going from Alaska to Montana. The hoarder blamed an overnight delay at the border for the dogs' grim shape. Additionally, a hoarder of twenty-four exotic birds, twenty dogs, and six cats, who had his animals seized due to their poor condition, explained he had problems with the heat and water, but the animals were well cared for. Even more, in a case in which a kennel operator was charged with neglect of her dogs (after four wounded pit bulls were found surrounded by excrement in a garage with no light or ventilation), her lawyer explained that the dogs created the "mess" while the owner was sleeping or away from the house.

A few hoarders fail to mention special circumstances and only focus on how the excuse-maker has done better. Mentioning good performances implies the existence of an accident; reference to those situations in which the subject has acted properly sets a favorable precedent. A poor performance is more likely to be regarded as an accident because it is considered to be atypical behavior, given that the subject is known to otherwise perform well. For instance, in a case where nineteen dead golden retrievers and eleven other severely malnourished dogs were found in a home, a friend and former client described the hoarder as a well known and respected dog breeder and trainer. "It floors me what happened," she said. By using this tactic, hoarders suggest that, unlike their poor performance in one situation, there are other places where they have performed well. Thus, the "questioned" subjects imply they should be held less responsible for a single bad performance in this particular situation. They seem to think they have earned some sort of "credit" for their good behavior in other areas of their life, and that this allows them to perform poorly in other situations without being held fully responsible for their behavior.

That hoarders excuse and justify their behavior is not surprising. What is surprising is that they go beyond neutralizing unwelcome or derogatory views to paint a flattering self-portrait firmly anchored in widely accepted and rewarded roles borrowed liberally from our general culture. They create an entire identity out of their neglect: it becomes the essence of who they are as people, it gives them their sense of self, it provides their purpose in life.[11]

SAINTLY ACCOUNTS

Animal hoarders tell themselves and others that they are *more* than decent and kind. They insist they are passionate and proud about their many animals and claim to "care" for them in self-proclaimed roles such as parent or shelter worker. Hoarders emphasize that, even if sacrifices are necessary, they can be counted on in tough situations to constantly keep in mind and help needy creatures. In other words, they present themselves as saints. They transform what others see as neglect into something positive by portraying themselves as saviors of unwanted and helpless animals for whom they make huge but worthy sacrifices so that these needy animals can have better lives. Although hoarders merely insinuate their saintliness, it underlies and informs how they characterize their feelings about and actions toward animals.

They portray themselves as saviors who are on a rescue mission to save animals from death or euthanasia. Barbara Erickson, for example, reported many amazing animal rescues; although hard to believe, they were definitely part of her presentation as someone who would go to great lengths, sparing nothing, for the sake of animals. Her rescue impulse was part of a larger belief that it was important to avoid the death of animals at all costs, although the irony was that doing so resulted in extensive and long-term suffering. In this way, Erickson and other hoarders believe that only they come through for animals in need, seeing themselves as the last outpost for many animals that would have nowhere else to go and no one else to care for them.

Most see this impulse to rescue animals from perceived death as a "duty" and feel "guilty" if they turn their backs. Barbara Erickson felt a duty to help and take in all needy dogs, never turning them away, perhaps because she saw them as her own and believed that without her the animals would surely die. Another hoarder viewed her acquisition of scores of dogs and cats as a "wake-up call" from a higher power to help animals. She said, "Well, God, this is the way you made me. You made me to love animals and I'm proud of it. It's not something that I need to make excuses for. I don't hurt people, you know." Hoarders see homeless animals as "abused" and say, in the words of one, they "cannot live knowing that they are being abused and not taken care of." Hoarders worry, indeed a few say they are "terrified," that something tragic will happen to animals—cars will hit them or "butchers" will sell them to medical labs—if they fail to act.

For example, a man found living with sixty dogs and two cats claimed that nine dogs were his, while the remainder belonged to people who asked him to care for them. "It was a goodwill gesture. I want those animals to live. I'd rather be put to sleep myself," he said. Another hoarder of thirty-one cats said he did not take the felines to the animal shelter because he did not want to see them euthanized. "I love animals and I don't feel any animal should be put to death," he said, citing religious reasons. And the owner of sixty-four pit bulls and a Rottweiler claimed: "That was my family. I took care of dogs people were trying to kill." For hoarders, then, death is an unthinkable option; any other possibility, not matter how horrific, is better for the animals.

Hoarders feel highly responsible for the welfare of all animals by maintaining vague and shifting boundaries between those in their home and others. Almost any animal they encounter can easily be seen as "their own" and one they feel an obligation to help. Their heightened sense of responsibility also comes from having a very broad and ambiguous definition of what constitutes a "needy" animal, and therefore one that should be helped. This perspective guarantees many situations that call for their intervention. There are always strays to be found and helped or unwanted animals from friends or strangers to be taken in. Shelters, too, offer unlimited numbers of animal "projects," as one hoarder calls them, to provide homes for the unadoptable. Some hoarders even feel responsible for the welfare of wildlife in need of shelter or care. Regarding the endless number of animals awaiting them, a hoarder commented, "It could go on forever. If one came to my door, I'd take it in." The result is that hoarders have endless opportunities to feel selfless, and they take advantage of many.

Hoarders provide dramatic accounts of rescuing and caring for animals. Their talk becomes very animated when they describe how much effort, emotion, patience, time, and money went into saving tragically injured, sick, or troubled animals that survive dire conditions. One hoarder recounted staying up all night to nurse stray kittens and another detailed how she followed one of her feral cats into its underground burrow and took food to it for over a month until it decided to come out. These excursions to save the cat from starving to death left the hoarder infested with fleas that she passed on to other people in her home. For weeks another hoarder nursed a dog with a broken pelvis, convinced that the local shelter would immediately destroy it if given the opportunity.

Many hoarders claim that they are operating an animal shelter or rescue organization. One said that she performed a "community service by taking in stray animals" and "saved quite a few lives of some of those cats." Several said that they were trying to place some or many of their animals in other homes, only temporarily keeping them until these arrangements could be made. In one case in which eighteen emaciated dogs were seized from a home, the hoarder explained to authorities that she was starting her own humane society. Sometimes, they claimed to do this because existing shelters provided poor animal care in their opinion. A hoarder of more than twenty-four dogs told reporters that after she rescues dogs from bad "pounds," she gives them shots and adequate nutrition. Other hoarders specifically use "no-kill" terminology to describe their animal work. When thirty-nine cats were discovered living in horrible conditions, the hoarder said she was trying to establish a no-kill shelter. "I am not a collector, people said I was a collector because I refused to associate with shelters that euthanize." By claiming to be rescue or humane organizations, hoarders frame their acts as kindhearted and benevolent, caring for animals that no one else will help or save. They tell themselves, and others, that their behavior is reasonable or, in some instances, morally admirable.

In keeping with their saintly presentation, hoarders make many sacrifices to rescue animals. In their own eyes, they are what Rosenhan (1970) calls "autonomous altruists," or those who—to a much greater degree than others—forgo many things and undergo great labor to aid people or, in this case, animals. Those who believe the hoarders' efforts at self-presentation might view hoarders in a positive light (Heckert 2003) and offer them social approval because hoarding, like the behavior of saints and good neighbors (Sorokin 1950) or the unselfishness of heroes (Scarpitti and McFarlane 1975), involves self-sacrifice and does not threaten society. However, it is more likely that even if people believe hoarders' accounts, they will still be regarded negatively because their sacrifices are so extreme.

The Ericksons certainly laid claim to this positive status. For one, they sacrificed their quality of life—indeed their very autonomy over everyday decisions—by relinquishing control of their home to the dogs who "took over." Indeed, at least one town resident, perhaps recognizing this relinquishment of humanity, referred to Barbara Erickson as the "dog woman." For another, they claimed to forgo self-care in the interests of their animals; in this regard, Barbara claimed to forgo expensive hip surgery to relieve chronic pain so that her dogs could eat.

One hoarder calls such sacrifices her "hardship" and lists not being able to go far from home, never having a clean and neat house or yard, never having undamaged material possessions, and having no social life. Another hoarder laments her inability to travel on vacation because no one can take care of her many animals, and because she would never use a kennel. Another cites the inability to have a "neat" house and yard because of her animals' habits, another the loss of her antique furniture and hand-knotted rugs because of urine saturation, and yet another the fact that the potent smell of her cats prevents visitors, including her best friend and sister, from entering her home. Indeed, several hoarders say that they miss their human friendships, although animal friendships replace them. In short, they diminish their horizons and forgo their desires, except those related to animals. Like saints, they eschew worldly wants and personal possessions in the name of having many unfettered animals. Spurning worldly or middle class desires for the greater good of helping animals echoes the belief in communist societies that renouncing the strife for individual property benefits others, though the one benefits animals and the other humans. To hoarders, curtailing everyday pleasures for the sake of their animals is not a political statement, it is just seen as "more worthwhile." As one hoarder says, she would rather spend all of her money on her animals than on herself.

One sacrifice, withdrawing from the social life of the community, is justified as necessary to protect animals from seizure by authorities. Hoarders explain, sometimes accurately, that humane law enforcement agents or animal control officers disapprove of their treatment of animals and want to remove them from their homes. They describe constant attacks by aggressive and insensitive officials, implying that the problem rests with those who seek to take their animals rather than with themselves. "Demonic" was the description of one local humane society. "I give those cats the best food money can buy. Whenever I'm away I have people taking care of the cats. Those people [humane society] are just out to ruin me...All was going well until the humane society moved in." Feeling harassed, one hoarder proclaimed, "Why don't they just leave us alone?" Another hoarder insisted that a humane agent threatened her, "saying he would get me and all of these animals would be euthanized." And another frustrated hoarder said, "They've been on us like locusts....He [a town official] just says anything. I have no sick or miserable animals here.... We're doing our level best."

They are victims, according to hoarders and their supporters. Friends of one hoarder considered her to be a "victim of constant hounding from county officials and neighboring ranchers—adversaries who color her strange for devoting her life to helping wayward animals." A neighbor defended another hoarder as someone who is eccentric but loves animals: "He's kind of different and sometimes people try to take advantage of him. In this case, he's kind of getting railroaded. It seems like the humane society is on a witch hunt." Hoarders claimed that officials or humane societies had personal vendettas against them.

Feeling unfairly persecuted by those who endanger their social world with animals, hoarders tragically depict what would happen if authorities seized the animals. These declarations testify to the importance of keeping their animals and the harm of losing them. A few even threaten to kill themselves or others if their animals are taken.

In response to perceived persecution, hoarders adopt a siege mentality, hiding from their neighbors and the community at large. One confided that she erected a seven-foot stockade fence as much to keep people out as to keep animals in. By having a low profile, they hope to keep secret the numbers of animals they have and the unsightliness of their property. Loss of social life, although psychologically costly, is one more worthy sacrifice in their eyes, although to some extent this low profile continues a life-long withdrawal from social interaction in general.

With an attitude of saintly martyrdom, hoarders bemoan these sacrifices but point out that it is not worth having nice furniture or taking long vacations if they come at their animals' expense. What they give up is justified in their opinion because they can do so much for animals. As one says, her sense of worth and happiness comes from "making their crummy lives decent." And they claim that animals do so much for them, even becoming their social life. In the words of a hoarder, "We just get our friendship from the animals. We don't miss the human friendship because we are always with the animals."

Hoarders resign themselves to these sacrifices and normalize them in their lives. Best typifying this attitude is one person who ceded her kitchen to thirty cats so they could have it as their territory for eating, playing, and excreting. She, nevertheless, still used the kitchen, at great inconvenience from an outsider's perspective but not hers. The woman grew accustomed to—in fact advocated the benefits of—no longer sitting down for meals in the kitchen and instead merely stood at the open refrigerator door and quickly grazed on whatever she grabbed "to get it over with," while her son had grown comfortable taking his food out of the refrigerator and closing himself in the adjoining bathroom with a hotplate and a juicer so that their cats would not interrupt his meals and soil his food, plates, and utensils.

Normalizing sacrifices leads hoarders to relinquish their human identity and become animalized. That their identity can be so profoundly affected is unsurprising, given the importance of animals to hoarders; it shapes who they think they are and how they behave. At one extreme are those who take on animal alters, although this falls short of the alternate animal personalities experienced by individuals with multiple-personality disorders (Hendrickson, McCarty, and Goodwin 1990).

Their animalization inverts the traditional priority placed on human concerns over those of animals, with greater importance placed on the latter. One hoarder showed an awareness of this inversion after a fire in her home killed some of her animals: "I wanted to die because I felt that I just wanted to be with them. It's funny that you would want to be with your pets more than your husband and kids but that's how I felt [near crying]. We lived near a lake. For a long time, I wanted to walk into the lake and drown." She also recalled a dream about another fire that gutted her home and some of the animals in it. "I said to my son, 'Oh thank God the dogs are okay.' You know, most people would say, 'Oh, your house didn't burn down.'" Inversion is also revealed when hoarders weigh the relative importance of human and animal life. Responding to a local tragedy where a woman killed her eighteen-month-old child and pets, the hoarder said, "When people say did you hear about that girl who killed her baby and her dogs, I would hear about that lady who killed her dogs and her baby? Do you follow me? I've got to watch myself because people who don't understand me might think that I don't value human life, which is not true. But to me, it was more devastating that she killed her dogs." Sometimes, this inversion is over more prosaic priorities. For example, one hoarder said, "When I punch the clock at night I don't think I'm going home to see my husband and kids. I think I'm going home and little Betty is going to be there and we're going to go out for a walk. She understands me."

This inversion resets the authority relationship between humans and animals and gives hoarders, compared with most pet owners in American society, much less control over animals. They relinquish some of their autonomy and decision-making ability, indeed a substantial amount in a few cases, for the sake of their animals' needs and whims and because they see their animals as having the right, like humans, to be free and exercise choice. One hoarder goes so far as to say that her animals "run" her life; another asserts that "their needs" determine everything she does. This treatment empowers animals and allows them to pursue their own identities unfettered by human restraint or preference.

Hoarders do not train animals and impose few rules on them so their authentic personalities can emerge. As one said, "I give them a lot more freedom than rules. I don't expect them to be something or anything in particular for me. I pretty much let them be who they are." By not regulating the behavior of animals, hoarders compromise the quality of their daily lives from the perspective of general community standards. For example, they might make one or two rooms off-limits to animals, but even these supposedly sequestered rooms are often overrun, disordered, and soiled by animals. Hoarders also hope to confine their animals' elimination to certain rooms, although typically there are scores of dirty litter boxes throughout houses and "mistakes" are common. In some cases, the floors of every room are completely soiled. Animals also may be allowed free run of kitchens, even when humans try to eat, resulting in massive swarming of both people and food. With no effort to train them or control their behavior, some hoarders strive to maintain a "peaceable kingdom" among their animals by monitoring and managing their aggressive behavior so that fellow animals are not harmed.

By not controlling their animals, hoarders challenge the cultural category of pets and the treatment of animals as lesser creatures. In fact, many flatly deny that they regard their animals as pets. As one hoarder maintains, people should not treat their animals as humanlike and "love" only a few. Although some hoarders claim to have a few "favorite" animals, and they can often identify many by name, they tend to relate to their animals as though they have a corporate identity rather than interacting with them as traditional pets. Not surprisingly, some hoarders admit they rarely play with their animals, also blaming this on the volume of animals or the difficulty of interacting with feral cats.

From the hoarders' perspective, having many animals is not a leisure pursuit, distinguishing them from people who collect things as hobbies. Of course, like hoarders, hobbyists can be deeply committed to their activities, but they do not lose sight of the fact that they are pursing leisure. And like hoarders, some hobbyists are involved in morally controversial activities; gun collectors, for example, are forced to develop various accounts and justifications for their interests to deal with public reproach for what they find fun to do (Eddy 1988). But they are hobbies rather than missions, passions rather than obsessions, diversions rather than causes.

According to hoarders, regular pet owners are hobbyists because their involvement with animals is just about "love" rather than part of a larger mission to care for them. Having companions is not the issue for hoarders. Some say that their feelings for animals "go beyond love." "I have a feeling," one said, "that you need to protect them because the need is great. You certainly can't keep them out there by themselves to fend for themselves. You can't do that." As another hoarder said about the dog her sister's family kept, "They have love, it's like their child. There's a lot of people that will love their animals and treat it like a human—there's a distinction, though. I mean, it's just not love, it's a caring, it's something deep."

Why do animal hoarders often create and cling to saintly identities? Hoarders are working through dilemmas they face in their everyday lives—dilemmas relating to the need to balance chaos with order, instability with stability. That their behavior provides this balance for their identity stems from the nature of animal hoarding as opposed to so-called rational hoarding. Rational hoarding has been observed in periods of uncertainty and scarce resources caused by economic failure or military siege. During the Great Depression in the United States, hoarding was a way to cope with the inability to obtain needed goods. The fear engendered by uncertainly and scarcity even continued among Depression-era survivors whose acquisition of material objects was less rational. A similar response to uncertainty and deprivation has been reported among those who withstand prolonged military invasion, like the residents of Stalingrad who faced an extended attack on their city by German soldiers, or those who have been forcibly ghettoized, like the citizens of Warsaw in World War II.

Animal hoarding's use is similar to the use of hoarding inanimate objects by people confined in institutions. In such circumstances, acquiring material objects is an identity-creating device that gives order, stability, and continuity to otherwise shapeless identities (Csikszentmihalyi and Rochberg-Halton 1981). People who are uprooted from familiar places and find themselves powerless, disoriented, and without possessions, can hoard objects to rebuild a new sense of self. Prisoners, for example, go to great lengths to acquire and keep almost anything following their dislocation from the outside world. Some of these acquisitions are rational, for example, if the item can be bartered or refashioned into a useful object, but acquisitions also allow prisoners to reestablish their identities by having something—and all the better if they and others regard the objects as important. Likewise, patients in mental institutions often become "pack rats" as a way to form an identity in a place that strips away their former selves without replacing them with new ones (Goffman 1961). The more possessions one acquires, the more identity one can amass under such deprived and changed circumstances. This is also true for uprooted survivors of natural disasters and for people placed in nursing homes who discover the meaning and use of possessions only after they are lost (e.g., Erikson 1976).

Amassing large numbers of animals reproduces and reinforces their earlier chaotic and marginal life. The disorder and isolation, however, can provide order and purpose in the personal lives of hoarders only if they define their activities in socially desirable ways. Accounts of saintly behavior toward animals provide a bridge to a larger culture that praises extreme instances of helping others, especially when they come at great cost to the helpers. Consumed by their consumption, hoarders build their saintly self-images in ways that transform what others see as appalling neglect into something that feels more familiar than strange, more comforting than distressing, more kind than cruel.

Far from typical pet owners, then, hoarders' saintly self-presentations starkly contrast with the press's negative portrayal of them as mentally ill, if not criminal or pitiful (Arluke 2002). No doubt, these contradictory images can confuse more than clarify the public's understanding of animal hoarding. Readers are likely to react to this inconsistent mix of information with shock and horror, but also with fascination. Understanding why people are so interested in animal hoarding reveals as much about ourselves and our culture as it does about hoarders themselves, as we see next.

PUBLIC FASCINATION

On their surface, animal hoarding cases make for good news stories because they are so extraordinary, baffling, and sad—scores of sick and starved animals being kept in filthy, cluttered homes, often by people who claim to "love" them. Following the rescue of Erickson's dogs, the press had a feeding frenzy with this case. Reporters spoke to humane society workers, veterinarians, and law enforcement officials and shot videos of what it looked like to be in the Erickson home, eventually playing this news story endless times. The Ericksons came across as monsters.

To understand why the public is fascinated with these cases, it is first important to see what journalists emphasize in their reporting. Many articles appear to de-emphasize the severity of animal neglect by providing few details about it. While there were reports of animals suffering from respiratory diseases, eye infections, heartworm, diarrhea, conjunctivitis, flu, ear mites, fleas, and malnutrition, articles rarely elaborated or emphasized these conditions. Instead, their emphasis on the disgusting or horrifying state of hoarders' homes and life-styles overshadowed animal suffering. More superlatives suggesting dismay and alarm were used to describe squalor and uncivilized behavior than were used to describe starved, sick, injured, and dehydrated animals. Similarly, when articles included photographs they were more likely to show the disarray of homes than the neglect of animals; rare exceptions showed a young horse with debris on its forelock and mane, a badly matted cocker spaniel, and a horse whose hooves were untrimmed and beginning to curl upward.

Other articles are mixed or ambiguous in their reports of animal neglect. Some note neglect in certain animals but not in others. According to the animal control officer involved in one case, nine cats were in "tough shape." "You could tell those animals were pretty sick," he said, "just by looking at them," because they had "severe ringworm" and "various respiratory ailments." Yet, six dogs and over twenty cats left in the home had "no serious ailments." In another case, a humane official said that the hoarder's dogs were "mistreated and badly cared for," but only twenty out of 249 seized dogs were "put down… because they were in extremely poor health." In other articles, it is unclear how many animals were involved, how many were neglected, or what their condition was when the case broke. For instance, one reported "dead from neglect and starvation," which in its brevity could make it hard for some readers to imagine the nature and extent of suffering experienced by these animals. Another article merely says that the animals "were not cared for properly and were living in dirty cages."

And some articles make no mention of animals' poor health or suffering, describing them as healthy and active, or at least not suffering serious health problems. One such piece notes that the hoarder's ten horses and nearly one hundred ducks, turkeys, and chickens "aren't in good condition....[But] most are suffering from the types of ailments you would expect from animals living without proper nutrition or medical care. None of these ailments are life-threatening." Photographs of hoarders' animals in their homes often feature animals that appear healthy and active and, less commonly, in "normal" interaction with hoarders. One article, for example, uses four photographs, all of healthy or active animals and a sign outside the hoarder's "sanctuary" reading, "Beyond These Gates Lies a Safe Haven for All of God's Creatures."

When victims get center stage in these reports, they are more likely to be human than animal. For example, child neglect by hoarders trumped animal neglect in both headlines and text. In one such article, the headline reads, "8 Children Taken from Squalid Home" and text describes a couple charged with child endangerment for letting their eight children live amid animal carcasses, excrement, and spoiled food. Toward the end of the short article, there is brief mention that the local humane society "was expected to cite the couple" because a horse and cow were found dead from neglect and starvation on their property. To some extent, these articles position animal hoarding as the cause of child endangerment or "environmental child neglect" rather than a problem in its own right. For example, one article entitled "Girl's Escape from Filthy House in Detroit Leads to Kids' Rescue: Animals and Garbage Filled Home" details the chaotic and unsanitary mess in this home, including "clouds of fleas," animals standing in feces and urine, caged animals, broken toys, human feces, and "crumpled religious pamphlets and posters." Most of the article chronicled the "pitiful" plight of the children, who were severely neglected by their parents. A single sentence notes the condition of the animals—an undetermined number of cats, hamsters, and a guinea pig were "so diseased that they were put to sleep."

That neglected animals receive short shrift is consistent with studies showing that the news in general focuses much more on criminals than on victims (Graber 1980; Sherizen 1978). Here, the "disaster" of squalor is given much more attention and detail than animal neglect, which appears to be a less important issue or even an afterthought. Because these articles focus on the hoarder's living conditions, readers may be less horrified about animal neglect than they are about squalor. To the extent that the press can rouse public interest for new issues and problems, articles de-emphasizing animal neglect may not elicit enough horror in readers to lead them to regard hoarding as a serious problem or prompt them to take action to prevent or better manage it.

Hoarders are pictured as extremely pathetic or sad people who live in nightmarish "squalor" that is hard for most readers of the news to comprehend. As the news describes the drama of the "worst" cases, it often concentrates on hoarders' lifestyles and living conditions in ways that might elicit pity or even disgust in readers. Such a strong reaction is likely because hoarders are reported to violate taboos against excessive filth and disorder. As such, their public identity becomes more animal than human.

Experts describe them as living in filthy conditions with a large number of animals—from dozens to hundreds—both alive and dead. These animals, most commonly cats and dogs, are frequently ill and malnourished to the point of starvation. The floors may be covered with feces and urine and the air so thick that it may be difficult to breathe inside (Patronek 2001). Such households are often heavily cluttered with trash and garbage, with unsanitary living and food preparation areas. These conditions may inhibit normal movement about the home and pose a threat to the hoarder's health and safety. In some cases, the residences are condemned as unfit for human habitation (HARC 2002). Additionally, involved animals suffer from serious health and behavioral problems that require euthanasia (Patronek 1999).

Articles about hoarders often paint a picture of domestic squalor. Typical headlines read, "Man Cited in Keeping 60 Labradors in Filth," "Cats Seized from Squalid Home," and "Menasha Woman Gets Jail Term for Keeping Pets in Filthy Home." The article headlined "Dog Lover Gets More Time to Clean" describes the case of a woman with 140 dogs (not reported as neglected) whose house was declared a "public nuisance" by health department officials because its floors needed scraping and scrubbing to get rid of the feces and roaches. Some of the articles noted that, in addition to being extremely unkempt and unsanitary, the hoarders' homes were abandoned, falling apart, or burned because of their owner's neglect. In one case, the hoarder had a candle on her television set that dripped on an adjacent plant that in turn ignited the television, causing it to explode, blow out the front window, and start a more general house fire.

Descriptions of stench-filled, dilapidated, rundown homes create an image of hoarders as pathetic, troubled people whose lifestyles clearly separate them from prevailing community standards. Details commonly describe feces, urine, and spoiled food found throughout hoarders' homes, defying conventional cultural norms that restrict domestic animals' movement, excretion, and eating to limited and specified areas. Not merely unaesthetic and chaotic, hoarders' homes were uncivilized. Homes and yards also were littered with animal carcasses, further contributing to the image of uncivilized chaos. A few reports describe scenes of carnage and death, with animal corpses scattered throughout the hoarders' homes in varying degrees of decomposition, sometimes partially eaten by other animals. One article describes a house "covered with feces, several inches thick in places" with "dead, dying, and half eaten cats" throughout. When humane workers arrived at one home with over two hundred dogs, they found "dead dogs hanging from windows. There were pieces of bodies of dogs. Some dogs were dead in their cages....Some adult dogs were feeding on puppies." Several articles report that animal cadavers were discovered in refrigerators. One, for example, reports that investigators discovered twenty-nine dead cats and a decomposed six-inch alligator in the hoarder's freezer. One bag of frozen cats was marked "S. Sauce." There was some question about whether five bags and a large pot of spaghetti sauce also in the freezer might have been made from cat meat. The result of the urine, feces, decomposed food, and cadavers was utter chaos and "overpowering stench," as though hoarders and their animals had sunk to a level of existence that was far below civilized standards. Articles suggest that this squalor was so bad that neither humans nor animals should live in such uncivilized conditions. Rather than simply describing this squalor, media accounts usually quote humane officials, house inspectors, or firefighters who recount in graphic terms the extreme clutter and stench they encountered, how it affected them, and the steps they took to overcome it.

Officials typically report that hoarders' homes and lives are "out of control," noting that animals "overrun" homes or have "total run" of them. Two headlines make this point: "Home Found Overrun with Birds [215 birds "in cages stacked from floor to ceiling in every room"] Resident...Found Dead" and "More Than 100 Dogs Take Over Home." The text of the accompanying articles elaborates this out-of-control image. In one case, the hoarder lived in the attic because she had turned over the rest of her house to animals. Another article says, "It was like a jungle in there. They had plenty of food, but the cats were living almost one on top of the other on one floor of the house. It was appalling." In another case, an animal official claims that the house is literally "running with cats...[They] were observed perched on top of appliances, living inside furniture and cabinets and ranging through the several rooms." In yet another case, cats were found living in the crevices of the walls. The animals appeared to be in control, free to do whatever they wished. Once the animals are in control, hoarders' homes lost their human nature in press reports, where they are instead described as "zoos," "menageries," or in one case a "feces clogged urban Noah's Ark" full of "strange creatures" including small birds, a wolf, foxes, hedgehogs, snakes, raccoons, guinea pigs, iguanas, fourteen dogs, and a baboon. Investigators also thought they saw an orangutan.

With animals "in control," hoarders' everyday habits appear less human. Their eating patterns, for example, could resemble those of animals. One article notes, "She eats dog food and grain along with her animals." Another article reports that the hoarder's son "has to eat in the loftier of the bunk beds to keep Spot, vaguely Dalmatian and the unquestioned leader of the pack, from picking his plate clean." Sleeping, too, became animal-like for some hoarders. Other articles describes this behavior in a hoarder who "sometimes slept" with her two hundred rabbits in "two cramped and filthy sheds," a hoarder who lived in a six-foot square rabbit hutch with her dozen cats and dogs, and a hoarder who said that she "used to sleep on the bottom bunk....but I kept waking up with too many dogs on my chest. They were cutting off my air supply."

Once hoarders lost control of their animals, their squalor and subhuman status suggested their acts were more pitiful than criminal, more sad than seriously mentally ill. Indeed, it was common for the press to quote people who felt "sorry" for hoarders. For example, in one case of dozens of sick cats living in squalor, a "code compliance officer" said "he felt sorry for the fifty-seven-year-old owner of the home....He said the man was probably just trying to care for stray cats and they multiplied to the point that they were no longer manageable."

The allure to readers of the upside-down and out-of-control world of hoarders is similar to the appeal of crime news in general. The value of these stories comes from their ability to raise questions and doubts about the social order rather than from their celebration of society's triumph over deviance and disorder. By raising fundamental questions about everyday existence, these stories can connect to and bear on reader's own lives and problems. They do this by providing material for a "ritual moral exercise" where, according to Katz (1987, 67), readers reflect on and mull over issues of personal competence and sensibilities that are often dramatized in crime news. From this reflection, people develop a moral perspective that can help them deal with the fear of miscalculating their own and others' abilities.

This moral exercise, however, can do more than merely shore up questions of competence. Crimes news also raises issues about personal and collective identity that key into everyday fears about how well people fit into their neighborhoods or work scenes, as well as more existential concerns about what makes them any better than anyone else. All of us, not just hoarders, face questions of belonging and identity. While the news will not tell readers who they are or how they are different from others, it provides the fodder to develop a perspective that will do so. This perspective is formed as readers locate themselves within a repertoire of emplotted stories. Such identity work is an ongoing dynamic between individuals and culture, or in this case readers and the news, where people come to know who they are by first comparing themselves with others and then by either excluding or including them in their own group.

Hoarding stories raise doubts about the sanctity of the social order. American values and beliefs that are assumed to be taken for granted cannot be, at least when it comes to hoarders. Thus, through these stories the media does not reproduce the status quo, as do other institutions (e.g., Foley 1990), but challenges it. Readers are reminded that things are not always the "way they ought to be" in society. Specifically, reports about hoarders question the endurance and importance of conventional values regarding human-animal relationships, domestic life, and civil obligation.

For one, news stories detail behaviors that blur interspecies boundaries, with hoarders routinely crossing lines that many people expect and uphold when it comes to presumed differences between humans and other animals. Indeed, their acts often violate taboos about inappropriate behavior toward animals. As they do so, hoarders become animalized, abandoning trappings associated with modern, civilized life. And these boundary crossings are likely to disturb many readers, despite growing interest in according animals ever higher moral status in society, whether by improving welfare standards, acknowledging sentience and intelligence, or granting legal rights (Franklin 1999).

These reports rarely reassure readers about this phylogenetic breech of the social order or reaffirm the traditional place of animals in society by clarifying moral and social distinctions between species. One story that did, however, involved a hoarder who allegedly owned fifty-four starving and dehydrated dogs and cats along with five dead cats, some of which were being consumed by other cats. The article suggests that the court's failure to punish this hoarder was due to the lesser social value of animals compared with that of humans. When the defendant argued that her animals "were like my children," the judge retorted, "If these were your children, you'd be going to jail for a long time." Of course, other reasons could account for this courtroom response; judges' inaction may reflect the fact that animal cruelty is considered only a misdemeanor in many states and that animal hoarding as a psychological problem is poorly understood at present.

Middle class norms also are commonly violated in news stories about hoarding, assaulting what mainstream America holds dear when it comes to standards of cleanliness and order, friendliness and civic duty, responsibility and moderation (e.g., Tittle and Paternoster 2003; Wolfe 1998). Details of hoarders' lifestyles defile what many readers assume is minimally civilized behavior in modern society. Indeed, their denial of middle-class morality is so extreme, readers might have almost a prurient interest in these reports because the behavior of hoarders verges on being a class obscenity.

For example, middle class expectations dictate that one has the right to privacy and exclusive control of personal items, while still being minimally responsible to oneself, one's dependents, and one's home. However, generally assumed standards of cleanliness and order (Hoy 1996), even when generously defined, are routinely violated in articles about hoarding. Reports also portray hoarders as irresponsible to family members, whether human or animal. Certainly, accusing hoarders of extreme animal neglect and abuse points to their violation of this norm; they have taken advantage of their privacy to harm others. And there are occasional reports of elderly parents or children who suffer neglect as well.

Also, there are middle class norms for being neighborly and civil. Yet, reports show hoarders disregarding the presence of others when it comes to maintaining physical property and the surrounding environment. They infringe on the lifestyles of neighbors, for example, when the dilapidation of their homes and yards spreads next door or their animals' defecation and destruction results unpleasant sounds, sights, or smells that easily offend those nearby. Hoarders also withdraw from neighborhood social life. Many accounts detail their clandestine ways, describing them as loners or reclusive people. They are guilty of alienation, having no acceptable excuse.

A final example is the middle class norm that encourages moderation over excessiveness. The numbers of animals kept by hoarders and the disarray of their homes grossly violate public expectations for the prosaic and moderate. Such practices tread on the belief that extremes of any kind are unacceptable. Even their apparent lying seems immoderate; there are middle class limits for tolerating deceitfulness, including the scale or extent of lying. Cover-ups that involve double lives, especially if the weak and helpless are exploited or harmed, are condemned. The very claim by hoarders that their actions are altruistic, if not saintly, is itself an affront to the value placed on honesty and may be seen as an admission of glaring irrationality that does not hold them in better steed.

Throughout these reports of species and class violations there is a lack of closure. Society does not triumph over this form of deviance and restore the social order. There is no great celebration or relief because hoarders have been caught; various authorities seem puzzled about how to deal with them, or even how to categorize them, and sometimes there is public outrage directed at law enforcement agencies or shelters. Reading articles about hoarders gives the impression that they rarely appear in court, and those who do are rarely punished, except for having future ownership of animals restricted, being required to undergo counseling, or being forced out of their homes to cleaner and safer locations. In part, this impression is due to the style of reporting crime news. "Breaking" stories that cover the apprehension of deviants and early criminal proceedings are favored over those that report trial outcomes. It also is due to the reluctance to impose sentences on hoarders either because the "crime" or "illness" is thought to be unserious or because court officials and other authorities are unsure how best to manage this problem.

The lack of closure leaves these reports raising more questions about the integrity of the social order than providing a sense of moral consensus or resolution. If they do not reassure readers, then what is their appeal? What is in them that readers find interesting to consider? Certainly, as a form of crime news, there is nothing to be gained. There is no information that can protect readers from harm, since few are likely to live near hoarders, and in the unlikely chance that some do, nothing is provided that can reduce the threat of harm to them. Indeed, it is not clear in the latter case that there is any danger posed other than possible damage to neighborhood aesthetics or real estate values.

Nevertheless, the public finds these news stories interesting at a personal level. There are moral tales within these reports that enable readers to work through existential dilemmas relating to boundaries thought to separate them from other people and animals. These reports provoke readers to ask questions about what it means to be human and civilized, to be a good and responsible neighbor, a fit parent or animal owner—questions far removed from the content of the news stories but close to their own anxieties and worries. How far should I go in trying to befriend the family next door? Am I going a little "overboard" by caring too much for my two cats? Does it really matter if I keep my lawn so well manicured? Why do I want certain things and not others? What do I keep secret and would others care to know? Do any of my actions harm others? And in asking and then answering these questions readers can sustain their belief that their own identities, as well as their place in society, are beyond reproach.

Finally, we are drawn to cases of animal hoarding—their drama, their unreality, their horror, their sadness—because they are mirrors of our times and culture. We see in them something larger. They are a stark reminder of the contradictions and conflicts about non-human animals that are shot through modern societies and writ small in the Erickson case and others like it. Indeed, paradoxes are plentiful when we examine human-animal relationships in general (Arluke and Sanders 1996), and hoarding is no exception. We can see these inconsistencies in the hoarders themselves—at one moment professing profound love for their animals only to turn their back on them in ways that cause as much or more suffering than encountered in intentional cruelty cases. And we can see these inconsistencies in our response to hoarding, some of which may be due to the lack of research into this topic. So in the news, animal hoarding in one report comes across as a light, even enduring human-interest story about the "daffy" cat lady, while in the next story it is reported like crime news as an "animal Dachau." In the animal shelter world, we find employees overwhelmed and heartbroken when having to euthanize the hoarder's sickened animals, then only to be chastised by an infuriated public that sees the shelter, not the hoarder, at fault. In the criminal justice world, we find some courts open to hearing cruelty cases and perhaps even finding against them, while in others, there is little interest in hearing such cases, let alone doing much about them. And then there are the animals themselves—if hoarders often take in unwanted animals—why are they ignored, who else is doing anything about them? And what does this say about our treatment of animals? Whether in the Erickson case, or others like them, these contradictions are about all of us and the non-human animals that are part of our world. Understanding why animal hoarding occurs and examining our response to it will take us one step closer to perhaps lessening these contradictions. This book asks us all—whether academic, policy-maker, humane worker, public official, or everyday citizen— to begin asking and answering these questions in earnest.

NOTES

1 For more information, see Arluke and others' (2002) study of press reports of animal hoarding from 1995 to 2002.

2 Founded by Gary Patronek at the Tufts Center for Animals and Public Policy, HARC eventually included a veterinarian, a humane official, a psychiatrist, a psychologist, three social workers, and a sociologist (Arluke).

3 However, not all their animals were that badly neglected; a number of outdoor dogs appeared healthy and had food and shelter, although they were lethargic, filthy, and needy for attention.

4 Severe upper respiratory infection can manifest as conjunctivitis, progressing to corneal ulcer, and in some cases, penetration of the eyeball.

5 Journalists who write these stories become significant players because they cull and report the views of various authorities. How we come to regard hoarders and assess their relationships with animals depends on the willingness and ability of journalists to capture the perspectives of these authorities as well as those of hoarders themselves.

6 Of course, we do not know whether hoarders genuinely believe their own accounts. The Ericksons' words were "heartfelt" and "delivered with utter conviction," according to Celeste Killeen. We also do not know whether these accounts, when heard by others, are believed. Jordan (1989) maintains that even skeptical listeners are normally reluctant to challenge or deny directly what an excuse-maker says. Snyder and Higgins (1988) concur, noting that the audience "collaborates" with an excuse maker to keep his self-esteem intact.

7 For more information, see Vaca-Guzman and Arluke's (2005) study of how hoarders neutralize negative portrayals of their behavior. Data for this research comes from content analysis of 163 newspaper articles representing 118 hoarding cases from 2000 to 2003 and from twenty-five semi-structured interviews with hoarders conducted by HARC between 1998 and 2003.

8 In the interests of privacy, the authors have not provided citations for quotations relating to specific hoarders.

9 A closely related justification is to reframe the hoarding as something that is considered socially acceptable, like being a breeder or pet shop owner. Barbara Erickson said that she was not a hoarder because, rather than keeping all her dogs, she let some go by selling them.

10 Hoarders more often excused rather than justified their behavior. This is not surprising. These cases are so grotesque and animal emaciation is so evident, hoarders may consider it easier to accept the wrongfulness of the behavior and deny responsibility for it, than to deny the wrongfulness of the behavior and accept responsibility for it. Also, by making accounts more credible, hoarders enhance their effectiveness as tools to create respectability.

11 When adolescents explain their prior cruelty, many are distressed by memories they cannot readily excuse (Arluke 2006). Although they recall their unsavory behavior as a way to "try on" adult identities, this view does not entirely numb whatever guilt or uneasiness they still feel. Others are indifferent, considering their memories as unimportant matters that neither help nor hurt their self-image, but they, too, compartmentalize their former abuse by linking it to a transition out of childhood. They have moved on; memories of abuse are just that. Their sense of self is not based on relationships with animals—whether positive or negative.

References

Alonso, A. A. 1985. An analytic typology of disclaimers, excuses and justifications surrounding illness: A situational approach to health and illness. *Social Science and Medicine* 21: 153-162.

Arluke, A. 2004. *Brute Force: Animal Police and the Challenge of Cruelty*. Lafayette: Purdue University Press.

Arluke, A. 2006. *Just a Dog: Understanding Cruelty and Ourselves*. Philadelphia: Temple University Press.

Arluke, A., R. Frost, G. Steketee, G. Patronek, C. Luke, E. Messner, J. Nathanson, and M. Papazian. 2002. Press reports of animal hoarding. *Society and Animals* 10: 1-23.

Arluke, A., and C. Luke. 1997. Physical cruelty toward animals in Massachusetts, 1975-1996. *Society and Animals* 5: 195-204.

Ball, S., L. Baer, and M. Otto. 1996. Symptom subtypes of obsessive-compulsive disorder in behavioral treatment studies: A quantitative review. *Behavioral Research and Therapy* 34: 47-51.

Berry, 2005. Long-term outcomes in animal cases. *Animal Law* 11: 167-194.

Campbell, C., and J. Robinson. 2001. Animal hoarding. In C. Bryant (ed.), *Encyclopedia of Criminology and Deviant Behaviour*, II: 11-15. Philadelphia: Brummer Routledge.

Colin, C. 2002. Loving animals to death. [Electronic version]. Salon.com. Retrieved June 6, 2002 http: //www.salon.com/people/feature/2002/03/08/hoarders/index.html.

Danzger, M. 1982. The use of newspapers. In R. Smith and P. Manning (eds.) *A Handbook of Social Science Methods, Volume 2: Qualitative Methods*, 197-218. Cambridge: Ballinger Publishing Company.

223

Earl, J., A. Martin, J. McCarthy, and S. Soule. 2004. The use of newspaper data in the study of collective action. *Annual Review of Sociology* 30: 65-80.

Foley, D. 1990. The great American football ritual: Reproducing race, class, and gender inequality. *Sociology of Sport Journal* 7: 111-35.

Franklin, A. 1999. *Animal and Modern Cultures: A Sociology of Human-Animal Relations in Modernity.* Thousand Oaks: Sage.

Frommer, S., and A. Arluke. 1999. Loving them to death: The blame-displacing strategies of animal shelter workers and surrenderers. *Society and Animals* 7: 1-16.

Frost, R. 1998. Hoarding, compulsive buying and reasons for saving. *Behavioral Research and Therapy* 36: 657-664.

Frost, R. 2000. People who hoard animals. *Psychiatric Times* 17(4): 25-29.

Frost, R., T. Hartl, R. Christian, and N. Williams. 1995. The value of possessions in compulsive hoarding: Patterns of use and attachment. *Behavioral Research and Therapy* 33: 897-902.

Graber, D. 1980. *Crime News and the Public.* New York: Praeger.

HARC 2002. Health implications of animal hoarding. *Health and Social Work* 27: 125-131.

Hoy, S. 1996. *Chasing Dirt: The American Pursuit of Cleanliness.* New York: Oxford University Press.

Hwang, J., S. Tsai, C. Yang, et al. 1999. Hoarding behavior in dementia: A preliminary report. *American Journal of Geriatric Psychiatry* 6: 285-289.

Jones, E. E., and S. Berglas. 1978. Control of attributions about the self through self-handicapping strategies: The appeal of alcohol and the role of underachievement. *Personality and Social Psychology Bulletin* 4: 200-206.

Jordan, N. 1989. When to lie to yourself. *Psychology Today* 23: 24-25.

Katz, J. 1987. What makes crime "news." *Media, Culture, and Society* 9: 47-75.

Lockwood, R. 1994. The psychology of animal collectors. *American Animal Hospital Association Trends Magazine* 9: 18-21.

Lockwood, R., and B. Cassidy. 1988. Killing with kindness? *The Humane Society News* Summer: 1-5.

Meagher, E., R. Frost, and J. Riskind. 1999. Compulsive lottery, scratch ticket, and keno gambling: Its relation to OCD, hoarding, impulsivity, and the urge to buy. Paper presented at the annual meeting of the Association for the Advancement of Behavior Therapy, Toronto, November.

Mills, C. W. 1940. Situated actions and vocabularies of motives. *American Sociological Review* 5: 904-913.

Nathanson, J. 2009. Animal hoarding: Slipping into the darkness of co-morbid animal and self neglect. Forthcoming. *Journal of Elder Abuse & Neglect*.

Orbuch, T. L., J. Harvey, S. Davis, and N. Merbach. 1994. Account-making and confiding as acts of meaning in response to sexual assault. *Journal of Family Violence* 9: 249-64.

Patronek, G. 1999. Hoarding of animals: An under-recognized public health problem in a difficult to study population. *Public Health Reports* 114: 82-87.

Patronek, G. 2001. The problem of animal hoarding. *Municipal Lawyer* 42:6-19.

Patronek, G., L. Loar, and J. Nathnason, eds. 2006. *Animal Hoarding: Structuring Interdisciplinary Responses to Help People, Animals and Communities at Risk*. Hoarding of Animals Research Consortium.

Poses, P., and K. Weishaupt. n.d. Catcher in the Rye: Animal collection syndrome and the borderline family system. Unpublished manuscript.

Rasmussen, S., and J. Eisen. 1992. The epidemiology and clinical features of obsessive compulsive disorder. *Psychiatric Clinics of North America* 15: 743- 758.

Rosenhan, D. 1973. On being sane in insane places. *Science* 179: 250-258.

Rotenberg, K. 1980. Children's use of intentionality in judgments of character and disposition. *Child Development* 29: 282-284.

Scott, M. B., and S. M. Lyman. 1968. Accounts. *American Sociological Review* 33: 46-62.

Shaw, M. E. 1968. Attribution of responsibility by adolescents in two cultures. *Journal of Adolescence* 3: 23-32.

Sherizen, S. 1978. Social creation of crime news. In C. Winick, ed. *Deviance and Mass Media*, 203-224. Beverly Hills: Sage.

Snyder, C. R. 1985. The excuse: An amazing grace? In B. Schlenker, ed. *The Self and Social Life*, 235-260. New York: McGraw-Hill.

Snyder, C. R., and R. L. Higgins. 1988. Excuses: Their effective role in the negotiation of reality. *Psychological Bulletin* 104: 23-35.

Snyder, C. R., R. L. Higgins, and R. J. Stucky. 1983. *Excuses: Masquerades in Search of Grace*. New York: Wiley-Interscience.

Stola Education Group. 2006 Animal hoarding: A hidden danger in the sport of purebred breeding? *IG Times*, Spring.

Strubbe, B. 2000. Clutter Busters: Deconstructing our acquisitive human nature. [Electronic version]. Metro Active Features.

Sykes, G., and D. Matza. 1957. Techniques of neutralization: A theory of delinquency. *American Sociological Review* 22: 640-670.

Tittle, C., and R. Paternoster. 2003. A typology of deviance based on middle class norms. In P. Adler and Pet Adler, eds. *Constructions of Deviance: Social Power, Context, and Interaction*, 19-29. Belmont: Wadsworth/Thomson.

Vaca-Guzman, M., and A. Arluke. 2005. Normalizing passive cruelty: The excuses and justifications of animal hoarders. *Anthrozoos* 18: 338-357.

Wilson, J., and G. Kelling. 1982. Broken windows: The police and neighborhood safety. *The Atlantic Monthly*, March.

Winsberg, M., K. Cassic, and L. Koran. 1999. Hoarding in obsessive compulsive disorder: A report of 20 cases. *Journal of Clinical Psychiatry* 60: 591-597.

Wolfe, A. 1998. *One Nation, After All*. New York: Penguin.

Worth, D., and A. Beck. 1981. Multiple ownership of animals in New York city. *Transactions and Studies of the College of Physicians of Philadelphia* 3: 280-300.

Index